A BISHOP'S MINISTRY

REFLECTIONS & RESOURCES FOR CHURCH LEADERSHIP

DAVID TUSTIN

Published by David Tustin
Publishing partner: Paragon Publishing, Rothersthorpe
First published 2013
© David Tustin 2013

The rights of David Tustin to be identified as the author of this work have been asserted by him in accordance with the Copyright, Designs and Patents Act of 1988.

All rights reserved; no part of this publication may be reproduced, stored in a retrieval system, or transmitted in any form or by any means, electronic, mechanical, photocopying, recording or otherwise without the prior written consent of the publisher or a licence permitting copying in the UK issued by the Copyright Licensing Agency Ltd. www.cla.co.uk

ISBN 978-1-78222-148-7

Book design, layout and production management by Into Print
www.intoprint.net
01604 832149

Printed and bound in UK and USA by Lightning Source

A Bishop's Ministry
*Reflections & Resources
for Church Leadership*

CONTENTS

Page

FOREWORD 4

1. Called to be a bishop 9
2. Changing gear 23
3. What consecration means 30
4. Getting into the job 38
5. Coming to grips with the role 49
6. The inner life 61
7. Outer lifestyle 69
8. Home and hospitality 81
9. Custody of time 87
10. Working together as a team 96
11. Caring for people within & beyond the church 110
12. Leading worship 132
13. Spreading the Christian message 146
14. Sending new ministers 163
15. Building bridges in society and within the church . 178
16. Fostering visible Christian unity 190
17. Review and professional development 201
18. Stepping into retirement 211

EPILOGUE 220

APPENDIX: Consecration sermon by Canon M. Mayne 221
SELECT BIBLIOGRAPHY 224
REPORTS 226
INDEX OF SUBJECTS AND KEY WORDS 229

FOREWORD

A generation ago Archbishop Michael Ramsey lamented the dearth of books about the office and work of a bishop. He pointed out that legions of books had been written about 'episcopacy', but hardly any about the inner life or practical problems of a bishop in our own times (see A.M. Ramsey, *'The Christian Priest Today'*, SPCK 1972, page 95).

THREE AIMS

a) My first and foremost aim in writing this book is to reflect systematically on the various facets of episcopal ministry, on the basis on my own theological understanding and practical experience. Dr Graham Neville rightly observed:

'... the intention of Christian theology is to examine and reflect on the whole of human experience in the light of the Christian revelation ... That theology is never 'timeless' but constantly changing, and its changes are related to the changes of its social setting. There must, therefore, always be a historical, and even a biographical, element in the description of any coherent theological scheme.' [G. Neville – *'Free Time: towards a theology of Leisure'*, **University of Birmingham Press 2004, page vi**]

Inevitably these pages are to some extent autobiographical, but their intention is to move beyond that to a framework of thought and action that could be widely relevant to those engaged in church leadership.

b) My second aim is to encourage other experienced bishops to set their reflections on record, and to stimulate new bishops of either gender to reflect more deeply on their own ministry as it develops in a contemporary context.

c) A third aim is to incorporate with these reflections some extracts that I have found useful from the writings of St Gregory the Great and St Bernard of Clairvaux. When studying in Geneva in 1959 I was first introduced to St Bernard's writings by Dr Douglas V. Steere, the American Quaker scholar (of Haverford, Pennsylvania). The insights from Bernard of which he made me aware have been a continuing stimulus throughout my ministry.

Bernard's vivid Latin is not easily put into readable English, and his clever word play is often untranslatable. I have selected a few extracts as a 'taster' for those who have not yet discovered Bernard, and freely adapted them to a contemporary idiom.

Bernard eventually led me back to Gregory the Great, though regrettably it was not until ten years after my consecration that I began studying his great work *'The Pastoral Rule'*. On discovering it during sabbatical leave in 1989 my initial delight soon turned to frustration and disappointment. I found the document off-putting for a number of reasons. Its style is at times repetitive and long-winded. Its use of biblical quotations, though generally very apt, is sometimes based on speculative exegesis that nowadays seems far-fetched and lacking in cogency. It addresses social conditions very different from our own day. The available English translations are not in modern idiom, and give the impression of a document that is dated and indigestible. Other modern readers may well have been tempted, as I was, to give up on reading Gregory. However, it would be a pity if such factors prevented his insight and practical wisdom from resonating with bishops today. This is why I began putting together a collection of interesting passages, freely abridged and paraphrased to render the material more lively and accessible – a task completed only in retirement.

The extracts from Gregory and Bernard will, I hope, convey something of the force and relevance of what those church leaders from centuries ago still have to say to bishops today.

MY PARTICULAR EXPERIENCE AS A BISHOP

At the outset I should indicate briefly what my experience of episcopal ministry has been, and in what contexts it has been carried out, since these factors inevitably colour my view of the subject.

For twenty-one years (1979-2000) I held the suffragan see of Grimsby. It was providential that I had spent four formative years (1963-67) on Archbishop Michael Ramsey's staff at Lambeth Palace in the Foreign Relations' department. This gave me an inside view of how his archiepiscopal household worked, as well as valuable experience of ecumenical relations at international level.

I was blessed with fifteen fulfilling years of parochial ministry in the West Midlands: three years as a curate in Stafford under Dudley Hodges (1960-63), and twelve years as an incumbent and trainer of several curates in Wednesbury and Wolverhampton (1967-79), latterly also as a rural dean. During these phases I was on the receiving end of *episcopé* as exercised by two contrasting Bishops of Lichfield – Stretton Reeve and Kenneth Skelton – and certain of their suffragans – Richard Clitherow and John Waine (both of Stafford) and Frank Cocks (of Shrewsbury). All these men in varying degrees have been amongst my episcopal role models, together with Michael Ramsey and the bishop who sponsored me as an ordinand – Leonard Wilson of Birmingham.

The strongest influence on my understanding of what it means to be a bishop has undoubtedly been that of the two Bishops of Lincoln with whom I served: Simon Phipps and Robert (Bob) Hardy. Their personalities and styles of ministry differed greatly, but each shared his episcopate with suffragan colleagues in a most generous and open manner. During these years my fellow suffragans within the diocese included three Bishops of Grantham – Dennis Hawker, Bill Ind and Alastair Redfern – whose friendship and support were invaluable.

My prime responsibility was the oversight and leadership of the pastoral area delegated to me – a territory covering some 1,300 square miles. This is roughly the northern half of Lincoln diocese, and comprises a wide spectrum of social settings. Various tasks were distributed amongst the senior staff, and re-shuffled from time to time. For ten years it fell to my lot to chair the Diocesan Board of Education and Training, which at that time covered not only church schools but also voluntary work amongst adults, youth and children. Later for nine years I chaired the Diocesan Pastoral Committee during a busy phase of pastoral re-organisation. I also had a hand in pioneering the Lincoln scheme for Local Ministry Scheme, and at two stages was involved in reforming diocesan structures – the Structures Review Group (1992-93) and 'Towards Total Ministry' (1999-2000).

Just as in parochial ministry, I struggled constantly to give a high priority to pastoral work. This engagement with clergy and their families remained my first love, reflecting the basic grounding I had received as a parish priest, and claimed the major portion of my attention and effort throughout the 'Grimsby' years – often in ways that were unseen.

Another major strand running through my ministry has been the active search for closer visible unity between Christians of different denominations at various levels – local, regional, national and international. The early training I received as a modern linguist and the experience gained in serving as an interpreter at several ecumenical gatherings in the 1960's provided a useful foundation for the responsibilities later laid upon me as a bishop in the field of Christian unity. These included co-chairing the Anglican-Lutheran dialogue body at world level for some twenty years, as well as conversations leading to the Meissen Agreement (1991) with the Evangelical Church in Germany and to the Porvoo Agreement (1996) with the Nordic and Baltic Lutheran Churches. On the home front I chaired both the Humberside Churches' Council and Sponsoring Body (1985-88) and the General Synod's Council for Christian Unity (1992-98). I also co-led preliminary talks between the Methodist Church and the Church of England in 1995-96, and throughout my 'Grimsby' years was closely involved with Roman Catholics through the three-way link between the RC dioceses of Nottingham and Brugge (Belgium) and our Anglican diocese of Lincoln.

This quick overview gives some idea of the actual circumstances in which I have experienced what it means to be a bishop in the Church of God, living with one foot in the local scene and the other in a wider one. This is the context in which my reflections are rooted.

Acknowledgements

The pages that follow would not have been written without the encouragement of my wife, Mary, and my late brother-in-law, Bishop Kenneth Stevenson, who initially persuaded me to distil the fruits of over thirty years' experience as a bishop. I have been greatly helped by those who generously gave their time to scrutinise earlier drafts: Mary, our son Nick Tustin, Archdeacon Roderick Wells, and three fellow bishops – Bob Hardy, Tony Foottit and David Hawtin. I record my warm gratitude to them for their constructive criticism and urging me to see this project through, and to those who have kindly let me to quote from their writings.

In pulling together various strands that are personally significant to me, I have become freshly aware of my indebtedness to many individuals with whom I have been privileged to work over the years – colleagues who have helped me in many practical ways, and contributed to my understanding of the Church's mission and ministry. I lay no claim to originality, and am conscious of St. Paul's words: *"What do you have that you did not receive? And if you received it, why do you boast as if it were not a gift?"* (1 Cor 4, 7).

Extracts from *'Common Worship: Ordination Services Study Edition'* are copyright © The Archbishops' Council, 2007, and are reproduced by permission – all rights reserved. Extracts from *'The Niagara Report'* are copyright © The Secretary General of the Anglican Consultative Council and the General Secretary of the Lutheran World Federation, and permission to reproduce them is acknowledged – all rights reserved. Scripture quotations contained herein from the New Revised Standard Version Bible are copyright © 1989 by the Division of Christian Education of the National Council of the Churches of Christ in the U.S.A., and are used by permission – all rights reserved.

For the extracts from Gregory's *'Pastoral Rule'* I consulted the translations by J. Barmby (1895) and H. Davis (1950). For Bernard's treatise *'On the Lifestyle and Duties of Bishops'* I worked from the original text in J.P. Migne's *'Patrologia Latina'*, and consulted the unpublished translation by Dr David Lightfoot of Louth which he graciously shared with me in 1981. For Bernard's work *'On Consideration'* I worked from M. Binetti's Latin text, and consulted the English translations by G. Lewis (1908), J.D. Anderson and E.T. Kennan (1976), and G.R. Evans (1987). Every effort has been made to acknowledge my sources, but for any inadvertent omission I apologise and will put this right in any future edition.

Description, not prescription

The demands of any job or way of life can only be fully understood from the inside, since only by doing it can you experience what the whole 'package' adds up to and what is required to sustain it. This account of the why, what and how of a bishop's ministry is meant to be descriptive, not prescriptive. I do not claim that my way is the best, or that I always lived up to my own ideals. Each of us has to tackle his or her own vocation in given circumstances and with a unique mix of gifts and weaknesses. There is no perfect or universally valid way of handling the various issues to be mentioned. A bishop's ministry has many similarities and parallels with other forms of Christian ministry and other walks of life. This just happens to be the particular challenge that I have had to address for a major part of my working life.

So here, for what it is worth, is my own take on a bishop's ministry. These reflections have been in gestation for many years. Clearing my head and consolidating my own thinking have been part of my therapy in retirement. As time goes by one's experience gets increasingly out of date, and becomes less relevant to the fast-changing circumstances of a new era. Nevertheless, there may be some value in recording what I thought I was trying to do 'on my watch', and I hope it will be of interest and help to others.

David Tustin

Wrawby
North Lincolnshire
August 2013

CHAPTER 1

Called to be a Bishop

WHAT SORT OF PERSON SHOULD BECOME A BISHOP?

Ideas have varied greatly from one time and culture to another about what sort of person ought, or ought *not*, to become a bishop.

The earliest surviving paradigm of how a bishop should be can be found in the Pastoral Epistles (1 Tim 3, 2-7 and Titus 1, 7-9), probably written around 110 A.D.. At that stage no single leadership pattern for local Christian communities had yet emerged. Many of the qualities expected of a bishop were similar to those needed for leading a synagogue or large household. However, by the time of late antiquity the main focus of a bishop's responsibilities had shifted from the local to the regional scene. Dr Richard A. Norris, the American church historian, has shown how the raised profile of a 4th or 5th century bishop demanded qualities more akin to those of a Roman prefect, magistrate or public orator (see R.A. Norris, *'The Bishop in the Church of Late Antiquity'*, pages 21-32 of the papers of the Anglican-Lutheran consultation on *'Episkopé'* at Niagara in 1987, published by the LWF and ACC, Geneva 1988). By that era a bishop had to be much more than a shepherd or focal person of his gathered flock. He needed to be capable of carrying out such roles as teacher or principal catechist; disciplinarian, enforcer of morals and arbitrator of disputes; administrator of property, church funds and welfare provision for the poor and needy; and liturgical celebrant and president of regular assemblies of the whole church community. This called not just for high moral qualities, but also for a considerable range of talents and experience.

GREGORY'S 'PASTORAL RULE'

The document that, above all others in patristic times, set a benchmark for the standard of church leadership was the *'Pastoral Rule'* of St Gregory the Great. It was largely inspired by the monastic rule of St Benedict, and published soon after Gregory became Pope in 591. He had given the subject much previous thought, and distilled the practical wisdom he had gathered first as the son of a senator, then as Prefect (i.e. executive mayor) of the city of Rome, and later as a monk, a church diplomat and abbot of a Benedictine monastery. He showed great insight into human character and motives, as well as into the temptations that arise from people's temperaments and circumstances.

This book was the main written guidance to bishops on how to carry out their ministry, and had a major impact on public life throughout the Western Church during the whole medieval period. Its structure, in four parts, is succinctly described in the introduction to Fr H. Davis's translation (*'Pastoral Care',* published by the Paulist Press, New York 1950 – see pages 4 to 9). The first part, on the difficulties and burdens of church government, includes a portrait of the ideal candidate to be a bishop:

> *'Here are some criteria for the sort of person who should become a bishop. He sets an example of good living. He is alive to the things of the Spirit, but dead to the passions of the flesh. He takes no account of worldly prosperity, and fears no adversity – his only desire is for inner riches. His body does not thwart his endeavours by reason of its frailty, nor does his spirit on account of not caring about itself. He is not disposed to covet other people's things, but freely gives of his own ... His compassion moves him quickly to be forgiving, but his uprightness never stoops to condoning more than is appropriate. He commits no unlawful deeds, but deplores those perpetrated by others as though they were his own. Out of affection his heart sympathises with anyone else's infirmity, and rejoices in his neighbour's advantage as though it were to his own benefit. He is such a good example in all he does that he has no cause to be embarrassed – at any rate not by reason of anything in his past life.*
> *His efforts are such that he is able to water even parched hearts with the rivers of his teaching. He has already learned through his own practice and experience of prayer that, whatever he asks God for, he can obtain ... If someone is too abashed to intercede with another person on whom he has no claim, what idea can he have about the role of interceding before God unless he himself lives in God's favour through the excellence of his own life? How can he ask God's pardon for others as long as he himself is not assured of peace with God? Something else to be anxiously feared is this: the one who is supposed to be competent to appease God's wrath should not provoke it on account of his own guilt.'*
>
> Condensed from Part I, chapter 10 (my own translation)

Gregory is equally clear about the sort of person who ought not to become a bishop. Though his analogy based on physical disabilities reads unacceptably in today's climate, he is right in saying that anyone must be regarded as unsuitable if he lacks consistency of behaviour, is undiscerning, or is too bogged down with worries or bad habits (**Part I, chapter 11**).

BERNARD'S ADVICE TO NEW BISHOPS

Six centuries later St Bernard of Clairvaux had much of value to say on this topic in his treatise to Archbishop Henry of Sens on *'The Lifestyle and Duties of a Bishop'*, written in 1126. This document was brought to my attention in 1981 by Dr David Lightfoot of Louth. It speaks of the need for chastity, purity of heart and humility – inner virtues that are a better adornment for a bishop than outward trappings. A number of extracts in my own translation will be quoted in a later chapter on questions of life-style.

Over the years I have similarly compiled a collection of extracts from Bernard's final work, *'On Consideration'*, which consists of advice to one of his former monks who had been elected Pope in 1145. The political circumstances were dire. Pope Lucius II had been killed in Rome during a popular uprising, and in this situation of unrest Bernard Pignatelli was elected. A native of Pisa, he had entered the monastery at Clairvaux in 1135, and later became abbot of the Cistercian community of St Vincent and Anastasius at the abbey of Tre Fontane in Rome. Although not a bishop, he was elected Pope and took the name Eugenius III. Immediately he had to flee the city, was consecrated at the monastery of Farfa, and had to keep on the move for most of his pontificate. He resided in Rome for only a few months before his death in 1153.

Bernard had serious doubts whether Eugenius was equal to the task. As soon as news of the election was announced Bernard wrote with typical frankness to all the Curia:

'God have mercy upon you! What have you done? ... What made you suddenly rush upon this rustic, lay hands upon him when [he was] in hiding from the world, drag him to the Palatine, place him upon a throne, and clothe him with purple and fine linen, and gird him with a sword? ... Had you no other wise and experienced man amongst you who would have been better suited for these things? It certainly seems ridiculous to take a man in rags and make him preside over princes, command bishops and dispose of kingdoms and empires.

Is it ridiculous or miraculous? Either one or the other! I have no doubts that this could be the work of God "who performs wonders as no-one else can", especially when I hear everyone saying that it has been done by the Lord ... I am not happy in my own mind, for his nature is delicate, and his tender diffidence is more accustomed to leisure than dealing in great affairs. I fear that he may not exercise his apostolate with sufficient firmness ... If you have any pity or compassion, support him in the work to which he has been lifted up by the Lord through you ...'

From B.S. James (transl.), *'The Letters of St Bernard of Clairvaux',*
(Burns Oates, London 1953), page 385

Though Bernard was astonished at this appointment, he did not doubt that it could be the work of God. At once he wrote to Eugenius to encourage him:

'This is the finger of God "raising up the poor man out of the dust, the beggar from his dunghill to sit among princes and reach the honour of a throne" ... The whole Church rejoices and glorifies God, because she has such confidence in you as she seems not to have had for a long time in your predecessors ... I do indeed rejoice, but confess that I do so not without trembling ... When I ponder on the honour that is yours, I fear the danger which is at hand ... You have been called to hold a high position, but not a safe one ... Have courage and be of good heart, ... but in all your actions remember that you are human.'

(Ibid, pages 277-278)

This episode from the dark days of the mid-twelfth century illustrates dramatically the paradox of all Christian ministry. Bernard's memorable retort, "Ridiculous or miraculous? One or the other!" emphasizes the huge gap between the glorious Gospel and our frail humanity; between the expectations of public office and our human limitations. He echoes St Paul's comment to the congregation at Corinth where the apostle's leadership had been challenged:

'We are no better than pots of earthenware to contain this treasure (i.e. the gospel), and this proves that such transcendent power does not come from us, but is God's alone' (2 Cor 4, 7 NEB)

Some examples of Bernard's wise counsel to Eugenius are included in later chapters, especially 6 and 7.

POLITICAL AND CULTURAL FACTORS

In many periods of the church's history bishops have exercised a strongly political role and, not surprisingly, rulers and statesmen have had a large say in episcopal appointments. This is illustrated, for example, in 19th century England where – according to Owen Chadwick – Lord Melbourne (Prime Minister 1835-41) 'took more trouble to discover the political views of candidates than to learn their pastoral capacity' (*'The Victorian Church'* – Part I, p 121). By contrast Lord Palmerston 'tried to choose bishops who were good for the pastoral work of the church without concerning himself much over their politics' (op cit – Part II, p 332). Owen Chadwick also observes:

'The queen's exercise of patronage was valuable ... for it produced a bench of bishops more eminent in wisdom, learning, personality and holiness of life than the Church of England had hitherto seen'

(op cit – Part II, p 340).

The church historian Dr Colin Podmore has published a fascinating survey of the changing means by which bishops have been chosen in the Early Church and in the Church of England (see *'Aspects of Anglican Identity'*, CHP 2005, chapter 9). Canon Malcolm Grundy has also summarised various models of the episcopal office through the course of history, as well as the present-day route to senior leadership in various denominations (see *'Leadership and Oversight',* Mowbray 2011, chapters III and IV).

Other cultural factors have had a major bearing on the choice of bishops, and continue to do so. When I lived in Greece and mentioned to my fellow students at Athens University that I hoped to be ordained, many asked the question: "Do you want to get married, or do you want to be a bishop?" They assumed that these were the only two options. To them it was unthinkable to break the 15 centuries' old Orthodox tradition of choosing bishops only from amongst celibate monks. A similar culture of celibacy prevails in the Roman Catholic Church, though prior to the Reformation married bishops survived in Iceland until Jón Arason, who was beheaded with his two sons in 1550. The current requirements for RC episcopal candidates are set out in Canon 378 of the 1983 Code.

I rejoice that a number of Anglican and Lutheran churches now include women in the episcopate, and hope that the Church of England will not delay much longer before doing so. Now that sexual orientation, as well as gender, has become the focus of cultural clashes within the Anglican Communion (as in other traditions too), the question as to what sort of person should become a bishop has clearly acquired a new urgency and importance, as well as an increased relevance to current debates in society as whole.

Contemporary criteria for selection

It makes no sense theologically to look at this issue in isolation from the general requirements for any kind of publicly accredited ministry. The report *'Criteria for Selection for Ministry in the Church of England'* drew attention to an important shift in the contemporary practice of ministry:

'A current major requirement of ministers is that they should be able to lead and to work collaboratively with others. The emphasis on collaboration ... is fed by an

understanding that ministry is the responsibility of the whole people of God so that the ordained ministry is to draw together the ministry of others and not to supplant it.'

(ABM Policy Paper No. 3A, October 1993, p 40)

Nowadays when selectors interview candidates for ordained or lay ministry, they are advised to explore eight main lines of enquiry:

A. Ministry within the Church of England
B. Vocation
C. Faith
D. Spirituality
E. Personality and character
F. Relationships
G. Leadership and collaboration
H. Quality of mind

These published guidelines contain several useful questions under each heading, such as:

How strong is their sense of the loving and saving purpose of God for the world?
How have they responded in the past to challenges to their faith?
Are their devotional lives disciplined and regular?
How do they cope with disappointment, criticism or opposition?
How able are they to acknowledge their vulnerability?
Do they show evidence of being prepared to handle conflict?
Do they have the ability to formulate aims and objectives for a church community and enable others to move together towards them?

(op cit pp 77-100)

If such questions are judged to be relevant to all ministerial candidates, they surely need to be raised all the more searchingly in regard to those who may become bishops. In the opening chapter of Bernard's treatise to Archbishop Henry of Sens he comments:

'To what great dangers must the life of a bishop be exposed? He has to put up with everyone's trials. If I, hiding in my cave or – as it were – 'under a bushel', cannot manage to avoid the blast of the wind and am worn out by the continual onslaught of various trials, what must it be like to be placed upon a mountain or on the top of

a candle-stick? I have only myself to look after ... What annoyances must bother a bishop? What injuries must trouble him on account of other people's outer struggles and inner fears, even if he has no private troubles of his own?'

('The Lifestyle and Duties of a Bishop', 1.1)

COLLEGIAL INTERDEPENDENCE

Bishops exercise their ministry not simply as individuals, but also in collegiality with other bishops. This corporate dimension was explored in *'Bishops in Communion'* (House of Bishops Occasional Paper, GS Misc 580, publ. CCU 2000), which speaks of a "connectedness of gracious belonging, operating at the local, national and international spheres of the life of the Church" – something rather different from day-to-day teamwork. The paper underlines certain qualities that are requisite for episcopal collegiality to be effective:

The bishops as a college have a special responsibility to nurture the unity and continuity of the Church. They also have a special responsibility for leading the Church in response to the complex issues of the contemporary world. This entails attentive listening to the challenges which come from new scientific knowledge and new moral dilemmas, as well as the questions posed to the Christian faith by other faith communities and new movements of spirituality. Collegiality entails listening to those on the margins of the Church, the prophetic voices, as well as to those outside the Church, in order to discern what should be the authentic witness to the gospel in today's world.

Episcopal collegiality involves leadership in the discernment of truth, bringing into focus matters of concern, and determining what level of the Church's life is the appropriate one for exploring them. It entails determining what needs to be said at any particular moment and after that continuing to show care for the response and reception in he ongoing life of the Church.

The exercise of collegiality requires that each bishop exhibit something of the following qualities:

- *faithful discipleship to Jesus Christ grounded in a life of prayer;*
- *a readiness to listen to the Church and the world;*
- *sound learning which springs from the study of Scripture, the tradition of the Church and contemporary theological research;*
- *a willingness to engage with new knowledge in various fields;*
- *an ability to weigh matters with wisdom;*

- *a recognition that the mystery of God is always seen 'as in a glass darkly';*
- *a patience to continue with difficult and seemingly intractable questions;*
- *a creative imagination to discern the signs of God's kingdom;*
- *a willingness to make room for different positions when matters are complex and answers as yet unclear;*
- *a humility to confess mistakes;*
- *the skill to communicate wisely;*
- *the courage to take the lead, even when it makes one unpopular;*
- *the readiness always to be attentive to the promptings of the guidance of the Holy Spirit;*
- *the willingness and ability to work in partnership with others.'*

('Bishops in Communion', pages 39-40)

This describes a leadership style that is not defensive or mainly concerned with enforcing a tight, cut-and-dried orthodoxy of whatever kind of churchmanship. Rather, it is outgoing and creative, ready to engage with life's complexities and to live open-endedly with unavoidable conflicts and anomalies. Leaders with these capacities are what the Anglican Communion needs at the present time.

Whose responsibility?

In the Church of England there is now greater openness in putting forward the names of potential bishops. Elected members of the Crown Nominations Commission have a specific brief to do this, and members of Vacancy in See Committees are also encouraged to send in their suggestions. For suffragan appointments, too, current practice allows room for broad local consultation. Not only do diocesan bishops put names forward at least annually to the Archbishops' Secretary for Appointments, but it is also open to anyone to submit suggestions in response to the advertisements that now appear at each vacancy in a diocesan see. It is important that the list of candidates should be drawn from various backgrounds.

However, individuals are not expected to put their own name forward – rightly so in my view. Nobody should presume to volunteer himself or herself. Rather, it is for others to judge whether they are the right sort of person to be a bishop. The onus for answering such questions as those mentioned above must rest in the first instance with *anyone* who plays a role in putting someone's name forward as a possible bishop. This wider involvement must be matched by a great sense of responsibility on the part of all who share in the appointments' process, not just the few who technically make the appointment.

Receiving the Call

As soon as anyone becomes aware that his or her own name is being actively considered for an episcopal appointment, a new onus falls on that person. It is one thing for a priest to wonder in a general way what it would be like to become a bishop one day, but quite another to receive a letter inviting him or her to explore a specific post! It can come as quite a shock to receive a 'call' that is unsought. I vividly recall getting just such a letter in summer 1978. At the time I was in bed at Tettenhall Vicarage, recovering from a severe bout of influenza. I did not recognise the handwriting on the envelope. The postmark was from Canterbury, where Simon Phipps was attending the Lambeth Conference. He wrote as follows:

'I am looking for a successor to the Bishop of Grimsby, who retires at Christmas. I am wondering whether you would think of discussing with me the possibility of being considered for the job ... It would be only fair that both of us should be free to be frank and say 'No' if we felt that was what was right to say ... It would be good if we could meet in Lincoln. I could then tell you and your wife about it all, and take you to see something of the northern part of this diocese ...
What sort of things am I looking for in the man? I know I can't have everything! But – a man who prays;
a man who reads and thinks, and can help the clergy do their theology;
a man who could chair a new board of Mission and Education ...;
a man who can relate to the secular powers-that-be;
a man who will be a reliable pastor to the clergy and their wives;
a man who can manage his share of routine diocesan administration ...
Your adult education experience greatly appeals to me, since resourcing the laity for mission, and the clergy too, is a key for the future. And your work with married couples is of great interest ...
Let me know if you are "moved"! and we'll start there. It would be lovely to meet you both, and I write with lots of hopes and best of wishes ...'

Exploring the Call

The first challenge that such an invitation raises is the uncomfortable one of searching one's own soul. The initial question is: knowing myself as I do, can I accept that those who think me suitable for this appointment may be right? Bernard stressed how vital it was know oneself. He advised Eugenius:

'Reflect on what sort of person you are ... this will certainly keep you within your limitations. It will not let you take flights of fancy from your real self, or 'occupy

yourself with great matters or things that are too high for you' (Ps 131, 2). Be true to your own self. Do not fall lower or lift yourself higher. Do not – so to speak – escape into greater 'length', or spread yourself out to greater 'width'. Stick to the middle course unless you want to lose the happy medium. The middle ground is safe ... Here I am talking of 'length' in the sense of promising ourselves a longer life, and of 'width' in the sense of involving our minds in more concerns than necessary. I am speaking of 'height' in the sense of people overrating themselves, and of 'depth' when they are too cast down ... Sensible people are not lured away by the uncertain prospect of a longer lifespan. Modest people limit their concerns and cut down on needless worries, though without ignoring what is necessary. Fair-minded people do not over-reach themselves ...

('On Consideration' II, 19)

The way you act when under pressure is something else I would not wish you to overlook. If you are steadfast in your own tribulations and sympathetic to those of other people, be glad about that ... What are you like when things are going well?

(Ibid II, 21)

Any call or invitation can receive various answers, and this freedom of choice is fundamental. There are dangers and risks both ways. If I decline, would it be evasion or disobedience? Would I be like Jonah who, when called to preach to the people of Nineveh, promptly took ship to Tarshish in the opposite direction! If I stay put, would I simply be playing safe? Would I regret it later? On the other hand, if I accept, where will it lead? Am I afraid of this unknown future, or can I trust God for it?

Gregory gives three Old Testament examples of struggling with vocation:

Isaiah, when the Lord asked whom He should send, offered himself spontaneously: 'Here am I – send me!' (Is 6, 8). Jeremiah, however, was sent, but humbly pleaded not to be sent. He said: 'Ah! Lord God; look, I do not know how to speak, for I am only a child' (Jer 1, 6).

Though different answers were heard outwardly from these two men, each response sprang from the same source of love within. For there are two precepts of charity: love of God and of our neighbour. This is why Isaiah, eager to benefit his neighbours through an active life, aspired to the office of preaching; whereas Jeremiah, longing to cling diligently to the love of his Creator through a contemplative life, protested against being sent to preach ... In both cases, it should be noted, the one who refused did not persist in his refusal, and the one who wanted to be sent received a vision of himself first being cleansed by a coal from the altar. This was for fear that one who had not been purged should dare to approach mysteries that were sacred, or lest one who had been chosen by divine grace should proudly resist under the guise of humility. Since it is very hard for anyone to be certain that he has been cleansed, the safer course is to decline the office of preaching. However, it ought not to be declined obstinately once God's will to undertake it has been recognised.

Moses fulfilled both requirements in a remarkable way: he was reluctant to be set over such a vast crowd, yet he obeyed. He would have been guilty of pride had he undertaken the leadership of that countless people without some trepidation; and clearly he would have been equally guilty of pride if he had refused to obey the Lord's command. So in both ways he was humble, and in both ways submissive. In the light of his own opinion of himself he shrank from being set over the people. Nevertheless, out of regard for the greatness of the One who commanded him, he consented ... Moses quaked at the thought, yet God persuaded him.

('Pastoral Rule' Part I, chapter 7)

Gregory goes on to point out the danger of ambition for personal prestige. He comments:

Those who hanker after the prestige of high office to feed to their own avarice often appeal to the apostle Paul's dictum: 'Whoever aspires to the office of bishop desires a noble task' (1 Tim 3, 1) ... We must, however, observe that this was said at a time when whoever was set over the people was the first to be led to the tortures of martyrdom. So it was indeed praiseworthy to seek the episcopate when, as a result of holding that office, its holder would doubtless encounter the most severe sufferings ...

(Ibid Part I, chapter 8)

Bernard, who remained Abbot of Clairvaux for nearly 40 years, was outspoken about the dangers of ambition amongst clergy:

Among the clergy of every age and rank, the learned as much as the ignorant, there is a general stampede for ecclesiastical responsibility, as though anyone might live without a care once he has secured a living ... How infinite is ambition, how insatiable is greed! ... For example, when someone has been made an archdeacon or something of the sort, he is not content with one honour ... He bustles about to find further honours, whether one or many. If the chance comes he would gladly prefer the honour of a bishopric. Will anything satisfy him? Once made a bishop, he desires to be an archbishop ... If people did these things for the sake of spiritual

> *gain, their zeal would be praiseworthy; but their presumptuous behaviour must be corrected.*
>
> *There are many who would not run with such confidence and haste towards positions of honour if only they knew the burdens involved as well. Indeed, they would fear to be burdened, and would not strive so energetically and dangerously after the insignia of all sorts of dignities. People nowadays look only to the glory, and not the cost ...*
>
> ('The Lifestyle and Duties of a Bishop' chapter 7, 25-27)

However, the opposite danger to ambition is to be too diffident. In the long history of the Church many have shrunk from accepting high office. John Chrysostom, Gregory Nazianzen and Augustine of Hippo all tried to dodge being ordained. In the 19th century William Ullathorne, who became the first Roman Catholic bishop of Birmingham, wrote in 1881 to another Benedictine monk who had just received an episcopal appointment:

> *'I may as well say that I have never felt grateful to those who made me a bishop. I refused three sees in succession and was, as it were, forced into the fourth by pressure ... I have never thought episcopacy a subject for congratulations.'*
>
> (Quoted in Judith Champ's biography, page 432)

Especially for those who might feel drawn to a quiet or scholarly life Gregory had this word of warning:

> *There are some people who are blessed with great gifts but, because they are keen on simply pursuing a contemplative life, they shrink from serving their neighbour's benefit through the [bishop's] ministry of preaching. They love to tuck themselves away in a quiet place, and long for a retreat in which to pursue their own thoughts. In regard to such conduct they must be judged guilty in proportion to the greatness of the gifts by which they might have been publicly useful. How can someone who could be of conspicuous benefit to others take the attitude of preferring his own privacy, seeing that the Only Begotten of the Father came from the Father's heart into the midst of us all so that He might do good to many?*
>
> ('Pastoral Rule' Part I, chapter 5)

Nearer to our own times Dietrich Bonhoeffer warns against the view that recognising God's will is simply a question of receiving an intuition that excludes any process of reasoning, or of naively grasping at the first thought or feeling that comes into one's mind:

'The will of God may lie very deeply concealed beneath a great number of available possibilities. It is something new and different in each different situation in life, and for this reason a person must always examine anew what the will of God may be. The heart, the understanding, observation and experience must all collaborate in this task. The voice of the heart is not to be confused with the will of God.
How does a person set about 'proving' the will of God (cf. Rom 12, 2)? Intelligence, discernment, attentive observation to the given facts – all these come into lively operation, all will be embraced and pervaded by prayer. Particular experiences will afford correction and warning. Direct inspirations must in no case be heeded or expected, for this could all too easily lead to self-deception. Possibilities and consequences must be carefully assessed. In other words, the whole apparatus of human powers must be set in motion. The Christian's gaze remains fixed entirely on Jesus Christ, since He is already present and active within us.'

(Condensed & adapted from *'Ethics'*, pp 161-6)

'SIX STEPS' TO CLARIFY A CALL

In summer 1976, when faced with an invitation to move to a new post, I devised a simple tool which I called the 'Six Steps'. On receiving Simon Phipps's letter I used it again, and subsequently recommended it to several clergy when they were confronted by a call to fresh work. The sequence of questions runs as follows:

1. In the light of my talents, experience, interests and concerns does this seem to be the right sort of job for me?
2. From the point of view of my family and myself, would it be right for me to move now?
3. From the point of view of my present parish and staff, would it be right for me to move now?
4. Does any other factor rule this possible new job entirely out of the question? If not, am I willing to look into it further?
5. Have I enough information on which to base a decision? If not, whom should I consult?
6. When enough is known, what is the balance of factors as between moving to the new job and continuing in the present one? Can I regard this as a serious call from God?

In regard to the fourth question there may well be factors that are unknown to those who put the person's name forward, or that are difficult to acknowledge openly. If so, the sooner a negative response is given, the better. This 'six steps' approach helped me to discern God's guiding hand through my circumstances and experience to date, and to regard the Grimsby proposal as a serious option. In later years I traced the same steps when invited to move to other spheres of episcopal work, though with negative conclusions on both occasions.

These, then, are some of the issues that need to be thought and prayed about when a ministerial call arises, especially if it be to a bishopric. The invitation, whether declined or accepted, has to be answered responsibly. The quality of decision is what counts. If it has been well made, its consequences can be lived with all the better.

After some three and a half years as a bishop, when making my self-assessment in July 1982, I made the following note:

'I feel I am in the right job. My fundamental reason for accepting this call when it came out of the blue was the conviction that Christian discipleship must mean giving up the safety and security of what is going well, and being ready to risk the unknown and tackle what is beyond me. I still see God's call in this way, and pray not to lose the sense of adventure and audacity. Temperamentally this is quite a struggle for me.'

CHAPTER 2

Changing Gear

The period between receiving the first approach about becoming a bishop and actually starting the new job is one of enormous pressure. This transitional phase involves coping with several unfamiliar factors, which I can best illustrate by telling my own story. The precise circumstances will vary for each individual.

SECRECY

The first practical difficulty is the secrecy that surrounds the appointment. Handling some degree of confidentiality is part of daily life, but the stakes go up when the matter is (literally) a state secret. To deal with apparently straight forward questions – Why are we visiting Lincoln? Where shall we be staying? Why are we looking at schools in Grimsby? – white lies and subterfuge became necessary not once or twice, but on a mounting scale. A few key people had to be told the real reason, even before the outcome was certain, and they too had to be sworn to secrecy. Whilst it is good that the appointment process is more open than it used to be, some degree of secrecy nevertheless remains. How complicated life becomes when one 'white' lie soon needs to be covered by another!

Though it is a great relief when news of the appointment becomes public, this event in turn launches even greater pressures, which fall into four categories: (a) those involved in leaving one's present post, (b) those that could apply to any family changing jobs and houses, (c) those related to the immediate practicalities of becoming a bishop, and (d) mental and spiritual preparation for episcopal ministry.

MOVING JOBS AND HOUSES

The hardest part, especially when you are a parish priest, is saying goodbye not just to colleagues and personal friends, but to one or more congregations and the wider community in which you have played a key public role. Their congratulations are tinged with sadness, and the element of bereavement is mutual. Mary and I received pressing invitations to 'one last meal' in so many households that our digestions nearly went on strike! We were overwhelmed with such kindness that we felt wretched about moving, and found this physically and emotionally exhausting. However, in retrospect it is clear that the huge amount of affirmation we received was a major ingredient in enabling us cope with the transition.

One's children have to be parted from their friends, too. A major worry for all parents is wondering how changes in their own lives will affect their children. Our children were aged eight and seven, and we thought it best not to burden them with our big secret until the day before it was announced. Nick, keenly interested in classical history, came up with an ingenious suggestion: "If Pompey was able to rule Gaul from Rome, couldn't you rule Grimsby from Wolverhampton?" He reluctantly accepted that this solution would not be workable, but was puzzled that the Church could not be more flexible! Juliet crayoned a picture of Daddy in his new cope and mitre, with a little note saying:

Dear Daddy,
I don't want to move house because I like Tettenhall a lot.
But just for your sake I will.
I hope you like our new house. I hope you like being a bishop.
Love, Juliet.

Housing can be quite a problem even though, as with most clergy jobs, it is provided by the church authorities. My predecessor, Bishop Gerald Colin, had lived 15 miles south of Grimsby in the market town of Louth, situated in the county of Lincolnshire. However, it had already been decided in principle that the next bishop should reside within the recently formed county of Humberside. The first suggestion was a disused vicarage in a remotely rural location, but it was quickly agreed that this would not be suitable. There was a rushed search for property in a pleasant residential area of Grimsby, served by good schools. We were shown a large semi-detached Edwardian house. When asked whether we were willing to live in it our answer was 'Yes', but if the question had been: 'Do you like it?' we would certainly have said 'No'. We made it our family home for the next eleven years despite its many practical disadvantages, but in common with many houses in the same road it proved to be structurally unsound, having been built on marshy ground near the fishponds of the former Augustinian Abbey of Wellow. Eventually an excellent new house was built near the edge of Grimsby. It was well designed, and the housing factor changed from being a hindrance to being a major help in ministry.

As with any family on the move, removals and decorations have to be arranged, and the options for the children's schooling need to be explored and chosen.

Run-up to consecration

On top of all the parochial and family factors already mentioned, a second group of concerns adds huge pressure to this period of transition. The run-up to consecration has several practical aspects that are time-consuming and unfamiliar:

(a) *Media*: preparing press releases, giving interviews and answering enquiries in connection with the new appointment. Nowadays a diocesan or national Communications Officer is generally available to advise diocesan bishops, but this is not always the case for suffragans and was certainly not so for me.

(b) *Correspondence*: acknowledging several hundred letters of congratulation, sending out invitations to the consecration service and distributing tickets to those who accept. This is a massive task needing extra secretarial resources.

(c) *Service planning*: coordinating the selection of hymns, anthems and a preacher with any others to be consecrated on the same occasion and with the authorities of the building where the service will take place.

(d) *Regalia*: ordering and being fitted for cope and mitre, rochet and two chimeres (red and black), ring and pectoral cross.

(e) *Reception*: arranging a reception after the consecration service. Nowadays more help is available, but in the late 1970s we needed to hire a room in Westminster and bring most of our own catering supplies in the car-boot!

Additionally, those who are to be diocesan bishops must attend the Confirmation of their Election and, before enthronement, do homage to the Sovereign.

Looking forward to the new job

It is generally recommended that an interval of at least a month should be planned between finishing the former job and starting the new one. Ideally this would be after moving house and before consecration, but this depends on housing being ready and available for occupation. In my case the purchase of a house was not completed until after the consecration, and we stayed in our previous vicarage for seven weeks after I had disengaged from ministering in the parish. We then moved, and I did not embark on public duties for a further fortnight. It is vital to leave sufficient time for mental and spiritual preparation apart from the mêlée of practicalities already described. This preparation is likely to take three main forms: mentors, reading and retreat.

a) Mentors

Nowadays the key person is the Bishops' Training Officer, who can impart a good deal of practical information. In my day neither this post nor the previous one of Archbishops' Adviser for Episcopal Ministry had yet been created, and I simply had brief conversations with the Provincial Registrar and the Archbishops' Secretary for Appointments. It is valuable at this stage if the new bishop can spend some time with a couple of existing bishops. The Appointments' Secretary or Training Officer may suggest whom to approach, but it should be a personal choice as well. A retired bishop, as long as he is not too out of date or out of touch, is more likely to have time available at short notice. If the new bishop has a spiritual director, this person may have a contribution to make, though he or she may not possess sufficient experience to offer appropriate advice on all aspects of a bishop's ministry.

Such mentors can help the new bishop on an individual basis in the following ways:

- Identify what new information he or she actually requires. This will vary according to previous experience or the lack of it. It is important to recognise the areas of deficit, and make plans to address them.
- Anticipate what pressures and expectations are to be faced, so as to enable him or her to cope with them better, with appropriate patterns to sustain spirituality.
- Enable him or her and the family to adjust personally to the changes in work, public role and place of residence.
- Suggest some initial goals, however provisional they may be, and some strategies for diary control and adequate time off.
- Think through the rationale of new functions.

Old colleagues and close friends will also be amongst one's mentors, and often have sound wisdom to impart. If they are encouraged to say what they expect of their own bishop, this can produce frank and well-grounded comments. It is important to accept blunt, honest advice without becoming defensive. I recall one close friend who was an experienced rural incumbent saying to me:

> *'I expect the bishop to relate to ordinary people when he comes to my parish. This is more important than a brilliant sermon. He must be able to get on with the squire as well as the labourer, and talk to them on their own terms. He must not only stay to the 'bunfight', but make himself part of it. Ordinary people remember the fact that the bishop stopped to speak to them. He must listen, and hear them out.*

I expect the bishop to support and encourage us clergy, but not breathe down our necks or interfere with each priest getting on with his own job in his own way. He should be available and accessible when needed, and let it be known that he is willing to visit clergy in their own homes by prior arrangement.'

Colleagues in my own former team stressed a number of practical points:

'Beware of being put on a pedestal by other people's attitude towards you. Avoid a feudal or despotic style, and above all remain a human being. Try to carry on sharing your ministry with other people's, and modelling a collaborative style of ministry.'
'Beware of power and the appearance of wielding power. At the same time remember that access to higher structures of society is an opportunity not open to many others.'
'Help clergy to clarify their own aims. Those in their first incumbency particularly need support. Help others to stand on their own feet and do their own job – you can't do it for them.'

It can also be useful to talk in confidence to someone with secular experience of a regional supervisory role. I was much helped by the comments of a former parishioner who held a senior position overseeing retail branch managers:

'Although you have been chosen to serve as a bishop, you are not yet personally known to those who will be in your care. To start with, therefore, you must earn their respect. You must show people in your new diocese that you can work hard, and that you exemplify integrity, fairness, objectivity, etc. People need an opportunity to get to know those who are set over them, and this process takes time.

You can greatly help people with their motivation. They need to be helped to set their own standards and targets, even down to small practical details. Yet the main incentive cannot be a financial one. It must be the individual's own commitment and desire to contribute to the total enterprise.

Follow the chain of command wherever possible, and enhance the authority of intermediate leaders. Refer any complaints back to the leader without undermining his standing. Encourage maximum discretion down the line, but also take conscious steps to foster communications upwards so that you know what people actually think. Remember that they do not just react as individuals; they also identify themselves as a group.'

b) Reading and reflection

It is vital that one's own theology of church and ministry should have been thoroughly thought out. In this transitional phase it is particularly useful to read or re-read some of the following:

A.M. Ramsey – *'The Christian Priest Today'* (SPCK, 1972) last chapter

P. Moore (ed) – *'Bishops, but what kind?'* (SPCK, 1982)

J. Halliburton – *'The Authority of a Bishop'* (SPCK, 1987)

M. Grundy – *'Leadership and Oversight'* (Mowbray 2011)

'Episcopal Ministry' GS 944 (Church House Press 1990) report of the Archbishops' group on the episcopate, usually known as the *Cameron Report*

'The Niagara Report on Episcopé' (ACC/LWF 1988) especially pp 45-110 and paragraphs 99-110

'Lambeth Conference 1988' (Church House Press 1988) paragraphs 151-153 & 164-174 and Resolution 41

'Baptism, Eucharist and Ministry' (WCC, 1982) paragraphs M 19-27, 29, 34-38, 41-44 and 52-53

'Documents of Vatican II' (Chapman 1967) especially *Lumen Gentium* paragraphs 25-27 and *Pastoral Office of Bishops* paragraphs 6-7, 11-19 and 37

A short burst of initial reading around the subject of episcopal ministry is a vital element in preparing to become a bishop. However, it is no substitute for subsequent study, especially in the formative early years of one's episcopate.

Another major element of preliminary study is what I would describe as 'getting the diocese into my head'. I found it useful to peruse the Lincoln diocesan handbook, and familiarise myself with the pattern of deaneries and committees. I also derived much valuable information from studying the Structure Plans for the counties of Lincolnshire and Humberside, containing a wealth of compressed facts about the demography and economic life of the diocese, e.g. Travel-to-Work areas, age structure, predicted population flow inwards and outwards, educational provision, projections for house building and small-scale industry, etc. All this was helpful in grasping the 'big picture' of those social realities within which the Church's mission must be played out. Then, too, by contrast I imbibed from the *'Bishop King's Spiritual Letters'* much about that good and holy bishop who stamped so much of his spirituality on Lincoln diocese during the 25 years of his episcopate, and whose portrait I was to encounter in one church vestry after another. Though he died as long ago as 1910, his presence is still felt and I spoke to several people who remembered being confirmed by him. Another book which I discovered later was *'Lincolnshire Towns and Industry 1700-1914'* by Neil Wright [vol. VI in the series on the history of Lincolnshire]. This social history shows what main strands have gone into making this area's distinctive character. Through such means one can develop a feel for the diocese's own special sense of place.

c) Retreat

It was a mistake to make my retreat immediately before travelling to London for my consecration. The Franciscan monastery of St Mary-at-the Cross, Glasshampton to which I went lies in remote rural Worcestershire, and was approachable only by a farm track. Light snow had already fallen, and heavier storms were forecast. Mary had to come a day earlier than planned to rescue me from being marooned there. Rather than having to cut the retreat short, it would have been better to leave a longer gap.

Fortunately the journaling that I usually find helpful to do on retreat was already complete. I had come to terms with leaving parochial ministry within such a remarkable parish and team, and outlined a provisional statement of what the main emphases of my new work should be. It was relaxing to dip into the communal liturgy and life of the friars. In preparing to dedicate myself afresh as a bishop, I found that Cardinal Newman's well-known prayer struck a chord deep within me:

O Emmanuel, O Wisdom,
I give myself to you. I trust you wholly.
You are wiser than I, and more loving to me than I myself.
Fulfil in me your high purpose.
Work in me and through me.
I am born to serve you; I am born to be yours.
I ask not to see; I ask not to know.
I ask only to be used.

When the prospect of embarking on such a ministry had seemed very daunting, I was much encouraged by Prebendary James Challis, the wise and kindly Vicar of Penn Fields, who, in true Evangelical style, sent me the following biblical text:

'Do not fear, for I am with you. Do not be afraid, for I am your God.
I will strengthen you, I will help you.
I will uphold you with my victorious right hand'

(Isaiah 41, 10)

CHAPTER 3

What Consecration Means

MY OWN CONSECRATION

It was Archbishop Donald Coggan who consecrated John Waller, Conrad Meyer and myself for the suffragan sees of Stafford, Dorchester and Grimsby respectively on 25th January 1979 in Westminster Abbey. The Archbishop was assisted by about 20 other bishops. It was the first occasion on which the revised ordinal, synodically approved in 1978 and due to be published with the Alternative Services Book 1980, was used. A congregation of about 1,000 worshippers attended, which was all the more remarkable since the country was in the grip not only of snow but also of national rail and postal strikes!

John Waller had suggested that the preacher should be Michael Mayne, who lived in his parish of Harpenden. I had known Michael at Cambridge in our undergraduate days, when both of us were much involved with the Franciscan friars and regularly worshipped at St Benet's Church. Michael later acquired an inside view of episcopal life as Mervyn Stockwood's domestic chaplain from 1959 to 1965, and subsequently he became Head of Religious Programmes at BBC Radio. Conrad and I readily agreed that he would be a suitable choice. This was several years before Michael's appointment as Dean of Westminster.

That day and that service are deeply etched in my memory. On each anniversary of my consecration I re-read the whole service and sermon, and spend some time pondering over them and renewing my vows. Each time I attend the consecration of a new bishop, which I have done on numerous occasions (Anglican, Lutheran and Roman Catholic), it is an opportunity to reflect further on the meaning of such an event. In this chapter I shall offer my own analysis of the layers of meaning to be found in the current Common Worship rite, approved in 2006 – see *'Ordination Services (study edition)',* published CHP 2007.

A NINEFOLD MATRIX

As with any sacrament, the initial focus is on the *vertical* dimension – what God is doing at this special moment. Yet the *horizontal* dimension is also significant in two ways:

(a) the corporate context of this event within the Church's life;
(b) the application to those who are consecrated.

When each of these elements is related to past, present and future, this forms a matrix of nine distinct aspects which can be identified in the meaning of the consecration rite, as the following chart indicates:

	Three Primary Aspects	Past	Present	Future
(vertical)	God's involvement	1	4	7
(horizontal)	Church's corporate life	2	5	8
	Individual application	3	6	9

PAST

1. GOD'S PURPOSE AND CALLING UNTIL NOW

Like any celebration of the eucharist, the consecration service proclaims the mighty acts of God through history. The Proper Preface recalls that God in his infinite love has *'formed throughout the world a holy people for (his) possession, a royal priesthood, a universal Church'*, and that Jesus *'having ascended into heaven, poured out your Holy Spirit upon his disciples, to give them power to preach the gospel to the ends of the earth and to build up your people in love'*.

This is the background against which the notion of 'vocation' can be fully appreciated – not as a self-chosen preference, but as the breaking in of God's calling. Jesus reminded his first disciples, *'You did not choose me, but I chose you'* (John 15, 16). Our God is one who repeatedly steps into people's lives, often radically changing their direction. What happens at a consecration service is consistent with many people's experience of God intervening in their lives over the centuries.

The Porvoo Common Statement (from now on "Porvoo") puts it this way:

'In the consecration of a bishop the sign [of the laying on of hands] ... bears witness to the Church's trust in God's faithfulness to his people and in the promised presence of Christ within his Church, through the power of the Holy Spirit, to the end of time ...'

(*'Together in Mission and Ministry',* CHP 1993, page 26, paragraph 48)

2. The Church's corporate life until now

Behind every celebration of the eucharist stands the Last Supper, and behind that stands the Passover – ordinances that have remained at the heart of the corporate life of God's People throughout the ages of history. As the Windsor Statement of ARCIC so clearly put it, the notion of memorial (*anamnesis*) is 'no mere calling to mind of a past event or of its significance'. It is the making effective in the present of an event in the past – see *'The Final Report'*, CTS/SPCK 1982, especially pages 14 and 20.

The congregation that meets for the consecration of a new bishop is no random assembly. It has been gathered for this purpose from within the living tradition of the whole community of faith. "Porvoo" states as follows:

> *'The primary manifestation of apostolic succession is to be found in the apostolic tradition of the Church as whole. The succession is an expression of the permanence and, therefore, of the continuity of Christ's own mission in which the Church participates (paragraph 39) ... In the case of the episcopate, to ordain by prayer and the laying on of hands is to do what the apostles did, and the Church through the ages ... [This sign] expresses the Church's intention to be faithful to God's initiative and gift, by living in the continuity of the apostolic faith and tradition ...'*
>
> (paras 47-48)

3. The individual's Christian journey until now

It is no mere formality when the Archbishop asks those who present the candidate: *'Do you believe him to be of godly life and sound learning?'* and *'Do you believe him to be duly called to serve God in this ministry?'* [This rite was worded for the male gender only.] These questions refer back to the candidate's track record as a Christian and as an ordained minister. Unless there is evidence that he has a credible Christian past, he is not considered fit to be consecrated. These earlier workings of grace in his life are a vital pre-condition. *'A gift of grace already given by God is recognised and confirmed'* (Porvoo, paragraph 47).

The Archbishop then asks the candidate: *'Do you believe that God is calling you to this ministry?'* This question is verifying that the process of discernment, already discussed in chapter two, has had time to occur and that the candidate is not being pushed to take an ill-considered step. The affirmative response expresses free consent – the equivalent of the bridegroom and bride saying *"I will"* before making their marriage vows.

One other preliminary element must also be in place – due authority for the consecration to occur. The appropriate form of authorisation, which varies from one church or country to another, must already have been given. In the Church of England this is expressed through the Royal Mandate, which is publicly read at the service.

These three initial aspects of the consecration service demonstrate with great clarity that the moment when it occurs cannot be seen in isolation, but that the past impacts powerfully upon the present. Let us move on to the new steps that ensue.

PRESENT

4. God's involvement now

The vertical element in the consecration service is made explicit when the Archbishop, having received the candidate's ordination vows, bids him: *'Pray earnestly for the gift of the Holy Spirit.'* All keep silence, and then sing the Veni Creator. After the Litany the Archbishop is joined by the other bishops who will lay on hands, and he prays: *'Send down the Holy Spirit on your servant N. for the office and work of a bishop in your Church'.* This form of words articulates the intention of the sacrament. The remainder of the ordination prayer spells out what particular qualities God is being asked to give the new bishop for his ministry:

> *'Fill this your servant with the grace and power which you gave to your apostles, that as a true shepherd he may feed and govern your flock, and lead them in proclaiming the gospel of your salvation in the world. Make him steadfast as a guardian of the faith and sacraments, wise as a teacher, and faithful in presiding at the worship of your people ... Give him humility, that he may use his authority to heal, not to hurt; to build up, not to destroy ...'*

5. The Church's corporate life now

The current ordinal strongly emphasises the Church's corporate life as the context within which consecration occurs. In his introduction the Archbishop speaks of the royal priesthood of the People of God. He reminds the congregation of the summons to all the baptised to witness to God's love and to work for the coming of his kingdom. This opening section concludes by stressing that: *'The Church in each place and time is united with the Church in every place and time'.*

The congregation's vocal assent to the consecration has long been a feature of the Orthodox rite. Our current ordinal re-interprets this element in the form of three questions that the Archbishop puts to the congregation:

'Is it now your will that he should be ordained?'
'Will you continually pray for him?'
Will you uphold and encourage him in his ministry?'

The symbolic importance of other bishops participating in the consecration received careful attention in the *'Niagara Report'* (especially paragraphs 49-53), where we built on the patristic material that Richard Norris's paper had provided at the consultation mentioned earlier.

In "Porvoo" we picked this up in the following way:

'... Thirdly, the participation of a group of bishops in the laying on of hands signifies their and their churches' acceptance of the new bishop and so of the catholicity of the churches ... The continuity signified in the consecration of a bishop to episcopal ministry cannot be divorced from the continuity of life and witness of the diocese to which he is called ...' (**paragraphs 48-49**).

In the 20th century such participation in the laying on of hands also became an ecumenical sign of 'communion' between churches belonging to different traditions. This ecumenical use of the sign was first proposed by the great Swedish ecumenist Nathan Söderblom in 1914 in connection with his own forthcoming consecration as Archbishop of Uppsala. However, it did not actually occur until September 1920 when, shortly after the 1920 Lambeth Conference, two English bishops (Hensley Henson of Durham and Frank Woods of Peterborough) were the first to join in laying hands on two Swedish Lutheran bishops (Einar Billing of Västerås and Viktor Rundgren of Visby). This use of the sign has since become widespread between Anglicans and those other churches with which we are in Full Communion. For me it has been a particular joy to represent the Archbishop of Canterbury at the consecration of ten Lutheran bishops in Sweden, Norway, Estonia and Lithuania. If becoming a bishop is understood as joining a wider collegiate body, inter-consecration makes clear that the body in question is not exclusively Anglican.

In addition to bishops 'in communion' who lay on hands, it is increasingly usual for other ecumenical representatives to attend with high profile. At my own consecration, for example, several representatives of the Orthodox, Oriental Orthodox and Lutheran traditions were robed and seated in choir. Broad ecumenical involvement is much to be welcomed and encouraged, as it enables the occasion to reflect the universal Church more fully. New bishops need to make known their wishes about which representatives should be invited, both from the area they are leaving and that to which they are going.

6. The individual's commitment & empowerment now

In several ways the revised rite brings a sharp focus to bear on the new bishop. The Archbishop's charge is addressed directly to him. He is required to express his personal commitment in the eleven specific undertakings that form the ordination vows. Hands are laid on him individually. The Archbishop also gives him the Bible and anoints him, and he is personally welcomed in his new capacity at The Peace. At the end of the service the Archbishop presents him with a pastoral staff, and leads him out amongst the people.

In the Swedish rite of 1987, which I have witnessed on several occasions, it is now customary for representative clergy and laity of the bishop's new diocese to share in the laying on of hands, and later to clothe him or her with the insignia of office – cope, mitre, pectoral cross and pastoral staff.

By the end of the service new bishops are very much aware not only of their new responsibilities, but also of the immense affirmation and support – divine and human – by which they are fortified.

FUTURE

A forward thrust is discernable within the service in the following ways:

7. God's future purpose and goal

A clear sense of movement and direction is conveyed by Jesus' words recorded in John's account of the Last Supper: *'During supper Jesus, knowing that the Father had given all things into his hands, and that he had come from God and was going to God, got up from the table...'* (John 13, 3). Like any celebration of the eucharist, the consecration service looks forward to the heavenly banquet in which God desires us to partake. In the Nicene Creed we affirm that: *'He will come again in glory to judge the living and the dead ...We look for the resurrection of the dead, and the life of the world to come.'* During the eucharistic prayer the people acclaim: *'Christ will come again'* or *'We proclaim your death, Lord Jesus, until you come in glory.'*

In the *Niagara Report* we drew attention to the sense in which the whole People of God is directed towards a heavenly goal:

> *'The journey on which the Church is engaged has a goal and a direction which shape the whole character of the mission of the people from the beginning. In the ministry, death and resurrection of Jesus the Church has been given a vision of the outcome of history ... It is, therefore to Christ that we look while running with*

resolution the race for which we are entered ... In him we have the confidence to view the future as the triumph of the Kingdom of God. We are the people who know the final outcome of the story, without yet knowing the details of the plot. Indeed, because the Church has been let in on the outcome of the story of the world, the Church's life and witness change the plot of history.'

(paragraph 35)

The hope of heaven and the Christian understanding of salvation do, indeed, touch the whole meaning of the universe – nothing less.

8. The Church's future expectation

As the new bishop stands on the brink of his new tasks, the Archbishop outlines what episcopal ministry will entail. All ministry has to be dynamic and forward looking. Ephesians 4 speaks of us all growing up in every way into him who is the head, even Christ. It talks of coming to maturity, to the measure of the full stature of Christ. The ordinal rightly underlines the corporate aspects of the bishop's job description. Chapter 5 will examine the main components of the bishop's ministry, and the right balance between them. At my own consecration Michael Mayne's sermon had some useful things to say about expectations (see appendix). It is crucial for new bishops to clarify at the outset of their ministry which right expectations they will play up to and which wrong ones they will reject. This stance will run through their whole style of leadership.

9. The individual's future accountability and hope

God is faithful, but there is no guarantee that each bishop will prove equally faithful throughout his life and ministry. The Archbishop's charge draws his attention to the accountability he owes to God:

'You are to ... prepare [God's people] to stand before him when at last he comes in glory ... Pray therefore that you may be conformed more and more to the image of God's Son, so that through the outpouring of the Holy Spirit your life and ministry may be made holy and acceptable to God'.

At the laying on of hands the prayer includes these words:

'Defend him from all evil, that he may, as a faithful steward, be presented blameless with all your household and, at the last, enter your eternal joy ...'

The element of spirituality will continue to be of vital importance for him. The second of the consecration vows responds to the question: *'Will you be diligent in prayer, in reading Holy Scripture, and in all studies that will deepen your faith ..?'*

The eleventh one asks: *'Will you then, in the strength of the Holy Spirit, continually stir up the gift of God that is in you ...?'* Each time the new bishop answers: *'By the help of God, I will'.* This pinpoints the vital necessity for him to remain in touch with God through all the time ahead, to be spiritually alive and to grow in personal holiness. There is no doubt that this was the inner secret of Bishop Edward King's remarkable ministry and its lasting impact on the parishes of Lincolnshire. People knew that they had been in the presence of a saint, and in this diocese we commemorate him as such. Any bishop must remain strongly rooted in Christ, or he is nothing. Chapter 6 will explore the bishop's inner life and discipline of prayer.

CATAPULTED INTO THE WIDER SCENE

When you are consecrated bishop, it is certainly a very special day and a major public occasion. It is, indeed, a moment that in a profound way touches the very meaning of the universe and the direction of human history.

'The Kingdom of God is served beyond the Church; ... and God may often have to work despite and against the Church. Because the Church betrays its mission it requires episcopé to recall it, rebuke it and reform it'

(Niagara Report, paragraph 40)

When consecration catapults a new bishop from the local into the wider scene, he or she becomes more of a public person than was the case as a priest. Privacy or keeping a low profile become no longer possible in quite the same way as before.

CHAPTER 4

Getting into the Job

Going public

After consecration the new bishop's initial phase of activity is mainly concerned with 'going public' in this role and becoming known in church and community life.

Some preliminary arrangements for this induction process will have been set up by colleagues. In my own case, for example, I was installed as a canon of Lincoln cathedral, and welcomed at special services in Grimsby and Scunthorpe, the two main urban centres of my pastoral area. Simon and Mary Phipps also hosted a party at Bishop's House for Mary and me to meet the two archdeacons and twelve rural deans with whom I would be working, together with their wives. A different pattern is appropriate when a diocesan bishop takes his place at the established hub of a see city, but at the periphery of the diocese suitable occasions need to be devised for a new bishop – whether diocesan or suffragan – to be seen and known locally. When Bob Hardy, Bill Ind and Alastair Redfern arrived, the senior staff arranged a series of corporate communion services for groups of neighbouring deaneries when the new bishop would preside and preach, and clergy, leading laity and community representatives at district level would have the chance to take part. This worked well, and enabled a wide circle of people to feel that they had met the new leader who had joined us, though sadly ecumenical participation was barely considered. An overall strategic pattern of induction needs to be set up for the new bishop to make initial contact with leaders of the community, the churches and other faith groups.

In Grimsby the Mayor laid on a formal luncheon when senior councillors and officers welcomed Mary and me. In Cleethorpes when I called at the Town Hall to sign the visitors' book the Mayor's welcome, though in a lower key, was no less warm. Other centres made no overtures, no doubt reflecting the fact that the office I held did not strike much of a chord with local leaders outside the Grimsby / Cleethorpes conurbation. Indeed, the public at large has little understanding of a bishop's territorial responsibilities. They seem to imagine that the Bishop of Lincoln can mostly be found at his cathedral, or his suffragans at the principal parish church of their see town. I lost count of the number of times that people told me, "I was christened at your church" (meaning St James' Minster, Grimsby). It would be churlish to respond, "Which of the 380 churches in my pastoral area do you mean?" Considerable time and effort are required to build up a network of effective links with congregations and communities right across the area, and to enable the bishop to express his or her direct concern for their well-being.

The local radio and press, Humberside Police and the Bankers' Institute were quick off the mark with various invitations. The largest local employer in Grimsby is the Health Service, and the hospital chaplain arranged an induction programme for me. Similarly, the team of industrial chaplains in Grimsby laid on an interesting day of visits and seminars for me to learn something of the docks and frozen food industry, whilst those in Scunthorpe provided something similar with British Steel.

In my first three months I carried out an initial round of visits to the twelve chapters of clergy covering my pastoral area, comprising about 150 clergy, and began to discover something about them and their families. The normal rolling programme of the Diocesan Synod, the Bishop's Council and various boards or councils brought me in contact with most of the specialist officers and key personnel of the diocese within my first year in post. However, ecumenical contacts were much slower to develop, and it became apparent how much we were all trapped within our own denominational structures.

DEVELOPING MUTUAL ACQUAINTANCE

Building up acquaintance and trust with people over such a wide area is bound to take some time, since frequent face-to-face contact is not possible. I was quite prepared to work at this steadily, but what came as a surprise was that most people perceived me only in my current role. They had little idea what experience I brought with me. One parish priest, for example, keen to introduce First Communion before Confirmation, was astonished to discover that I had explored this topic several years earlier; he had scarcely begun to address many of the issues raised by the Ely Report (1971), which the Tettenhall team ministry had fully debated and with which it had experimented. One Sunday when I officiated during an interregnum the churchwarden commented that "he had never seen a bishop conduct the whole service", and wondered if I could manage by myself! Another parish priest was having problems with his new deacon, but clearly had no inkling that I had already trained eight deacons. In two team ministries difficulties arose over team vicars from district churches conducting weddings at the main parish church – a matter we had satisfactorily resolved at Tettenhall. These are examples of pastoral issues of which I had a wealth of experience. The challenge now was to share the fruits of that experience gently and appropriately, whilst avoiding self-importance.

At the same time I had much to learn or re-learn, since building up acquaintance is essentially a mutual process. There were lots of new names and places to be discovered, as within any large organisation. About half the population of Lincoln diocese is urban and, having worked in the industrial West Midlands, I felt quite at home with many aspects of urban and suburban ministry. However, there were other realities to address, such as high seasonal unemployment along the coast, pockets of acute poverty, and social deprivation in the deeply rural scene. It would have been foolish to push my own preconceived agenda. I was largely unaware of corporate diocesan policy, and did not yet know the mind of the diocesan bishop. My ignorance was brought home to me vividly at a deanery synod meeting when the rural dean invited me to share my previous experiences. After my talk the first few questions from the audience showed that the situation I had described was so far removed from theirs as to make my comments barely relevant, e.g. structuring a marriage preparation programme for 60 couples a year, whereas most of the clergy present would be lucky to conduct six weddings a year. I had described how the leadership of a confirmation scheme for 100 participants had been devolved to two dozen lay helpers, but this deanery was working with much smaller and less viable numbers. I had discussed the training of house-group leaders, yet few Lincolnshire parishes at that time had any house-groups. I needed to look and listen very attentively to understand the dynamics of this very different scene.

In some respects the diocese to which I had come struck me as being twenty years behind the times. Yet in other ways I discovered that Lincoln was leading the field nationally in terms of pastoral re-organisation, local ministry, women's ministry and some aspects of ecumenism. Gradually I grew aware of the privilege of belonging to a great diocese with a long history, its own personalities and its own distinctive 'feel'.

TAPPING INTO ONE'S RESOURCES

Adjusting to this new environment felt like joining a motorway in the fast lane. It was a stressful experience, and one I had to face in greater isolation than when previously surrounded by the day-to-day support of a parochial team ministry. When one is under pressure, there is always a danger of taking refuge within an earlier and more familiar role. Cardinal John Heenan described in his autobiography *'Not the Whole Truth'* how, in his early days as Bishop of Leeds, he sought solace in reverting inappropriately to the role of a parish priest. I was quickly driven to ask: what are my resources? It was important to identify and re-assess them, so as to be able to draw upon them consciously and to the full. They seemed to me to lie in six main directions:

- a) God himself
- b) My immediate family
- c) Key people
- d) Equipment and set-up
- e) Stored knowledge and experience
- f) The personality that God has given me

a) Relating to God through private prayer

The second of the ordination vows has already been mentioned: *'Will you be diligent in prayer, in reading Holy Scripture, and in all studies that will deepen your faith and fit you to bear witness to the truth of the gospel?'* Such diligence requires a bishop always to give private prayer and Bible reading a high priority. In my experience there are three main difficulties in achieving this. First, patterns of devotion that worked well at theological college and in parochial life no longer fit one's circumstances if there is no chapel in which to find peace and quiet, and if there are no colleagues with whom to pray the daily office. Some bishops have the opportunity for weekday worship in their cathedral or with their chaplain, but for suffragans this is generally not the case. Furthermore, the pressures on one's time and attention are far greater than before. Finally, travel that often involves starting out early, getting home late or being away overnight renders impossible any standardised daily routine. A more flexible strategy has to be devised, based partly on regular patterns that are achievable some of the time, and partly on opportunities, alternatives and ways of compensating. When the right balance cannot be achieved within a particular day or group of days, time-slots for preparation and recovery must be built in beforehand and afterwards.

When living in central Grimsby I found it necessary to create my own makeshift oratory in an outhouse next to the back garden during the summer or, during colder seasons, in a spare bedroom. Otherwise, it was impossible to escape domestic noises and the telephone. It became my normal practice to set aside about an hour each day on average, in one or two chunks, with three staple ingredients: meditation, the daily office and intercessions. A separate chapter is later devoted to the inner life of the spirit.

b) Immediate family

Anybody who has to move house on account of changing their job is fortunate if they can be supported by their nuclear family. Doing it alone could be very hard. When plucked from the soil where you have previously flourished, you are vulnerable until fresh roots can be established.

When we moved to Grimsby Mary was 37 years old, and our children were aged 10 and 8. It meant major changes for us all, and at first we needed one another more than ever. As I settled into episcopal ministry my family proved to be a huge resource, not least in keeping me earthed in the realities of ordinary life. At that stage some of our neighbours were unfriendly and of no real help, though in later years at Irby our neighbours became good friends.

It was providential for Mary and me that we were actively involved in the Association for Marriage Enrichment from the mid 1970's, and jointly took part over several years in 'workshops' to develop and strengthen our marriage. Mary also trained as a Marriage Guidance counsellor (or 'Relate' as it is now called). This gave us some of the tools we needed to cope with added strains in our marriage. I wrote in my journal:

'At first Mary was meeting too few people and I too many for comfort. We are developing separate circles of acquaintance – hers mostly local and mine spread across the northern part of the diocese. This is inevitable, and similar to the experience of most normal families. Most men do not work from home, and their associates would not usually be closely involved with their wife and family ...

We have found ourselves less in step with each other than usual, and responding in different ways to all the changes. Partly through increased pressure of outward circumstances and partly through the difference between our personal responses to our new situations, we have discovered ambiguities in some of the decisions made on what we each believed was a corporate basis. I am glad that this has not pushed us apart, and that we have the will and capacity to work through these new pressures together. I hope that during our month's holiday we can clarify various issues of communication between us. Mary is giving me excellent support, and being very understanding about the new issues I am facing ...'

There is a huge difference in moving from the kind of shared ministry that is possible in a parish, where there are many callers at the vicarage, to working from the comparative isolation of a suffragan's house. The bishop's wife can be on her own a lot, and much less involved in her husband's job than before. If he was previously an archdeacon or sector minister, the difference for his wife may be far less. A later chapter will explore more fully the longer-term issues affecting home and family.

c) Key people

The new bishop also needs to identify other human resources, and to connect with them as soon as possible. The first line of advice and support is the senior staff group, especially the archdeacons and other bishops. They are all busy people, and may be based some way off. It is vital to work out how best to consult them quickly and easily. Rural deans and deanery lay chairmen are a strategic link in the chain of communication across the diocese, and combine local knowledge with a pastoral overview. A handful of leading people in various aspects of community life needs to be identified with the aid of one's colleagues, such as Members of Parliament, chief officers of local authorities, police commanders, senior representatives of industry and education, etc with whom to become personally acquainted. Early contact is desirable with one's ecumenical counterparts and, where other faith communities have a significant presence, with their leaders.

A local congregation needs to be found where the bishop's family can worship regularly and he or she can also attend when not engaged in public duties. This is a delicate matter, as some clergy can feel very threatened. We were fortunate to find two churches where we could appear in the congregation without giving the clergy a nervous breakdown! One was St James' Grimsby, and the other was St Lawrence's Church Stretton near our holiday cottage in Shropshire. It is vital for the bishop's family to be able to belong somewhere as ordinary Christians, and not feel rootless.

As part of my in-service training I was required to set up my own Support Group, with whom to share confidentially the content and focus of my ministry. They met several times over a two year period, and were chaired by a United Reformed minister who was an industrial chaplain. The other members I invited were Mary, a team rector, the diocesan bishop's PA, a woman counsellor and social worker who belonged to a New Life Church and an Anglican layman who was a senior manager at Courtauld's. This group of people was challenging and supportive in equal measure, and I found their help invaluable. Every new bishop would do well to have such a group in the early years of the episcopate. In the long run it can also be useful to belong to a cell group or regional bishops' group, but these are unlikely to offer so much detailed attention to one particular bishop's agenda whilst he or she gets established in the job. Maintaining personal links in other parts of the country is also important, but this requires conscious effort if one happens to live where friends are unlikely to pop in. An open invitation to "look us up next time you are passing through Grimsby" did not produce much response!

d) Equipment and set-up

At the time of my consecration there was no house or office for the Bishop of Grimsby. My predecessor, who lived in the market town of Louth, passed on three items: a car provided by the Church Commissioners, a pastoral staff and an old red chimere. There were no papers or records, nor any office equipment. From Tettenhall came my own library and desk, and a few personal filing cabinets. I had to start from scratch in purchasing a dictating machine, long-carriage typewriter, intercom telephone and set of filing cabinets, and to find a part-time secretary. The Diocesan Secretary and Church Commissioners' Bishoprics' Department were helpful, but I received no guidelines as to what I was entitled to request. Only years later did such useful technical aids as a photocopier, shredder, mobile phone, electric typewriter, fax machine, word processor, laptop or the internet become available to people like myself. Securing a basic office set-up and plugging into diocesan information systems are pre-conditions of effective episcopal ministry. Most bishops nowadays have a BlackBerry or iPhone, and computer literacy has become essential.

In the 1970's I regarded a car radio as a luxury, but was grateful to another bishop for urging me to get one. Driving about 14,000 miles a year on the roads of Lincolnshire I enjoyed many informative programmes and learned much from them, not least in the field of current affairs.

Mary and I brought from Tettenhall enough cutlery and wine glasses to cater for about 40 people. We supplemented our own crockery with a stock of dinner plates, soup/coffee mugs and ramekin dishes, as well as several stacking chairs. New bishops should receive clear guidance on the equipment needed to do the job properly and, where necessary, be reimbursed for the cost of obtaining it as official property of the see.

e) Stored knowledge and experience

A bishop needs to be well resourced in his or her own thinking and knowledge. To be constantly giving out involves drawing upon the fund of knowledge and experience that have been accumulated over many years, as well as continuing to build it up. This point is well made in Bernard's sermon on the Song of Songs:

> *'If you are wise, you will show yourself to be a reservoir and not an irrigation channel. A channel empties out as fast as it takes in, but a reservoir waits until it is full before it overflows and so shares its surplus ... We have all too few such reservoirs in the Church at present, though we have plenty of channels – those who wish to pour out when they themselves have not yet been filled up. They are readier to speak than to listen, eager to teach what they themselves do not yet know, and keen to exercise authority over other people though they have not yet learnt how to control themselves ... Be filled yourself; then pour out your fullness – but discreetly, mind!*
>
> ('Song of Songs', pp 45-46)

Three distinct issues are at stake here: how to store knowledge, how to access it and how to apply its fruits. There can be no substitute for the habits of sound learning: to keep a record of books actually read, to summarise points noted, to write down one's reflections from time to time, to collect interesting lectures or articles, and to retain one's own sermons, reports and papers. If these materials are indexed for easy retrieval, it becomes possible to emulate that *'master of the household who brings out of his treasure what is new and what is old'* (Mat 13, 52).

The bishop must make a habit of browsing repeatedly over the range of information that he or she has already stored away. It is helpful, too, to think laterally: seeking parallel situations or issues, distilling what principles are involved and what choices of action are available, and pondering what So-and-so would have thought, said or done. It is wasteful if one does not bring one's accumulated wisdom to bear, yet in applying and sharing this there is need for sensitivity and humility. In one of Edward King's early letters to a trainee teacher he stressed the distinction between 'knowledge' and 'wisdom':

'Get all the knowledge you can, labour to become a perfect master of all the subjects you may have to teach. You must have this knowledge, but always remember that 'knowledge' and 'wisdom' are different things. "Knowledge is proud that she knows so much, Wisdom is humble that she knows no more". Look out St James 3, 17 and remember it when your blackboard and chalk are ready. [This verse reads: 'The wisdom that is from above is first pure, than peaceable, gentle, willing to yield, full of mercy and good fruits, without a trace of partiality or hypocrisy'.]

(*'Bishop King's Spiritual Letters'*, **page 2**)

Kenneth Stevenson has commented how, when amongst colleagues in the House of Bishops, he could often spot which defining job someone had held before becoming a bishop and how this impacted on the way he approached the matter under debate:

'Some bishops are obviously former parish priests; others were theological teachers; some have been involved in lay training; others have worked a good deal with ordinands; some ran cathedrals, which could give them a strong liturgical sense, or a convincing civic awareness; while others again were archdeacons, who seemed to know the ropes rather better than many of the others ... When people are made bishops, they need to be aware of those shaping ministries. This can help them to get into their new role, and not remain what they were ...'

(Final presidential address to Portsmouth Diocesan Synod, June 2009)

f) God-given personality

When Simon Phipps first approached me in August 1978 about becoming Bishop of Grimsby, I had one big worry. If I took on this office, could I remain a human being? This was my real and deep concern – an apprehension lest the pressures and expectations of the role might force me to be less true to myself than I had been as a parish priest. Amongst the factors that helped me was a memorable phrase from Michael Mayne's sermon at my consecration: *"It's <u>you</u> we want, not a de luxe version of you".*

Bernard advised Pope Eugenius that consideration of one's own self fell into three divisions: **what** you are, **who** you are and **what sort** of person you are – i.e. your nature, your role and your character. On this last point he made some useful observations:

> *'Strip off the disguise of this fleeting honour ... so that you may consider yourself in your bare nakedness. For naked you came from your mother's womb (Job 1, 21). Were you then wearing a sacred stole? Did you then have glittering gems about your person? Were you robed in flowery silks? ... If you scatter all these things like morning clouds, what you will see is a human being – naked, poor, wretched and miserable. Whilst thinking of yourself as Supreme Pontiff bear in mind that you not only were, but still are, worthless ashes.*
>
> *Carefully distinguish how far you are what you are through your own efforts, and how far through the gift of God. See whether you have advanced in virtue, in wisdom, in understanding, in loveliness of character; or whether – God forbid! – you have regressed. Are you more or less patient than usual? Are you more quick-tempered or more good-natured? Are you more arrogant or more humble? Are you more approachable or more austere? Are you more easily persuaded or more stubborn? Are you more diffident or more large-hearted? Are you more conscientious, or more slipshod? Are you more fearful or more confident than you should be? What a vast field this opens up for your consideration! These are just the seeds of a few ideas for you to work on.*
>
> **(Condensed from** *'On Consideration'*, **Book II, 18 & 20)**

One of Simon Phipps' strengths was to be thoroughly realistic about what he could and could not do. In his early years at Lincoln he worked out what kind of diocesan bishop he had it in him to be, and then concentrated on making that contribution. He was a modest and godly man, true to the gifts God gave him (see my essay in *'Simon Phipps – a Portrait'*, edited by D. Machin, Continuum 2003). Following this example I have tried, in reviewing my ministry from time to time, to assess my personality honestly. For example, in July 1982 I wrote:

> *'I see myself as open and friendly; conciliatory rather than confrontational; sensitive to what needs doing in a situation rather than insisting on "my way"; prayerful, dependable and flexible; efficient, but less fussed at imperfections than*

I used to be; loving and prepared to make allowances for other people. But I also have a psychological need for orderliness, a shrinking or tendency to detach myself from emotional involvement, and a strong inclination to stay safely within known limits. I am also very much affected by lack of sleep or food.'

The Myers-Briggs type indicator [MBTI] can be a useful tool for understanding one's own personality and the way it works. Whatever type of personality one may have, it is important to dance to one's own tune rather than someone else's, to acknowledge the pressures and frustrations of ministry as well as its joys and satisfactions, and to hang on to the 'real me'. I found talking through these factors with my Support Group a constructive and liberating exercise. It is important to sustain one's vision and energy over a span of many years, and to find in responsibilities beyond the diocese some refreshment from the regular round of duties within it.

Time and again I have recalled with gratitude Michael Mayne's words at my consecration:

'... to care passionately for the people and for the Kingdom; but still to be able to laugh at yourself with that laughter which is healing and redemptive, for it means viewing yourself with a sort of loving forgiveness which is an echo of God's loving forgiveness of you.'

To a new woman bishop I would wish to say:

You bring to this new office considerable experience and gifts. Remember that we have 'gifts that differ'. You don't have to be a bishop in just the same way as the men. You will represent Christ to us in a different way – your own distinctive way. God wants you, as a bishop, to be your own person, not some episcopal clone. Entrust your ministry and your style of ministry to God. Rely on Him. Be who you are, and He will enable you.

PROVISIONAL GOALS

When the moment comes to make a start as bishop, a key question is: am I going to run this job, or is it going to run me? A balance has to be struck between being proactive and responsive. A pace has to be found that is sustainable. I freely admit to a number of mistakes and misjudgements over priorities and time management at first, from which I learned some useful lessons about diary control and pastoral priorities – points to be dealt with more fully later.

Two essential practices are to keep a *record of activities* and to set a *time-scale for review*. My own approach was to record all interviews and home visits carried out, services conducted, sermons and talks given, meetings attended, parishes/

deaneries or other organisations contacted, letters posted, etc. Without this factual basis one's subsequent analysis was bound to lack specificity and rely too heavily on subjective impressions, which are notoriously unreliable. For my first review I set the horizon at one month after starting the job. Then it was every six months for the next seven years, and annually thereafter.

CHAPTER 5

Coming to Grips with the Role

WHAT ARE A BISHOP'S MAIN RESPONSIBILITIES?

If many church members have only a hazy idea as to what the bishop's role amounts to, the general public's grasp of it is even hazier. There is no unique blueprint stored up somewhere, uniformly applicable to every era and culture. The historic episcopate has evolved over time and space. As the 1888 Lambeth Quadrilateral recognised, it has been 'locally adapted in the methods of its administration to the varying needs of the nations and peoples called of God into the unity of the Church' (Resolution 11d). Overviews of this development can be found in the following reports:

> *'The Niagara Report'* (Church House Publishing 1988), §§ 41-59
> *'Episcopal Ministry'* – the Cameron Report (CHP 1990), §§ 26-337
> *Episcopal Ministry within the Apostolicity of the Church'* – the Lund Statement (Lutheran World Federation 2007), §§ 5-26

In this chapter I start by reviewing a dozen contemporary examples of the bishop's job description. This may save new bishops time and trouble in tracking down sources which they may not have readily available. My focus then moves to a more personal distillation – i.e. how I initially saw, and later came to re-envisage, the shape of this ministry. In the light of experience and reflection my own ideas of the episcopal role changed, and I try to track how my mental picture of it developed and how this worked out in practice.

A SELECTION OF RECENT JOB DESCRIPTIONS

a) Revised Catechism 1962

A brief and inadequate description is given in the Church of England's Revised Catechism (clause 16):

> *The work of a Bishop is -*
> *to be a chief shepherd and a ruler in the Church;*

to guard the Faith;
to ordain and confirm;
and to be the chief minister of the Word and Sacraments in his diocese.

This gives no clue as to the bishop's proper concern with society as a whole, or to a prophetic element in his or her ministry. This is a regrettable omission.

b) Canons of the Church of England (revised in the 1960's)

Canon C.18 entitled 'Of Diocesan Bishops' picks up similar points, expanding them in such phrases as the following:

§1 *Every bishop is the chief pastor of all that are within his diocese, as well clergy as laity, and their father in God ...*

It appertains to his office to teach and to uphold sound and wholesome doctrine, and to banish and drive away all erroneous and strange opinions ...

... himself an example of righteous and godly living, it is his duty to set forward and maintain quietness, love and peace among all men.

§2/3 *Every bishop has within his diocese jurisdiction as Ordinary ... exercised by the bishop himself or by ... (another) commissary ...*

§4 *Every bishop is, within his diocese, the principal minister, and to him belongs the right ... of celebrating the rites of ordination and confirmation; of conducting, ordering, controlling and authorising all services in churches ...; of instituting to all vacant benefices ...; of admitting by licence to all other vacant ecclesiastical offices; of holding visitations ... that he may get some good knowledge of the state, sufficiency and ability of the clergy and other persons ...; and of being president of the diocesan synod.*

§6 *Every bishop ... shall provide, as much as in him lies, that in every place within his diocese there shall be sufficient priests to minister the word and sacraments to the people that are therein.*

§7 *Every bishop shall correct and punish all such as be unquiet, disobedient or criminous, within his diocese, according to such authority as he has by God's Word and is committed to him by the laws and ordinances of this realm.*

c) Second Vatican Council

The Roman Catholic Church updated its theological rationale of the Church and the episcopate in two main documents: the dogmatic constitution on 'The Church' (*Lumen Gentium* 1964), and the decree on 'The Pastoral Office of Bishops in the Church' (1965). Both documents combine considerable theological vision and pastoral experience. Though centred round the Roman Pontiff and Curia, they contain a good deal of material that is none the less relevant to all bishops, including those not of the papal obedience. The shape of the bishop's ministry follows the traditional pattern of Christ's threefold office as Prophet, Priest and King. This pattern of thought can be traced as far back as Eusebius and John Chrysostom, and its later development by Calvin and Newman has been well summarised by Paul Avis (see *'Beyond the Reformation?'*, pages 9 and following). Vatican II sees the bishop's principal duties as: to teach, to celebrate the eucharist, and to govern the diocese (see *Lumen Gentium* §25-27). The whole tone of the document on Bishops is practical and pastoral, and shows sensitivity to widely varying situations. The last chapter stresses the need for bishops to work collegially for the wellbeing of the whole church – a new emphasis that enhanced the status of Roman Catholic and Uniate bishops vis-à-vis the papacy, despite leaving unchanged the teaching of Vatican I on the Pope's infallibility and universal jurisdiction.

d) Lambeth Conference 1968

The report of Section 2 (*'Renewal in Ministry'*) reflected on the nature of the episcopate:

'The service of the bishop has its centre in the liturgical and sacramental life of the Church, in his celebration of the Eucharist and in ordination and confirmation. It is developed in his work of teaching and safeguarding the faith and in his general care for the up-building and equipping of the Church. It is concerned with deepening and broadening ecumenical relationships and reaches out in service, witness, and prophetic word to the life of the human community as whole.

Christ who is the Servant is also Lord. The bishop is called to exercise an authority which is rooted in the authority of the risen Christ. This authority has to be exercised according to the pattern that he gave (John 13) ... The bishop has to lead people in their obedience to Christ, leading them and taking them with him. As a teacher he must try to evoke the creative thinking of his people. As an administrator he must call out and train their varied gifts so that the Church may move forward as one in its varied mission.

The commission of Christ is given to the whole Church. The bishop is therefore to exercise his ministry in fellowship with others. In his own diocese he must guide, teach and serve in an ordered fellowship with clergy and laity. He can fulfil his role as focus of authority in his diocese only because his ministry is exercised in partnership with brother bishops and with the regional and universal Church ...'

(pages 108-109)

Where the diocese is so big that the bishop needs to share his responsibility with a suffragan or assistant bishop, the report recommends that such a colleague 'should exercise all episcopal functions and have an equal place in the Councils of the Church'.

The report of Section 3 (*'Renewal in Unity'*) responded to Vatican II with a characteristically Anglican understanding of collegiality and primacy:

> 'The collegiality of the episcopate must always be seen in the context of the conciliar character of the Church, involving the 'consensus fidelium', in which the episcopate has its place.'

(page 138)

e)   Lambeth Conference 1978

The ensuing conference voiced its urgent concern that the Church should engage with moral issues affecting contemporary society, and make its urban and rural mission more effective. In this context it passed an important resolution about the bishop's ministry amongst the general public, not just in church circles:

> '... a bishop is called to be one with the apostles in proclaiming Christ's resurrection and interpreting the Gospel, and to testify to Christ's sovereignty as Lord of Lords and King of Kings. In order to do this effectively, he will give major attention to his public ministry. Reflecting the ministry of the prophets, he will have a concern for the well-being of the whole community (especially of those at a disadvantage) not primarily for the advantage or protection of the Church community. The bishop should be ready to be present in secular situations, to give time to the necessary study, to find skilled advisers and to take sides publicly if necessary (in ecumenical partnership if at all possible) about issues which concern justice, mercy and truth. Members of the Church should be prepared to see that the bishop is supported in such ministry.'

(Resolution 18, page 44)

This added a new dimension to what the previous Lambeth Conference had said about the bishop's functions. The report of Section 2 (*'The people of God and ministry'*) reiterated the earlier insights, and added fresh material about the vital inter-connection between episcopal authority and synodical government (see pages 76-77):

> '...Christ is the Head of the body, the faithful are the members. The bishop receives his authority from both Head and members, and neither without the other. This authority is not to be exercised without the Church, that is, without collegial consultation at proper times with brother bishops, and without ensuring

that it has the support and consent of the rest of the Church as far as possible. This authority cannot be evident in its fullness as long as the Church is divided ...

Within the diocese, the bishop's authority is interpreted and expressed in the missionary pastoral situations, liturgical and teaching activities, and through his leadership and participation in the synods and councils of the Church.

The guardianship of the faith is a collegial responsibility of the episcopate. Synodical government should make provision for this responsibility to be fulfilled ...

Anglicanism has firmly committed itself to constitutional episcopacy in which the government of the Church by the bishop is limited and supported by synods, canons, and other methods whereby the whole Church – clergy and laity – participate in its government and mission.

The bishop is the sign and agent of unity and continuity within the diocese and within the whole Church.'

f) Revised Ordinals

The Church of England's ordinal was revised in 1978 ready for inclusion in the Alternative Services Book 1980. It was first used in January 1979 at my own consecration. A significant feature is the inclusion of a paragraph describing the bishop's job [see § 13, page 388], where the following components are named:

> leading and overseeing the Church
> furthering unity, upholding discipline and guarding the faith
> promoting mission
> praying for those committed to his charge
> teaching and governing in God's name and interpreting the gospel
> knowing his people and being known by them
> ordaining, sending and enabling new ministers
> leading worship
> administering discipline with firmness and mercy
> caring specially for the outcast and needy
> declaring forgiveness

A generation later in 2006 a second revision was completed as part of the 'Common Worship' series. It added an introduction to the service, placing the bishop's ministry firmly in the context of the royal priesthood of the whole people of God. It also augmented the job description to take account of such new factors as the burgeoning of lay ministries and the global dimension of Christian social responsibility:

'(Bishops) are to baptize and confirm, nurturing God's people in the life of the Spirit and leading them in the way of holiness. They are to discern and foster the gifts of the Spirit in all who follow Christ, commissioning them to minister in his name ... Following the example of the prophets and the teaching of the apostles, they are to proclaim the gospel boldly, confront injustice and work for righteousness and peace in all the world.'

g) World Council of Churches' Lima document 1982

The report *'Baptism, Eucharist and Ministry'* was the fruit of some 50 years' multilateral ecumenical dialogue on Faith and Order issues. Certain paragraphs in the Ministry section are particularly relevant to bishops. §26 identifies three aspects of ministry that need to be held together: the *personal*, the *collegial* and the *communal*. §29 summarizes the functions of bishops. §34 spells out what is meant by the apostolicity of the whole Church. §38 speaks of episcopal succession "as a sign, though not a guarantee, of the continuity and unity of the Church". These ecumenical formulations produced considerable resonance and have been endorsed in several agreements.

h) Niagara Report 1987

This report of the world-wide Anglican-Lutheran dialogue body did not just re-evaluate the historical development of episcopacy. It also focussed on the bishop's role in leading and sustaining the Church's mission, and posed a number of key questions aimed at helping bishops to be self-critical about the renewal and reform of their ministry (see especially §§ 99-110).

i) Lambeth Conference 1988

The report of Section 1 (*'Mission and Ministry'*) listed ten distinct aspects of the bishop's office:

'Under God, the bishop leads the local church in its mission to the world. Amongst other things, the bishop is:

- a) *a symbol of the Unity of the Church in its mission;*
- b) *a teacher and defender of the faith;*
- c) *a pastor of the pastors and of the laity;*
- d) *an enabler in the preaching of the Word, and in the administration of the Sacraments;*
- e) *a leader in mission and an initiator of outreach to the world surrounding the community of the faithful;*

f) *a shepherd who nurtures and cares for the flock of God;*
g) *a physician to whom are brought the wounds of society;*
h) *a voice of conscience within the society in which the local church is placed;*
i) *a prophet who proclaims the justice of God in the context of the Gospel of loving redemption;*
j) *a head of the family in its wholeness, its misery and its joy. The bishop is the family's centre of life and love.'*

(§151, page 61)

j) Materials from Sweden

The Church of Sweden at its Synod in 1987 adopted a new ordinal, which was first used the following year. It had many similarities to the Church of England's ASB ordinal, including a paragraph describing the bishop's job. The Swedish Bishops' Conference then produced a comprehensive document on the ministry of the Church in 1990, *'Bishop, Priest & Deacon in the Church of Sweden'* (in English). Its exposition of a bishop's responsibilities on pages 22-25 and pages 42-46 is a worthy Lutheran counterpart to Vatican II's document on 'The Pastoral Office of Bishops in the Church', and contains some memorable phrases – e.g.:

> '... *to be a bridge-builder, with the calling to work for the visible unity of the Church;*
>
> *to participate in public debate and give voice to the faith and values of the Church;*
>
> *to administer the spiritual heritage of the Church in such a way that it is not dissipated but increases;*
>
> *to pray for humility of the heart in accord with the example of Christ and, in faith, to seek forgiveness at the cross and new fortitude from the Risen One and, in spite of human weakness, to be the servant of divine unity.'*

(page 25)

The main responsibilities are seen as: doctrine, oversight, leadership and ordination. Administration is to be shared and delegated (see page 46).

k) Full Communion agreements between Anglicans & Lutherans

Building on the insights of the Niagara report, three regional agreements were reached which led to the establishment of Full Communion between Anglican and Lutheran churches in parts of Northern Europe and in North America (*Porvoo 1996, Called to Common Mission 2000 and Waterloo 2001*). In each case an integral element in achieving this closer relationship was a shared understanding of the ministry of bishops and an acknowledgement that *'the episcopal office is valued and maintained'*. The fullest theological rationale was that in "Porvoo", chapter IV. A summary of the bishop's job description in the ordinals of each of the British, Irish, Nordic and Baltic Churches was given on pages 165-176 of *'Together in Mission & Ministry'* (Church House Publishing 1993, GS.1083).

l) Lutheran World Federation 'Lund statement' 2007

In April 2007 the Council of the Lutheran World Federation adopted a statement summarising how its member churches understood the ministry of oversight in the Church. This was the fruit of studies that had been taking place since 1983, and was largely based on material gathered from those ecumenical dialogues in which Lutherans had participated. Of particular interest are §§ 43-64.

On the issue of safeguarding sound doctrine a distinctively Lutheran emphasis emerges in the Lund statement that stands in marked contrast to Roman Catholic teaching on the *'magisterium'*, i.e. the right of the hierarchy to teach authoritatively:

> *'In the church there is no absolute distinction between the directed and the directing, between the teaching and the taught, between those who decide and those who are the objects of decision. All members of the church, lay and ordained, exercising different ministries, stand under the word of God; all are fallible sinners, but all are baptized and anointed by the Spirit. Mutual accountability binds together ordained ministers and other baptized believers.*
>
> *According to Lutheran understanding, the church exercises responsibility for its doctrine and practices through open, critical deliberation and transparent ecclesial processes. These processes, which can often be tension-filled, involve persons and church bodies with different responsibilities, aiming at the building of consensus and consensual action. Together with teachers of theology, pastors in congregations, persons called to a ministry of education and committed lay persons, episcopal ministers are especially called to judge doctrine in the life of the church, and to reject teaching that is contrary to the gospel ...'*

(§§ 51-52)

These twelve examples from recent decades illustrate what a plethora of models and images is available for describing the ministry of a bishop. It also shows that shifts of emphasis have occurred even within so short a period as my own working life.

My own distillation

a) Initial approach

No human being could fulfil all the expectations cited above, or be equally effective in carrying out the entire range of roles. Each bishop has to choose what his or her priorities will be. He or she must decide what the main headings are; what makes a good overall shape, and secures a fair balance between the elements; and, above all, what is personally sustainable.

A suffragan bishop's approach to the job is largely conditioned by what his or her diocesan bishop asks or implicitly expects. Some suffragans have spoken of feeling constrained and frustrated. For example, one told me that at his previous staff meeting the number of points for action by him were five and by his diocesan were thirty-five! Another, after seven years as a suffragan, had not been invited to conduct an ordination. This was not my experience at all – quite the opposite. Both Simon Phipps and Bob Hardy shared responsibility generously and delegated extensively, enabling their suffragans to exercise the full episcopal office, not just a thinned down version of it. The Lincoln model, as Bob once described it, was "one episcopate exercised by three bishops collegially".

I remember John Yates' advice when talking to me about the role of an area suffragan as he had experienced it in his days as Bishop of Whitby. His counsel was: 'Never think of it as *my* ministry. Think of it as Simon's and mine. No good purpose is served by trying to corner your own bit of the market.' I recall, too, what John Hammersley said when presenting me with a shepherd's crook on behalf of the Tettenhall team ministry: 'Never forget that all ministry is shared ministry'.

In March 1979 I publicly shared my reflections on the nature of the task before me through a sermon at St James', Grimsby and an article in the Grimsby Gazette. The following paragraphs condense and conflate the two:

> *'A bishop is not much use without the clergy and the laity. We all depend on one another, and I cannot hope to make any sense of my job apart from the total mission of the Church in this area. So my first task, as I see it, is to strengthen the Church's corporate ministry and to try to help each Christian (ordained and lay) to grow stronger in his or her daily ministry, wherever that may lie.*
>
> *This is not everyone's idea of a bishop. Recently a priest in Wolverhampton told me that people expect a bishop to be like a meteor – one who shines brightly for a short time and then disappears, perhaps never to be seen again! That is not my idea of a bishop. I have no ambition to be the dazzling solo performer,*

*and certainly no wish to be thought remote. Mine is a homelier aspiration: to be accessible, to be one of you, and to attach as much importance to informal, personal contact as to the big special occasion like a Confirmation. No meteor, but a human being and a Christian **like** you and **with** you. Together we must carry forward the work of Christ, and of course it will take a little time to get to know and trust each other. This is what corporate ministry is about. The bishop belongs firmly in that corporate context – hopefully as a leader, certainly as a fellow-member of the Christian team.*

It would be a mistake to spend all my time in church circles. God is not just concerned with the Church, but with the whole of life. It is a parody of religion to confine it to a separate compartment. This is why an integral part of my work as a bishop must be to interest and inform myself about the major aspects of life in South Humberside and North Lincolnshire. Here I have a lot to learn: about fishing, industry and commerce; local government and education; the media, health, leisure and the arts; unemployment, crime – in short, social needs and problems of all kinds. People expect the bishop to be a spokesman for the Christian point of view in public life. Before I can speak I must listen, and find out the complexities of the local situation. My hope is to support and encourage all those who are trying to ensure a Christian presence within the various sectors of community life. The secular world is the right and proper concern of us all.

A special part of the bishop's job is to be a friend and adviser to the clergy and their families. They come under a lot of pressure, not just out in the parish but right into their own homes. It often does not occur to parishioners that their clergy have personal needs of their own. Priests and their wives should have someone who cares about them. It is not just a question of trouble-shooting or picking up the bits when things go wrong, but an ongoing relationship. I want to help clergy and lay leaders in this part of the diocese to have a clearer vision of what they are trying to do, and greater courage to stand on their own feet in doing it.

*In all spiritual work undertaken by any of us what matters most is its quality, and the commitment to God that lies behind it. I shall try to spend a due proportion of my time in reading, studying and praying, so as to maintain the right foundations. Please remember me and my family in your prayers. I look forward to getting to know you and to working with you. Please come and say hello whenever you see me around in Grimsby. I am conscious how many of you there are who can help and share in Our Lord's work. **Together** we must worship God, love and build one another up, proclaim the Gospel and serve our community.'*

In July 1980 when I looked back over my first full year in office, I jotted down some observations. There had been many good occasions of public worship, including 55 services of Confirmation, 6 institutions of new incumbents and 2 ordinations. I had managed to join in the life of 110 different congregations.

With some sectors of the community I had built up links in that first year as opportunity arose, but it was not yet clear to me what initiatives to take next or what principle of selection to follow. A start was made on helping individual clergy to develop self-awareness about their gifts and limitations, and to be realistic about their targets. I encouraged a few to be bolder in experimentation. Their morale seemed to be strengthened by encouraging regular review and a carefully thought-out approach to continuing education. Such counselling as I undertook in person turned out to be mostly with clergy couples in marital difficulty.

Regarding staff work I made a false start by meeting the two northern archdeacons (Bill Dudman and David Scott) together each month, but soon found that it was better to handle separately the agenda of their different territories and their contrasting personalities. Between us we developed a more systematic approach to appointments and vacancies, of which we normally had about 20 in our terrain at any one time, and encouraged parishes to approach an interregnum not just as a gap to be filled but as a creative opportunity.

It took me some while to work out how to relate appropriately to diocesan field officers and specialists, especially those serving boards and committees that I chaired. The three major policy areas that I was asked to tackle in the diocese were: launching our Local Ministry scheme, re-structuring the whole Education set-up (150 Church Schools plus voluntary education with adults, young people and children), and developing links with the Roman Catholic dioceses of Brugge and Nottingham. At one stage I was under huge pressure when acting as chairman of five diocesan bodies. This involved a 70-mile round trip for every meeting, and vetting all the agendas, background documents and draft minutes. However, these responsibilities were later redistributed and became less burdensome.

b)   Re-stating the essence of 'episcopé'

In April 1983 after four years on the job I tried to re-state what I understood to be the essence of church leadership and pastoral oversight. Through study shared with other bishops and ecumenical colleagues, and through reflection on my own experience, my model had developed to a new level. The next page indicates the shape that I chose to put on the role in my middle and later Grimsby years. This shape structures the ensuing chapter headings, and each aspect is cross-referenced to the chapters that address it. As will quickly become clear, certain aspects of *episcopé* stand in perpetual tension with one other.

Episcopé has the following aspects:

1. **It is personal** – is the right kind of person: human, Christ-like; has firm roots in the Gospel and current church tradition through prayer & study; stands for faith and hope; and is committed to regular review and continuing professional development; *chapters 6-9 and 17*
2. **It is corporate** – not individualistic, but skilled in and committed to collaborative leadership; delegating, sharing in corporate consultation, and administering the Church's human and material resources professionally and competently; *chapters 10, 11 and 14*
3. **It is accountable** – to God for living up to one's calling and the vows of consecration; to the Church for obeying and upholding its discipline and canon law; and to all those with whom one is bound by a common purpose; *chapters 10 and 15-17*
4. **It cares systematically** for people within and beyond the church, in partnership with others, on a continuing basis and in crisis; *chapter 11*
5. **It encourages**, affirms, inspires, builds trust, floats ideas; equips and enables the ministry of others; and exemplifies by one's own ministry; *chapter 11*
6. **It challenges**, discerns and criticises prophetically, risking conflict and engaging seriously with contemporary realities; *chapters 11, 13 and 15*
7. **It leads** the offering of prayer and praise, including the sacraments; *chapter 12*
8. **It teaches**, proclaims, guards and interprets the Christian faith; explores and makes sense of current issues in the light of that faith; ensures that theological resources are available to laity and clergy sharing in ministry; and co-operates with those providing public education at all ages and levels; *chapter 13*
9. **It promotes mission** and sends new ministers, wisely deploying those already available and nurturing new life for all forms of ministry; engages with the secular world, and has a special concern for the outcast and needy; *chapters 14-15*
10. **It unifies** diverse views and contributions; minimises and overcomes divisions; and promotes ecumenism and catholicity. *chapters 15-16*

CHAPTER 6

The Inner Life

INNER CONSECRATION

This chapter deals with the inner core of the bishop's life as I have come to know it. The most essential aspect of *episcope*, as of all Christian discipleship and ministry, is to be rooted in God through prayer, reflection and study; to draw one's inspiration continually from the very heart of the gospel; and so to exist within the Church's living tradition as to be uplifted and borne along by its flow.

Before the archbishop ordains a new bishop he speaks of that inner consecration that is so necessary:

> *'We pray that you may offer to [God] your best powers of mind and spirit, so that as you follow the rule and teaching of Our Lord you may grow up into his likeness, and sanctify the lives of those with whom you have to do.'*

The following question introduces the second of the vows:

> *'Will you be diligent in prayer, in reading Holy Scripture, and in all studies that will deepen your faith and fit you to bear witness to the truth of the gospel?'*

Later the archbishop exhorts the candidate in these words:

> *'Pray that you may conformed more and more to the image of God's Son, so that through the outpouring of the Holy Spirit your life and ministry may be made holy and acceptable to God.'*

GREGORY'S ADVICE

In his *'Pastoral Rule'* Gregory commends two practices: constantly entering and leaving the tabernacle of God's presence, and meditating daily on Holy Scripture. Writing under the heading of 'Compassion and Prayerfulness' he says:

> *'Moses frequently went in and out of the tabernacle. Whilst inside he was caught up in contemplation; whilst outside he devoted himself to the concerns of the weak. Inwardly he pondered on the hidden things of God; outwardly he shouldered the burdens of earthly-minded human beings. In matters of doubt he always returned to the tabernacle to consult the Lord in front of the Ark of the Covenant. In this*

he undoubtedly set an example to bishops. When they are uncertain how to settle a secular matter, they should always go back for reflection as if to the tabernacle. Standing there – as it were before the Ark of the Covenant – they should consult the Lord as to whether a solution to their problems may be sought within the pages of the sacred Word.
He who was the Truth itself, revealed to us by taking on our human nature, engaged in prayer on the mountain as well as working miracles in the towns (cf. Lk 6, 12-19).

(*'Pastoral Rule'*, part II, chapter 5)

In the final section of Part II Gregory concludes:
'If the bishop meditates diligently and daily on the teachings of the sacred Word, the words of divine counsel will restore his sense of responsibility and his concern for the heavenly life, which are constantly worn down by frequent human dealings. One who spends long years in secular society should heed the twinges of his conscience and constantly be renewed in the love of his spiritual homeland ... David says: 'Lord, how I love your law: all the day long it is my study' (Ps 119, 97).'

I mentioned earlier the three staple ingredients for my daily time of private prayer: meditation, the daily office and intercessions. Let us examine these in turn.

Meditation

Usually I spend the first chunk of quiet time simply "being with God", unloading whatever is on my mind, and trying to restore my perspective on life. This may take only a few minutes or, on other days, over half an hour. The busier I am, the more I need it. The pressure is far less in the more spacious and reflective circumstances of retirement.

Does it really count as 'prayer' if I spend time before God mulling over thoughts that include problem-solving, prioritising and planning? What enables me to answer that question affirmatively is Bernard's idea of 'consideration'. It is worth looking in detail at what he wrote in *'On Consideration'*, his extended letter to a new Pope:

'Let me offer you my advice. If you give all your life and all your wisdom to action and none of it to consideration, should I commend you? In this matter I certainly do not commend you, nor would anyone who pays attention to Solomon's words: 'Only the one who has little business can become wise' (Ecclesiasticus 38, 24). *Action does not turn out well unless preceded by consideration. If you wish*

to give yourself entirely to others, like him who was made all things to all people (1 Cor 9, 22), I commend your human compassion, but only on condition that it is complete. How can it be complete when you yourself are left out? You, too, are human. Find room for yourself as well. What does it profit you if you gain the whole world, but forfeit your own life? (Mt 16, 26) ...

You are under an obligation to the wise and the foolish. Are you the only one to whom you deny yourself? The foolish and the wise, the slaves and the free, the rich and the poor, men and women, the old and the young, clergy and laity, the just and the unjust – all alike have some part in you. They all drink from the public fountain of your heart. Will you yourself stand apart and go thirsty? ... 'If one is mean to himself, to whom will he be generous?' (Ecclesiasticus 14, 5). So I say: not always or often but at least sometimes, remember to restore yourself to yourself.

I have warned you not to give yourself to action totally and continuously. Set aside some portion of your heart and of your time for consideration ... Do you ask what piety is? It is making time for consideration. You may perhaps tell me that I differ on this point from those who define piety as 'the worship of God'. Not really ... What could be more relevant to the worship of God than what the psalm encourages us to do: 'Be still and know that I am God' (Ps 46, 10). Surely this is the main object of consideration. Is there anything so influential in every respect as consideration? Does it not helpfully look ahead, and divide up our active life into sections, rehearsing what needs to be done and arranging it in advance? This is highly necessary in case, by any chance, things that are expected to turn out well are fraught with danger ...

First of all, consideration purifies the very source from which it springs – namely, the mind. Then it regulates our affections, directs our actions, restrains our excesses, moderates our behaviour, brings integrity and order to our lives and, above all, develops our knowledge of things both human and divine. It is consideration that brings order out of disorder, makes connections, pulls things together, searches out the unknown, discerns the truth, weighs one thing against another, and explores what is bogus or false. It is consideration that arranges in advance what needs doing and reviews what has been accomplished, so that nothing faulty or requiring correction may lodge in our minds. It is consideration that in prosperity feels the sting of adversity, and in adversity is as though it did not feel it ...'

(Extracts from Book I, sections 6 & 8)

This kind of meditation helps me to form a 'right judgement in all things', as the Whitsun collect calls it. This includes discerning the right timing of pastoral work, e.g. discerning when to confront, when to let be, when to initiate, when to move on, etc..

It is after brooding on such practical matters that I feel able to move on to contemplating the 'Things Above', about which Bernard writes so movingly. In the last chapter of Book V, completed shortly before his death, is the climax not only to Bernard's final work, but also to his entire ministry. Here he explores in what sense it is possible for human beings to comprehend *the depth of the riches and wisdom and knowledge of God* (Rom 11, 33), and teaches that there are four kinds of contemplation:

> *'The first and greatest kind of contemplation is to* **wonder at God's majesty**. *This requires a heart that has been cleansed, so that it is free from its faults and pardoned from its sins. It can easily be raised up to the things of heaven. Sometimes, even if for only a short interval, the beholder can be transfixed in ecstasy and wonder.*
>
> *The second kind of contemplation is also needful: namely,* **to gaze upon God's judgments**. *This has a terrifying aspect that strikes awe into our hearts, drives away our faults, builds up our virtues, opens to door to wisdom and keeps us humble. Indeed, the sure and stable foundation of our virtues is humility. If that should weaken, the whole accumulation of our virtues collapses in ruin.*
>
> *The third kind of contemplation is to spend time* **remembering God's blessings**. *This prevents us from being ungrateful, and encourages us to love the Giver of all good things. As the Psalmist says: 'They shall pour forth the story of your abundant kindness'* (Ps 145, 7).
>
> *The fourth kind of contemplation is to forget what lies behind, and rely solely on looking forward to what we have been promised. This means* **meditating on God's eternity**. *It fosters our patience, and reinforces our perseverance.*
>
> *... It is easy to associate the four kinds of meditation we have described with the four dimensions identified by the Apostle [i.e. 'the breadth and length and depth and height' Eph 3, 18]. Meditating on what is promised takes in God's length. Remembering his blessings takes in his breadth. Contemplating his majesty takes in his height. Investigating his judgments takes in his depths. God still has to be sought after. He has not yet been fully discovered, and it is impossible to seek Him too much. It is through prayer rather than debate that God is most appropriately sought and most easily found. Though this is the end of my book, let it not be the end of our searching.'*

(Book V, section 32)

Daily Office

To recite the Divine Office is not just a daily duty, enjoined upon all clergy by Canon C.26. In my experience it is also a great mainstay and source of inspiration.

I began using Mattins and Evensong from the Book of Common Prayer over 50 years ago, followed in later years by the shorter form in the Alternative Service Book. Early in the 1990's I switched to the Franciscan form of the office, *'Celebrating Common Prayer'*, but found it rather complicated. The pocket edition distributed at the 1998 Lambeth Conference was better, and I still find this is a handy option when travelling or on holiday. Since *'Common Worship: Daily Prayer'* appeared this has been my norm. It is a delight to use, and a constant source of enrichment. I sometimes combine with the readings for Mattins or Evensong those for the Daily Eucharist.

I have grown used to saying the office alone for many years, and appreciate being able to pause for deeper thought when verses of scripture jump out of the page – the practice often referred as *'lectio divina'*. This ties in with Gregory's earlier comment about the value of meditating daily on Holy Scripture. The NRSV is my favourite English translation, and from time to time I like to read the New Testament lessons in other languages as an aid to reflection and fluency.

The sacramental dimension of the bishop's ministry will be dealt with in chapter 12.

INTERCESSION

The other main ingredient of private prayer, namely intercession, has always struck me as being particularly vital to the bishop's ministry.

The gospels show that Jesus' earthly ministry was shot through with his prayer for other people in their various needs. Two obvious examples spring to mind. *'Simon, Simon, I have prayer for you that your own faith may not fail'* (Luke 22, 31), and *'Holy Father, protect in your name those whom you have given me'* (John 17, 11). The epistle to the Hebrews gives us the picture of Jesus as our great high priest who always lives to make intercession for us (Heb 7, 25). The other epistles, too, contain many glimpses of intercession as normal element in the life of the apostolic church: see Eph 1, 16-19; Phil 1, 3-5; Col 1, 3 and 9-12; 1 Thess 1, 2-3; 1 Tim 2, 1-6; and James 5, 16). The priestly role of the whole people of God is expressed in I Peter 2, 5 and Rev 1, 5. In Acts we read of the local church in Jerusalem praying fervently for Peter during his imprisonment (Acts 12, 5) with astonishing results. Against such a rich background how could any bishop fail to see intercessory prayer as a prime obligation?

Bob Hardy often used the phrase *'holding the diocese to God'.* In his essay *'The Challenge of Holding the Whole'* (Magazine of the Cambridge Society, 1994) he wrote of *'holding the clergy, the people and their common life so that they feel cherished, nourished and understood'* - an emphasis that comes close to Gregory's conjunction of 'compassion and prayerfulness', quoted above.

A similar thought was expressed by Bill Ind as follows:

'One of the privileges of being a bishop is to know that we are prayed for by name daily in so many churches up and down the diocese. The parochial clergy and the parishes need to know that the bishops also pray [for them] and that indeed, the people and the parishes are 'inside' the bishops. In other words, what is at stake is not just a form of management, but an understanding of the reality of the life of prayer.'

(From an unpublished talk to a clergy cell, 1991)

Although in retirement I am content to follow the diocesan cycle of intercession, during my Grimsby years this did not feel adequate. The names and places did not come round often enough. My aim was to pray at least once a month for each of the parochial clergy in my pastoral area, as well as for their spouses and children. The method I followed was to allocate the first twelve days of the month to the deaneries of my pastoral area, i.e. one deanery per day, keeping a balance between church life and public life in those communities. For example, on Day 8 I would pray not just for the clergy families of Deanery 8: *'Calcewaithe and Candleshoe'* (the coastal strip around Skegness and Mablethorpe), but also for those engaged in the tourist industry, the hundreds of holidaymakers, the lifeboat crews and beach guards, those seasonally unemployed, those flying helicopters to and from oil rigs, those piping in gas supplies from the North Sea, etc. Two further days were allocated to team ministries in the conurbations of Scunthorpe and Grimsby. This left enough other days to cover such topics as: industry, agriculture, education for various age-groups, health and those with special needs, national and local government, housing, the voluntary sector, social justice, leisure and the arts, world peace, human rights, other faiths, Lincoln cathedral, the staff of the Diocesan Office and Registry, ecumenical partnerships and leaders of other denominations, the General Synod and its agencies, missionary societies, the world-wide church, etc. For the international scene I found the World Council of Churches' prayer handbook exceptionally helpful – originally entitled *'For All God's People'*, now revised as *'Into God's Hands'*. I greatly value the latter, as well as the daily prayer topics published quarterly by the United Society (formerly USPG).

Bishop W.H. Frere, one of the founders of the Community of the Resurrection, gave some fine teaching about how our circle of prayer should always be expanding. He put it like this:

'The duty of intercession is an ever widening element in each individual life: as a man's interests and experience widen, so must his prayers. At first his horizon is narrow, limited to a small home circle. Then he goes out into the larger world, and

that too claims his intercessions. Bit by bit, as friends, acquaintances and interests grow, he must keep pace with all this expansion, not only in the activity of his outer life, but also in the hidden energy of his life of devotion and supplication ... If he is a man of God, he finds that he accomplishes more of God's purposes and of his own best hopes by a short, quiet half-hour of prayer than by days of restless activity.'
(Condensed from *'Sursum Corda'*, p 1)

As an amateur horologist, I liken intercession to lubricating the movement of a clock: everything runs more easily, and each wheel or pinion engages better with those next to it. Intercession changes the way we interrelate with people. In a phrase from the American novelist Kathryn Stockett, *'it is like electricity – it keeps everything going'* (from *'The Help',* Penguin 2010, page 23). If, for example, a priest from my pastoral area has not seen me for several months yet I was praying for him or her only last week, we are half-way towards meeting one another. One benefit of intercession is to sharpen our conscience and memory about what we should be doing for those on our spiritual radar-screen. Another benefit is to be freed from too fixed an image of other people. One of the great spiritual leaders in the days of East Germany – the so-called German Democratic Republic – was Pastor Johannes Hamel, who had trained in the Confessing Church. He wrote tellingly that:

'...in praying for those with whom we come into contact, we receive them anew from God's hand as they really are: human beings for whom God intends good ...'
(J. Hamel, *'A Christian in East Germany'*, page 83)

SPIRITUALITY IN BROAD TERMS

In addition to these basic components of devotional life I am convinced that 'spirituality' has to be viewed in its broadest terms. It covers everything that energises me spiritually, and that keeps me open to God at various levels: as a *human being*, as a *Christian* living the life of the Spirit, and as a *bishop* sustaining the tasks and expectations of public ministry within the Church and at large in the world.

This means being more than a competent functionary, but someone who is alert, sensitive, creative, inspired and inspiring to other people. 'Spirituality', therefore, is about what nourishes me, what puts me on my mettle, what takes my mind off work, what energises, etc.. To understand and honour these factors is crucial to survival, and to flourishing as the person God intends me to be.

Recreations and hobbies obviously vary from person to person. Some of them, like gardening or going to the theatre, may be shared with one's spouse. Others, like foreign travel or entertaining guests, may involve the family. I remember how much pleasure I found in skating with our children every week when they were young, but this stage did not last long. Sport has never interested me. Perhaps because I was an only child and entertained myself for much of the time, my preference is for individual pursuits. Turning over the compost, mending a clock, translating an article or balancing the household ledger can all refresh me in different ways. Music – be it my own limited efforts at the keyboard or attending concerts with others – touches parts of me that nothing else can reach. Journaling is a favourite way of exploring my own thoughts or fixing in the mind some recent trip or experience. Whatever leisure pursuits appeal to our differing temperaments, they are a vital element in accepting who we are under God and letting ourselves be continually re-created. In this connection the Myers-Briggs type indicator can yield helpful insights.

Styles of spirituality are largely a matter of personal preference, whether Benedictine, Carmelite, Celtic, charismatic, Franciscan, Ignatian or whatever you care to name. One type is neither necessarily better than another, nor guaranteed to bring us automatically nearer to the Kingdom of Heaven. God sustains our inner life by an amazingly wide variety of means. The whole matter was well summed by the wise words of Bishop Edmund Morgan (formerly of Truro):

> *'It is by the bishop's godward life that his ministry will bear fruit and be controlled. In order to guard against overwork, to counteract the snare of activism, to curb his concern for his reputation, to overcome the temptation to love the praise of men more than the glory of God, his life must be a continual 'Sursum Corda'; he must be ever groping, fighting, leaping Godwards. He must in fact give priority to spirituality, abiding in the certainty that God – and not merely the 'things of God' – is central in life ... It is not the amount of work he does that counts, but its spiritual quality and the way he does it ... His daily quiet time and period of study have place of privilege'*
>
> (From *'Bishops'*, Faith Press 1961, pp 23-25)

I give the closing word on this theme to Bishop Edward King, who wrote:

> *'I hope the next set of bishops will be better, and say their prayers and read, instead of rushing about'*
>
> (From *'Edward King and our Times',* Lord Elton, Godfrey Bles 1958, page 105)

CHAPTER 7

Outer Lifestyle

The following question is put in the eighth vow that a bishop takes before being consecrated:

"Will you endeavour to fashion your own life and that of your household according to the way of Christ, and make your home a place of hospitality and welcome?"

This can serve as a framework for exploring three principal aspects of the lifestyle expected of bishops: the bishop's own way of life [in this chapter], that of his or her family and household, and the use and ethos of the bishop's home [in the next chapter].

THE BISHOP'S OWN WAY OF LIFE

Any bishop's manner of life inevitably reflects his or her own personality and attitude. What matters most is to be the right kind of person – one who is fully human, well-rounded and integrated, and fashioned according to the way of Christ. This is not a question of putting on a public face to make an impression, nor is it about style or technique. It is a far deeper issue – namely, about the heart and core of who you really are, whether male or female, and about struggling to be committed wholly to God. The truism that 'what you *are* speaks louder than what you say' is magnified by high office.

The New Testament epistles contain plenty of general advice to all Christians about how to conduct themselves in daily life, both within the community of believers and in the eyes of those outside the church. These moral guidelines apply all the more to church leaders since, the higher the public profile, the greater is the need to be Christ-like. The requirements for a bishop specified in 1 Tim 3, 1-7 were mentioned earlier (see above, page 9).

GREGORY'S ADVICE

In the late sixth century Gregory the Great devoted the second part of his *'Pastoral Rule'* to the manner of life expected of a bishop. He originally addressed this work to John, Bishop of Ravenna in 591 AD, and also sent it to his friend Leander of Seville for the benefit of the church in Spain. Augustine brought it with him to England in 596 AD. It was soon translated into Greek by Anastasius, Patriarch of Antioch. In a series of councils held in Gaul during the ninth century (Mayence, Rheims, Tours and Châlon-sur-Seine) the study of it was enjoined on all bishops. A copy of it, together with the Book of Canons, was often presented to new bishops at their consecration. Alfred the Great had a paraphrase of it made in the West Saxon language to be sent to every bishop within his kingdom. Thus Gregory's observations were hugely influential far beyond his own life-time. (Further background is given in the introduction to H.J. Davis's translation).

Gregory opens Part II with a summary of the right demeanour for a bishop:

'The bishop is under a duty to consider how necessary it is for him to live uprightly. He must be:

a) *pure in heart; exemplary in action;*
b) *discreet in keeping silence; able to speak to good advantage;*
c) *a near neighbour to everyone through his sympathy; pre-eminent in prayerfulness;*
d) *a close friend, in all humility, of those who lead a good life; but strict in his zeal for righteousness as regards the vices of evil doers;*
e) *not slack in his concern for inward things whilst occupied with outward things; nor neglecting to provide for outward things whilst concerned with what is inward.'*

(Pt II, ch 1)

These carefully balanced pairs of phrases are characteristic of Gregory's style, and highlight the inevitable tensions with which bishops have to wrestle constantly.

He warns bishops not to get carried away with self-importance – what might be called 'bishopitis':

'All who hold high authority should view themselves not in the light of their rank, but according to the equality of their human nature. They should find their joy not in lording it over people, but in helping them.

By virtue of his superior position over others a bishop may become conceited. Because everything is at his service, because his orders are quickly carried out in accordance with his wishes, because those under him praise him for what he has done well but lack the authority to criticise what he has done amiss, and because they usually praise even when they ought to blame! – for all these reasons the bishop may get above himself. While he is surrounded outwardly by plenty of favourable comments, the true situation within himself is belied. He forgets what he is, gets drawn away by other people's compliments, and believes himself to be what others tell him – rather than what he should judge himself to be. He puts himself on a pedestal in his own estimation.'

(from Pt II, ch 6)

Gregory speaks wisely about maintaining a balance between inward and outward realities:

'The bishop should not slacken his concern for inward things whilst occupying himself with outward things; nor should his concern for what is inward make him neglect what is outward. If he is totally engrossed in external matters, he will be ruined inwardly. If he is pre-occupied with what concerns only his inner self, he will not bestow on his neighbours the external care they need.

It is often the case that some bishops concentrate all their attention on secular concerns, and even take a delight in being weighed down with such matters. They disregard those interior matters about which they should be teaching others. Consequently the life of their people is debilitated. When the head is sick, the members cannot thrive. Moses was rebuked by Jethro for wearing himself out with other people's earthly affairs (Ex 18). He advised him to appoint others to sort out people's disputes, so that he himself might be freer to learn the secret of spiritual matters for teaching to the people. Engagement in secular activities is sometimes to be endured with a generous heart, but never pursued for the love of it.'

(from Pt II, ch 7)

Gregory also warns about the dangers of trying to please people:

'The bishop should not be eager to please people, and yet should pay attention to what <u>ought</u> to please them. He should aim at being loved in order that he may be listened to, but not seek to be loved for his own sake. This is well indicated by St Paul, when he reveals to us the secret of his endeavours: "I try to please everyone in everything I do" (1 Cor 10, 33). But again he says: "If I were still pleasing people, I would not be a servant of Christ" (Gal 1, 10). So Paul both pleases and does not please. In wishing to please he was seeking not to please people, but rather that the truth communicated through him might please them.'

(from Pt II, ch 8)

Though Gregory was addressing social conditions very different from our own day, his remarks are informed by a close acquaintance with the Bible and with shrewd insights into human nature, and can still resonate with bishops today.

BERNARD'S ADVICE

Bernard of Clairvaux laid a similar stress on the need for bishops to have the right inner dispositions and motives. Their core virtues would then express themselves in right actions. Bernard's advice on lifestyle was sought by Henri Sanglier soon after he had been consecrated as Archbishop of Sens in 1122. This was a very senior post in the French Church, carrying seniority over the bishops of seven other dioceses including Paris. The young abbot Bernard, still only in his mid-thirties, responded in 1126 with his treatise *'On the Lifestyle and Duties of Bishops'* (Letter no 42, Benedictine edition), which had a powerful effect. At Bernard's bidding Archbishop Henri renounced his worldly way of life, and withdrew from the self-indulgent court of King Louis VI, as did Bishop Stephen of Paris. This offended the King, who then persecuted the Archbishop for his newly found religious fervour!

Bernard pitched in with typical forthrightness:

'The honour and glory of ecclesiastical dignity consist not in outward splendour, but in the glory of morals and virtues. You will not bring honour to your ministry by concern for clothing, pride in horses or spacious buildings, but by distinguished morals, spiritual studies and good works.

(from ch 2)

Such things as I have mentioned seem to show honour, but only to the eye that looks on the outward appearance, not to that which is secret.

The most powerful and honourable ornaments for religious leaders are their chastity, love and humility. Chastity is an ornament of such beauty that it worthily brings honour. The memory of the bishop lives on not in his physical descendants, but in the spiritual benediction he leaves behind. Yet chastity without love is like a lamp without oil: remove the oil, and the lamp does not light. Remove love, and chastity is not pleasing.

Purity of heart consists in two things: seeking the glory of God and the good of one's neighbour. It is clear that a bishop, in all his deeds and words, should seek not his own advantage, but only the honour of God or the salvation of his fellow human beings, or both. By doing this he will fulfil the office of 'pontiff' in the true meaning of that word, by making himself a bridge between God and his fellow human beings. He offers to God the prayers and vows of the people. He carries back to them God's blessing and grace.

(from ch 3)

Humility is contempt for one's own pre-eminence, and contempt is the opposite of hankering after something. The one who knows how to think humbly of himself cannot allow his opinion of himself be fooled. He cannot think that he is something greater than he is, or that what he is actually comes from himself. He patiently manages without that which he knows he lacks, and he humbly glories in what he actually has – not in himself but in the Lord. When people find themselves being praised about the good that happens to be in them, they are anxious to repel the dart of favour from themselves with the shield of truth. They give glory to God saying: 'By the grace of God I am what I am' (1 Cor 15, 10). Pushing any sneaking suggestion away from themselves, they say to the Lord: 'Not to us, Lord, not to us but to your name give the glory' (Ps 115, 1)'

(from ch 5)

Bernard criticised three types of shortcoming amongst the clergy of his day: an excessive concern over apparel, the use of costly ornaments (such as gold trimmings on the horse's bridle), and the prevalence of ecclesiastical ambition. A few short extracts from his letter give the flavour of his remarks:

'Let those be ashamed who take pride in the handiwork of weavers and furriers, rather than in their own actions. The things that these men carry about their persons like martyrs are not the marks of Christ.'

(from ch 2, §4)

'The naked and the hungry cry out, "What is gold doing on your bridle, Bishop?" Does the gold that adorns your bridle drive away cold or hunger? Your vanities are at the expense of our necessities.'

(from ch 2, §7)

'For you, Most Reverend Sir – you especially – I judge that humility is all the more necessary since you have at your disposal so great an opportunity of being haughty. Your ancestry, your mature age, your learning, your episcopal throne and, what is more, the prerogative of primacy – to whom would such things not be the occasion of pride? Yet they could also be the occasion of humility.'

(from ch 7, §25)

'When you were first dragged to your episcopal throne, you wept. You shrank from it. You bewailed your power, saying that it was a great burden for you and altogether beyond you. You cried out that you were wretched and unworthy, not fit for so sacred a ministry, not up to such great cares. Why now, therefore, have you put aside your modest dread, and do you strive of your own accord for higher positions? Why are you not content with your own affairs, and have the irreverent audacity to meddle in other people's. Why do you do this? Is it perhaps in order to save more people? But it is harmful to put your sickle into someone else's harvest. Such an increase of one diocese at the expense of another does not please Him who is the bridegroom of all the churches.'

(from ch 7, §27-28)

Towards the end of his life Bernard wrote in similar vein to Pope Eugenius III, again emphasising the cardinal virtues and castigating current abuses in the church. The following extracts are from *'On Consideration'*, his final work.

*'Patience is certainly a great virtue, but I could not wish you to be patient about all the demands of your office. Sometimes it is more commendable to be **im**patient! ... Patience is not a good thing if you let yourself become a slave when you should be free. Be under no illusion about the slavery to which you submit on a daily basis without even realising it ... Tell me: when are you ever free, or ever safe, or ever your own person? Everywhere there is noise and uproar. Everywhere the yoke of slavery is chafing you.'*

(I, 4)

'It would be worthier of your apostolic office, healthier for your conscience and more fruitful for the Church of God if you heeded what Paul said: 'You were bought with a price; do not become slaves of human masters' (1 Cor 7, 23) ... When are we to pray? When are we to teach the people? When are we to build up the Church, or meditate on the Law of the Lord? Spare yourself from the demands made on you.'

(I, 5)

'Notice how beautifully and harmoniously the cardinal virtues [viz. temperance, justice, prudence and fortitude] combine with one another and are mutually dependent. Consideration sits like an umpire of the tug-of-war between our pleasures and our necessities. It fixes the limits on either side, allowing enough for our necessities and taking what is excessive from our pleasures. From both of these it fashions the virtue known as temperance. For consideration judges people who deny themselves what is necessary to be no less intemperate than those who indulge themselves to excess. Temperance consists, therefore, not only in cutting down our excesses, but also in allowing for our necessities ... This agrees with the philosopher's maxim: 'Moderation in all things'.

(I, 9)

'As regards justice, another of the four virtues ... it does not stand by itself. Notice how beautifully it connects with, and is consistent with, temperance ... The Wise One says: 'Do not be too righteous' (Ecclesiastes 7, 17), showing that he disapproves of justice that is not moderated by temperance ... The task of fortitude is no light one: it is to restrain our likes and dislikes between the extremes, i.e. too little and too much. In this way our wills can be at ease with the middle way that is stripped to basics, pure, detached, self-consistent and self-sufficient ...'

(I, 10)

'What if you suddenly dedicate yourself to this way of thinking? It has not been the custom of your predecessors. You will annoy a great many people if, all of a sudden, you do not follow in your forefathers' footsteps. Indeed, you will be regarded as insulting them. You will be picked on as the odd man out. It will look as if you are trying to draw attention to yourself. You cannot suddenly put

right at one go everything that is wrong, or cut excesses down to moderation. The chance will come for you to do this bit by bit, as God in his wisdom gives you the right time and as you seek opportunity. Meanwhile, turn other people's wrongdoing to good effect as far as you can.'

(I, 12)

'We cannot get away from the fact that you have been promoted, but ask yourself: what for? Not for lording it over other people, as I see it ... We should be aware that it is a burden of service that has been laid upon us, not the privilege of lordship that has been bestowed on us. By the grace of God you are what you are ... If you are wise, you will be content with the measure you receive from God ... Learn to exercise your influence not with the object of ordering people about, but of doing what the occasion requires. If you are to do the work of a prophet (cf. Jer 1, 10), what you require is not a sceptre but a hoe – not to dominate, but to root out the weeds.'

(II, 9)

We have already seen that Bernard did not mince his words when attacking outward show or luxury. The same emphasis comes out in the following:

'How seldom do you come across people who in time of prosperity do not relax their vigilance and self-discipline, at least to some extent. When did prosperity not undermine self-control, just as fire melts wax or as sunshine melts snow or ice? David was wise and Samuel even wiser, but the flattery of great success made fools of them both ... Anyone who does not bestow too much attention upon dress or on pampering the body in times of prosperity is truly great.'

(II, 21)

'Peter never processed about dressed up in jewels and silks, covered with gold, mounted on a white horse, attended by a guard and with servants milling round him. Yet without these trappings he believed he could fulfil well enough Our Lord's command: 'If you love me, feed my sheep' (Jn 21, 15). In all this pomp you are the successor not of Peter, but of Constantine ... Whilst you may tolerate it for the time being, you must not claim it as a debt to which you are entitled.'

(IV, 6)

These snippets give us a glimpse of Bernard, the radical reformer, who did so much to renew the church in his own times. Both documents from which I have quoted were addressed to bishops who had been recently consecrated, and were getting to grips with the spiritual and practical challenges of their new responsibility as senior church leaders. A bishop in any age would be fortunate to have such a mentor!

Simon Phipps' comment

Soon after my arrival as Simon Phipps' suffragan I asked him what was most important in the life and ministry of a bishop. His answer was simple and instantaneous, and clearly the question was one to which he had given much previous thought. He replied:

'Like the first apostles, a bishop must stand for the resurrection. His main task is to bring hope, affirmation, encouragement and reassurance to people in a wide range of situations.'

In the memorable sermon that he preached on the 25th anniversary of his consecration Simon made a similar point:

'The resurrection tells us that we cannot put an end to things where God is concerned ... What the resurrection says to us is that God is to be trusted in calling us into the Kingdom, in spite of its costs and risks ... God is to be trusted in calling us into his future, the future that is always there as a possibility in every new situation which life continually unfolds ... The 'end' is something that belongs to God and not to us ... Infinite love comes to us in proportion as we open our lives in trust to God. That is our Faith. That is our Hope. That is the Love in which both are grounded ...'

He truly and deeply believed that this should be the main thrust of any bishop's ministry, and it certainly was for him.

Some contemporary issues

In each generation bishops have to work out how best to inhabit their role in ways appropriate to their own culture and times. The manner in which we dress, or relate to people, or travel, or conduct our own lives has to send out the right messages. How far do we reflect Christ, our servant-leader?

a)   Dress

The purpose of any uniform is to signal to others, especially those who do not know us, what role we carry. The 18th century style of gaiters and aprons was largely abandoned by church dignitaries in about 1970. Nowadays the basic marks by which the general population recognises an Anglican bishop are a clerical collar, a purple shirt or cassock and a pectoral cross, or – in a liturgical context – a mitre. Some bishops choose to dress in 'black crow' to look like ordinary priests, but there is a danger that, when their identity emerges, people may feel tricked. There is much to be said for coming out in our true colours, but with modesty and simplicity. Canon C.27 simply states that a bishop's dress shall be *'suitable to his office*. Some flexibility is needed to adapt to a range of social situations. No good purpose is served by bishops wearing rings and pectoral crosses that are overly ornate. A jacket or pullover is sometimes more appropriate than a sombre business suit, and can look perfectly presentable.

b) Titles

'How should I address you?' people often ask. The 1968 Lambeth Conference recommended that bishops *'should radically examine the honours paid to them in the course of divine worship, in titles and customary address, and in style of living'* (Resolution 41). Though few formal changes have occurred, there is noticeably less my-lording and a more informal style. There is also widespread ignorance of correct modes of address anyway. I believe that we should patiently tolerate people's faltering efforts to show courtesy and respect to the office we bear, but neither expect nor demand such formalities. In the liturgy bishops are customarily prayed for by their Christian name, and I am content to be addressed by mine. Whilst in office I signed most letters "+David" to clergy colleagues and people I knew personally, and "+David Grimsby" on other correspondence and official documents. It is salutary to have a family who are amused by grandiloquent titles.

c) Travel

Since retirement I have been glad to resume carrying a passport in my personal name instead of one marked *'The Lord Bishop of Grimsby',* which sometimes caused delay when security staff noticed that it did not match the name on my air ticket! Several bishops have set a good example in minimising their carbon footprint by restricting air travel, but practical questions of time and cost are also involved. For many destinations to which I travelled world-wide on behalf of the Anglican Communion there was no alternative to flying.

When visiting the Greek Orthodox Church in 1983 I was amazed to find that bishops' cars carried CD number plates, and seemed to be treated by traffic police as above the law.   In general I believe that we should beware of special privileges and symbols of superiority. Michael Ramsey gave up the pennant on his car bonnet in the mid-1960's. His driver did, though, retain the ivory lozenge permitting vehicular access to and from Whitehall via the Horseguards' archway, which was of real practical benefit. I suppose that today's equivalent of the 'gold on their bridles', condemned by Bernard (see above page 73), would be a flashy car, but bishops tempted to indulge themselves in that way are effectively constrained by the Church Commissioners' guidelines and the level of tax allowances. Another entirely practical question is whether a bishop needs a driver. A few bishops cannot drive for various reasons. Some find real difficulty in concentrating on driving whilst weightier matters are on their minds, and actually need someone else at the wheel. Normally I preferred to drive myself, but Lincolnshire traffic was comparatively light. In some areas parking and traffic jams are so difficult that a driver is a huge help. There are also questions of age, tiredness and pressure of time to be weighed. With the help of a driver a number of senior bishops make prudent use of several hours a week in the car for reading documents, dictating letters, preparing addresses, and even a bit of 'shut-eye'. This can be justified as a practical necessity, not a status symbol.

On trains I nearly always travelled second class. Only on a handful of occasions did I travel first class, when it was absolutely necessary to use this time for work and the train was noisy or so crowded that I could not spread out confidential papers. I aimed to work on the way to London, but relax on the way back.

d) Moral standards

Canon C.26 deals with the manner of life of all ordained Ministers, and ends by saying that they are to be *'wholesome examples and patterns to the flock of Christ'*. 1 Tim 3, 7 mentions that *'a bishop must be well thought of by outsiders'*, and the duty to live at peace with all people is urged in 2 Tim 2, 22 and Hebrews 12, 14. Beside speaking of the positive value of virtuous behaviour, the same Canon indicates what any Minister should avoid – advice that applies all the more to a bishop:

'(he) shall not give himself to such occupations, habits or recreations as do not befit his sacred calling, or may be detrimental to the performance of the duties of his office, or tend to be a just cause of offence to others'.

If the behaviour of bishops is unworthy, it damages not just their personal reputation but the good name of the church. In particular, it harms their own clergy and laity. When any crime has been committed, the courts rightly come down harder on those in positions of trust and public responsibility. It is not so much a question of double standards as of the dictum: *'From the one to whom much has been entrusted, even more will be demanded'* (Luke 12, 48). This puts the pressure of higher expectations on bishops to be law-abiding and exemplary citizens. They must be transparently honest in regard to their working expenses and, if required to administer charitable funds, do so conscientiously. They must behave appropriately towards children, vulnerable adults and members of the opposite gender, especially in the light of recent sexual abuses of the clerical office and of the centuries-old association of episcopal office with power and domination. Paul's advice to Timothy is still relevant: *'Set the believers an example in speech and conduct, in love, in faith, in purity'* (1 Tim 4, 12).

Paul appealed to the church at Thessalonica not only to *'hold fast to what is good',* but also to *'abstain from every appearance of evil'* (1 Thess 5, 22 AV). Appearances and perceptions cannot be ignored, and care must be taken to avoid giving the wrong impression. In our Grimsby days the window-cleaner always called on my day off, and could have gathered the impression that I was lazing around whenever he called. Since he was not to know that I had had a hectic week or been working late the previous evening, I made a point of being up and about in the week he was due to come. To give another example, it has long been my practice to interview unaccompanied women only when my wife or secretary can be around. The female visitor becomes aware, when some other woman answers the door or brings in a drink, that I am not alone in the house – an arrangement that is as much for my protection as the visitor's. Prudence in such matters is always advisable. Women bishops, too, must set similar standards in their own way.

THE BISHOP AS SERVANT

In 1965 the Second Vatican Council promulgated its Decree on the Pastoral Office of Bishops, which in paragraph 15 stressed that:

'Bishops should be mindful of their obligation to give an example of holiness through charity, humility and simplicity of life'.

In 1968 the Lambeth Conference reflected similarly on the nature of the episcopate. The report of Section II under the theme *'The Renewal of the Church in Ministry'* said:

'Christ requires those who exercise leadership in the Church to be servants of all. Our way of exercising the office of bishop has often obscured this truth. What we do, and the way we do it, should remind people of Jesus the servant. This true of all ministry in the Church; it should be especially true of a bishop ... Simplicity in life, humility in manner, and joy in serving should be the marks of a bishop's life.'

(pages 108 and 110)

The motivation for such service was spelt out memorably by Paul in Philippians 2, 1-11. Nothing less than Christ's own self-emptying is its inspiration.

A servant is expected to be reasonably accessible when needed. One question which my Support Group raised with me early in the Grimsby years was: 'What are the limits of your availability?' It was salutary to be made to reflect on the need both to have some sensible boundaries but also to avoid seeming remote or inaccessible. I recall what a negative impression was made on the clergy of another diocese when they found that they could never get in touch with their archdeacon between Friday and Monday. They expected him to be no less available to them for pastoral emergencies than they were for their parishioners. A careful balance has to be struck.

The essence of humble service is well captured in a modern prayer by Lusmarina Campos Garcia from Brazil, who reflects movingly on Mary Magdalene bathing Jesus' feet with her tears:

> 'By her example you show us how to serve one another,
> not out of superiority, competence or strength
> but out of humility, inferiority and weakness,
> not because we have more resources,
> are more powerful or in a better situation,
> but because we have no other option
> than to bend over and wash your feet and the feet of all you love.'
>
> (from *'Into God's Hands',* WCC, pages 246-7)

This servant model is what leads me, in trying to capture the essence of this chapter and the next, to describe the primary aspect of episcopé in the following terms:

It is personal - is the right kind of person: human and Christ-like;
- has firm roots in the Gospel and current church tradition through prayer & study;
- and stands for faith and hope.

CHAPTER 8

Home and Hospitality

FREEDOM TO MARRY OR NOT

It is not just the bishop whose life is to be fashioned *'according to the way of Christ'*, but – to take up the words of the eighth vow – also that of the episcopal family and household, whatever that may comprise. In the Roman Catholic, Orthodox and Oriental Orthodox communions a bishop does not have a wife or children, though he generally maintains a household of some kind. For Anglicans, however, and other traditions with which we are in full communion (e.g. Old Catholics, Lutherans, etc) our bishops are free to follow their individual calling over the question of marriage, as is any church member, ordained or lay. This freedom was classically expressed in Article XXXII:

> *'Bishops, Priests and Deacons are not commanded by God's law, either to vow the estate of single life, or to abstain from marriage: therefore it is lawful also for them, as for all other Christian men, to marry at their own discretion, as they shall judge the same to serve better to godliness'.*

The critical issue is whether being married or not enables you to 'serve better to godliness' – that is, to be a better person, to render a more effective ministry, and to be more pleasing to God. To marry or remain single is, therefore, a matter of personal choice that should be exercised in the light of one's vocation as a Christian. Most of our male and female bishops in the Anglican Communion are married, though a few are not.

As one who is married, I am conscious how much I owe to my wife and family in sustaining my ministry as a bishop. They support me, keep me grounded in normal daily life, challenge me when necessary, and help me to be a rounded human being with a sense of proportion. The nuclear family is one of the strongest influences in shaping all of us as persons, and in providing us with emotional and psychological support.

SHARED VOCATION

Most bishops' spouses look upon their marital partnership as a shared vocation, however much their roles as individuals may diverge from one another. Mary and

I benefited greatly from our active involvement in the Association for Marriage Enrichment (of which we were founder members) for about ten years. Through regular training events and individual exercises we had the chance to deepen and strengthen our couple-relationship. This process involved helping each other to become more self-aware; to explore and share feelings and affections; to communicate with greater emotional intelligence; and to deal with conflicts and problems in a climate of openness and trust. This was a nurturing experience that enabled us to grow and change, and helped us to value ourselves and each other more fully.

In our shared role as an 'accredited Leader Couple' we undertook a number projects jointly, such as running workshops and residential courses on marriage enrichment, mainly for ordinands or clergy and their spouses, and providing remedial counselling for some clergy couples under stress. These were specific bits of joint work which we chose to undertake over a period of several years, not necessarily linked to the roles of bishop or bishop's wife. In many respects, however, we chose to follow our own separate paths, though they intersected and partly overlapped. Each of us took particular care to preserve our own professional confidentiality, even if that meant people occasionally getting a blank look when they wrongly presumed that we had shared with each other information deemed to be private.

Whilst I travelled round the diocese and the world, Mary was anchored in the local scene. During my frequent absences she 'held the fort' at home, as I did during her occasional absences. If a child was ill, it would sometimes be my turn to stay at home if Mary's professional commitments were more pressing. There are many different ways of having a 'shared ministry', and each couple has to decide what is appropriate for them and juggle with the various factors in their own way. There is no perpetually valid 'right way' to do this, since the balance of factors has to vary continually in response to changing demands. Each spouse has to be ready to act as 'blotting paper' to the pressures in the other's life, and to support the other's personal and professional development. This is the essence of their partnership. It can be tragic if the pressures of public ministry 'gobble up' any bishop, priest or deacon so much that he or she becomes an unsatisfactory spouse or parent, leaving only the dregs of themselves for the family.

To set a life-style for one's family and create the ethos of one's home is a joint undertaking. This embraces bringing up children, handling money carefully and responsibly, looking after the official house and garden (which are to some extent public property), shopping and eating ethically and healthily, avoiding waste and extravagance, engaging in suitable leisure activities, taking appropriate holidays, and so on. Mary and I found that handling these issues at Grimsby was not fundamentally different from our earlier experience when based in a vicarage at Wood Green or Tettenhall. Nevertheless, the higher the profile of our jobs, the greater the pressure of public expectations.

THE BISHOP'S SPOUSE

Nothing makes Mary crosser than to be introduced as the 'bishop's wife', as if she were some mere appendage. She is a person in her own right, carrying a number of roles, only one of which is to be married to me! For many years she was a full-time parent. She has also pursued three different professional careers as nurse, probation officer and Family Court officer, and exercised a wide range of voluntary tasks in church and community life, such as 'Relate' counsellor, playgroup leader, house-group facilitator, pastoral visitor, fund-raiser, organiser of adult classes and Village Hall lunches, PCC member, etc..

In parts of the Anglican Communion, especially Africa, the bishop's wife is still often regarded as 'mother' of the diocese. In this country, however, there is no clear statutory role for a bishop's spouse, though being married to the bishop offers endless scope for exercising a useful ministry according to personal vocation and choice. In the early 90s Grace Sheppard's *Handbook for Bishops' Wives* was circulated to those who came new to the role. She set out some of the expectations and pitfalls, and stressed the importance of choosing one's own style and communicating it clearly. After the 2008 Lambeth Conference Jane Williams collated accounts of the experiences of those married to bishops.

Bishops' wives and husbands (the latter category does not yet exist in the Church of England but is expanding elsewhere) are so diverse that, apart from their spouse's work, they do not readily form a common interest group. This may explain why some of them are reluctant to be clubbed together. Among the choices a bishop's spouse has to make is where to worship, and when to accompany the bishop on public occasions. Years ago it was widely assumed that the bishop's wife would be looked after by the vicar's or churchwarden's wife, but this cannot be taken for granted. The bishop's spouse may prefer to remain anonymous.

PROTECTING THE FAMILY

Quite apart from taking 'time off', there is a value in having some 'family time' for its own sake. A couple of hours of 'downtime' need to be kept for family purposes within every working day, in addition to meal times, as mentioned already. A major practical issue is the handling of unscheduled intrusions. During the three hours that my secretary was at Bishop's House on Mondays, Wednesdays and Fridays she normally fielded incoming calls. Otherwise I generally answered them except during 'family time' or 'time off', when Mary would deal with them if she was available. Genuine emergencies are a different matter, and take priority when they occur.

On John Waine's advice we decided to follow a firm policy over Sunday lunch, especially during the years our children were at home. I normally declined invitations to stay for lunch in the parish where I was officiating on Sunday morning, but made it clear that I would not rush away. I tried to meet everyone over the usual 'bun fight', but would make a point of returning home for lunch even if it meant our family not eating until 2 p.m.. This line of action was understood and respected in the diocese, and safeguarded Sunday lunch as an important focus of family life.

Canon C.26 states that:

'At all times [the minister] shall be diligent to frame and fashion his life and that of his family according to the doctrine of Christ, and to make himself and them, as much as in him lies, wholesome examples and patterns to the flock of Christ'.

A key phrase here is *'as much as in him lies'.* This proviso wisely recognises that there are limits as to how far Christian ministers should impose their convictions and life-style on their spouses and children. Each family member needs 'space' and privacy in which to be true to himself or herself, and should be protected from excessive parental domination or public expectations. It can be bad enough being the vicar's children, let alone the bishop's! To be marked out in that way adds one more complication to the business of discovering their true selves. Christian parents naturally hope that their children may make a Christian commitment of their own. Often clergy children are glad to take part in church life, but this is not necessarily the case. Bishops' children are at particular risk of being overwhelmed with too much churchiness. Teenage independence, even rebellion, is a natural part of growing up, and each young person's path to autonomy deserves the utmost respect. It is particularly important to make room for doing ordinary things together as a family, and to be in touch with the agenda of one's children's friends and their parents and, at a later stage, of one's grandchildren.

A PLACE OF WELCOME

A few bishops have their main office in the diocesan headquarters, but the majority operate from home, like most parochial clergy. This is a great advantage in my view, and helps to give the bishop a pastoral identity that is distinct from the administrative machinery of the diocese. Sharing your home is a way of sharing yourself, and hospitality is 'a basic means of following Our Lord's command to love our neighbour as ourselves. It is a way of ... making the stranger welcome'

(*'Something to Celebrate'*, CHP 1995, page 94). When bishops welcome people into their own home, it is a chance for their guests to become more aware that they are known and affirmed.

One of the scriptural requirements of a bishop is to be hospitable (see 1 Tim 3, 2). A report by the relevant department of the Church Commissioners estimated that a diocesan bishop and his wife would 'typically welcome over 800 guests a year to their home for meetings and hospitality' (*'Called to be a bishop'*, November 1999, page 10). Modest financial assistance is provided to enable bishops to meet this expectation. Most suffragans operate on a smaller scale that is tailored to their geographical area, to the domestic facilities at their disposal and to the time that the bishop's wife can devote to entertaining alongside her other commitments. Our first house at Grimsby, in Abbey Park Road, was so fraught with practical difficulties that we usually entertained no more than 60 people a year. After moving to the new house at Irby-on-Humber in 1990 we could accommodate lunch or dinner for eight in the dining room, or a sit-down buffet for up to 30 by using the inter-connecting lounge as well. As Mary was working full time, the most we could manage in a 6-8 week period was one dinner party, one buffet party, and a few odd meals for ones and twos. In 1992 we put on 18 events at the new house, and welcomed over 200 people. We made a similar special effort in 1999 prior to retirement, but in the mean time a sustainable target was more like 120 people a year. Depending on local circumstances it can be appropriate for the bishop's house and/or garden to be made available for occasional charitable events or communal gatherings.

A RANGE OF AIMS

Within the general purpose of all hospitality we identified the following specific aims:

- to welcome new clergy, lay workers and spouses into the diocese
- to build bridges by bringing different groups together
  (e.g. civic and community representatives, those sharing a particular role or concern such as deanery leaders, ecumenical colleagues, foreign visitors, etc.)
- to encourage particular clergy, lay workers and their spouses
- to foster acquaintance across deanery boundaries
- to thank individuals for work done and, in some cases, to bid them farewell
- to deepen our friendship with particular people, and enjoy their company.

Choosing how to entertain

Successful hospitality requires a good deal of mental energy and careful planning. For dinner parties we tried hard to get the human chemistry right, and bring together people with interests in common. Some clergy couples are simply not at home with the 'art form' of a dinner party, and for buffet gatherings we made sure that everyone was already acquainted with two or three others present. Rather than invite deaneries *en bloc* we mixed together groups of people from adjoining deaneries.

We did all the shopping, preparation and catering ourselves, preferring to serve our own guests, though we sometimes recruited our children and their friends as washers-up for extra pocket money. The style of anyone's hospitality is a highly individual matter, but in addition to our family upbringing we owed much to one particular influence. In the early years of our marriage I had been on Michael Ramsey's staff at Lambeth Palace, where we lived in a cottage within the grounds. We came to admire Joan Ramsey's style of catering: warm, simple and well done; always in good taste, with a touch of style; but never posh, ostentatious or lavish. This was the ideal we embraced. The real issue is not style but substance – endeavouring to receive people into one's home *'according to the way of Christ'*.

CHAPTER 9

Custody of Time

BALANCING THE BASIC ELEMENTS

However much one may try to do justice to all the aspects of episcopé, the fact remains that "everything has to be paid for in the only universal currency of mankind, the currency of time" (A. Somerset Ward – *'A Guide for Spiritual Directors'*, Mowbrays 1957). Fine principles have to be boiled down to an actual schedule, and choices made between conflicting claims on time.

For any Christian the first basic principle about the stewardship of time is that the whole of our time comes from God, and is a trust from Him. Nothing we do lies outside His concern. Every hour we spend, like every pound we spend, matters to Him, and we are answerable to Him for the way we use *all* of it.

Those of us who trained for the priesthood at Cuddesdon under Edward Knapp-Fisher can recall how often he used to speak of "the custody of time". This somewhat chilling phrase was intended to remind us that clergy enjoy more flexibility over their use of time than many other professionals, and that this carries both a danger and a heavy responsibility. Parish priests face more demands than it is humanly possible to fulfil, and can never say that their job is done. They must, therefore, learn to set time boundaries for the sake of their own survival and spiritual welfare, and recognise that they are duty-bound to allocate their time sensibly and use it well.

Bishops, too, need to budget their time in order to strike the right balance, as the 1968 Lambeth Conference observed:

'[The bishop's] use of time will involve and be conditioned by:

- *a) pastoral oversight and administration of the diocesan family;*
- *b) service to the whole community, including those of other faiths, within the area of his diocese and beyond;*
- *c) care of his own family and household;*
- *d) strict limitation of the number of engagements and responsibilities which he undertakes, with a readiness to delegate to others so that he may have unhurried time for individuals;*

e)   his own reading, recreation and rest.'

(Section II, 'Renewal in Ministry', page 110)

MEASURING THE USE OF TIME

To quantify the pace and volume of one's work it is indispensible to keep actual records, which is not as easy as it may seem. The mere act of noting exactly how much time is spent on specific activities involves a degree of experimental contamination. When your awareness is raised, you do things in a subtly different way.

When I was parish priest of Tettenhall I saw nearly every day a public clock on the Upper Green that bore the motto: *'For every hour there is a record'*. During that period I began experimenting with a form of time-sheet used by many solicitors. Each hour is divided into ten units of six minutes each. The duration of each interview, letter or telephone call is jotted down, and can later be charged to the appropriate client account. I found this method too fiddling and intrusive, and unsuited to some aspects of priestly work. Nevertheless, it helped me to evolve my own way of logging time-use to the nearest quarter of an hour, and to keep an eye on the balance between such categories as public worship, private prayer, pastoral visits and interviews, sermon preparation, other study and professional training, routine administration, planning, staff work, meetings, family time and time off. Over a two month period in summer 1975 I found that I was working an average of 55 hours a week, but feeling too strained and pressurised. This prompted me to take a smaller share of the numerous weddings and funerals, to cut down the number of meetings I attended and my non-parochial commitments, to use the parish secretary's help more effectively, and to get a retired computer operator to prepare the quarterly schedule of services involving five clergy and fifteen lay assistants at our three churches. These measures enabled me to spend more time on prayer and study, pay more visits and still reduce my work package to 52 hours a week – probably to everyone's benefit!

Later, at Grimsby, I did something similar as part of a training course for bishops run by the Urban Ministry Project. Each participant kept a careful record of time-use for a three month period in autumn 1982. We divided each day simply into three sessions (morning, afternoon and evening), and roughly quantified the time spent on agreed categories of activity. This was a better method because it avoided too much hair-splitting over the inevitable interruptions and odd jobs. The object was not only to monitor time-use but also to identify our pressure-points. At the subsequent residential conference with our peers and consultants we found much value in comparing our experiences, and each of us was later able to explore this subject-matter in more detail with our own local support group.

This yielded some interesting findings. Each new sermon took me about three hours to prepare. I visited 100 parishes over the course of that year, and on average each visit took about four hours (including travel and meeting people afterwards, but excluding preparation time). Nearly half of these occasions were Confirmations, usually with First Communion and sometimes with Baptism as well (though in my first year I had conducted 55, the later annual average was around 40). In the same year I linked into 28 non-church community events, each taking an average of three hours. This covered voluntary organisations (7) such as the hospice or Marriage Guidance / Relate, visits to schools (6), civic events at borough and county levels (4), setting up a local radio station (5), and various other public gatherings (4).

Because of the distances involved I tended to conduct short pastoral consultations by telephone whenever appropriate, but to fit more substantial face-to-face encounters into slots of 45 minutes or an hour. Throughout the year I carried out 238 interviews lasting three-quarters of an hour or more, which represents an average of 5 per week or 21 per month excluding August. Of these 130 were with the clergy of my area (often home visits), 24 with ordinands (usually in my study), and the rest miscellaneous.

To this must be added the time spent in conferring regularly with my fellow bishops of Lincoln and Grantham, the archdeacons of Stow and Lindsey, and the whole senior staff, as well as with the heads of those departments for which I held a particular responsibility – education, local ministry training and ecumenical relations. This worked out at 132 hours for the year. I must admit that before becoming a bishop I had little idea of what went into running a diocese, even though as a parish priest I had been on the Bishop's Council for ten years and served as rural dean and chairman of the diocesan house of clergy. I *thought* I knew what was involved, but the full reality came as quite a revelation.

Then there was the inevitable desk-work. Each week I received about 80 'real' letters, i.e. excluding committee papers and circulars, and despatched 40 to 50 replies. This was before the days of e-mail. My secretary normally worked for 9 hours per week, mostly typing letters and documents but also filing. My own desk-time in a typical week was spent on 6 hours' dictating, 3 to 6 hours' telephoning, and 4 hours in devouring the contents of my in-tray, signing letters and marking up items for my secretary to file. On average it took me an hour to deal with an inch of in-tray papers, though this varied according to the subject-matter.

As for the inner life, I set aside about 470 hours in the same year for prayer, study and sermon preparation.

This gave me a clear and realistic picture of how my time was actually being spent. In January 1983 I noted the following amongst the pressure-points felt in my ministry:

1. Needing to keep myself on top form for numerous special occasions – partly a question of good health and enough sleep, partly a question of pride in matching people's expectations.
2. Preparing sermons 'against the clock' for major public events.
3. Needing to think, plan and commit myself a long way in advance – up to two years ahead on specific dates.
4. Remaining accessible – and appearing so – without being swamped or diverted from the right priorities.
5. Finding dates for emergencies or other priorities that crop up at short notice.
6. Responding to letters and messages that flood in faster than I can deal with them.
7. Finding time to travel to all parts of an area covering 1,500 square miles.
8. Participating in complex corporate decisions often requiring consultation with colleagues based 30 miles away.

All this will sound familiar to anyone who has been a senior leader at area level in any organisation. There were, however, a number of other pressure-points that were not to do with time-use, but inherent in the nature of a bishop's work. These will be discussed later in the appropriate chapters.

In the early years of my episcopate national and international commitments were minimal, amounting to just a few days per year. In later years these responsibilities expanded considerably. For example, in 1996 international duties claimed 15 days and General Synod work (I was then carrying 'cabinet' responsibilities) shot up to a massive 45 days. At the heaviest point extra-diocesan work was taking up about 7 working days per month (77 per annum) – a huge pressure.

Four stages in planning time-use

In the light of such information it is highly necessary to step back and adjust one's allocation of time so as to spread and balance the elements better – an exercise which I repeat at least annually. My own approach to the planning of time is by no means original, and moves through four stages:

a)   noting given factors
b)   creating space
c)   budgeting and scheduling 'set workload'
d)   fitting in 'flexible workload'

The first stage is to schedule into next year's diary *given factors* beyond one's control. These include major festivals and Bank Holidays, school terms and half-terms, and inevitable activities such as staff meetings, attendance at Diocesan Synod and the Bishop's Council, attendance at General Synod and the House of Bishops, and other national and international commitments. Birthdays and other significant anniversaries are built in at this stage, though the manner of observing them will not be decided until nearer the time.

The second stage is *creating space* by blocking off an annual holiday, other short breaks (e.g. post-Christmas and post-Easter), regular days off, times away for retreat or conferences, and 'catch-up days' after busy spells. Blocks of time for creative study and planning need to be built at this stage. All this generally amounts to about 100 days – essential for survival and safeguarding 'quality time'.

The third stage is to list what I see as my *'set workload'* for the coming year, and to estimate the number of hours required for each category of activity. This will probably total about 900 hours, which I then split down in "sessions" of 3 to 4 hours' duration – mornings, afternoons and evenings. Possible dates are earmarked for events that will need to happen (e.g. ordinations, confirmations, institutions, regular consultations with archdeacons and heads of departments, etc), taking care to spread the load and avoid bunching too much into any week. I would generally earmark roughly the required number of Sunday mornings for confirmations and commissioning Local Ministry teams, Sunday mornings or evenings for ordinations, and Tuesday / Wednesday / Friday evenings for institutions and licensings. Most dates are negotiated several months or weeks ahead, and just a few at short notice. The general plan for hospitality is shaped at this stage, with specific invitations following nearer the time.

The fourth stage is to fit the *'flexible workload'* into the remaining sessions – interviews, home visits, extra hospitality and other discretionary events. Essential though it is to have a balanced overall plan, it does have to be flexible. This can be achieved in various ways, such as swapping one thing for another, referral to colleagues, the occasional cancellation, or consciously compensating after too much or too little of anything. No two weeks are ever quite the same, but keeping the notion of an ideal standard week in mind does help to build up a familiar rhythm, which is more sustainable than a totally irregular existence.

Useful tips for diary control

The following strategies, suggested by a range of bishops, proved useful in handling the diary:

a) ***Emergency slots*** Reserve two emergency slots per week for urgent needs that will not become apparent until they happen, such as personal crises, funerals, unexpected developments, media attention, etc. Until two or three days beforehand these slots are treated as already booked. Then they can either be used for an emergency, or exchanged for another slot, or adapted to some different purpose.

b) ***Preparation time*** When accepting any engagement, book the specific time slot when preparation can be done.

c) ***Week full up*** When 15 sessions have been booked, mark the whole week "full" and resist further bookings, if possible.

d) ***Allow for secular events at short notice*** Invitations to events in the wider community often arise on a much shorter timescale than church events. It is hard to fit in the former if you are too booked up with the latter.

e) ***Deanery rationing*** Work out how many public engagements you aim to carry out in each deanery over the year, in rough proportion to the population and number of clergy. Those who invite you often or early cannot always be accepted. Where invitations are slow to arise they must be initiated. Smaller churches often hesitate to invite the bishop because they doubt their ability to put on a 'big occasion', and need encouragement.

f) ***Leave your diary at home normally*** If asked when out and about, "Are you free on such-and-such a date?", you run the risk of accepting engagements on the spur of the moment without due consideration. However, the exception to this is, when future meeting dates are likely to be fixed, always take your diary, thereby minimising recurrent absences.

g) ***Don't peak too often*** To preach effectively the adrenalin must flow. Limit the number of times this occurs within a few days, e.g. only twice between Friday evening and Monday morning. Pacing and sustainability must be related to one's energy levels.

h) ***'Four-fold filter'*** Invitations should normally meet the following criteria before receiving a 'Yes':

(1) Could I realistically be available on the date requested?
(2) Does that week allow room for preparation and travel as well as the actual event?
(3) Would this fit into the deanery ration (see **e.** above) and the desired balance and spread of my work?
(4) Is this the type of activity that I should do, or want to do?

i) **Consolidate travel time** Avoid making long excursions more than once a day. An engagement far from home can often be balanced by another that is nearer. Mileage and travel can be much reduced by combining calls. Minimise long journeys when the weather is likely to be bad or the traffic heavy, e.g. February fog or seaside destinations at Bank Holidays.

j) **Family time** In every working day keep at least a couple of hours, in addition to meals, as 'downtime' for various family purposes.

k) **Two votes** With the rare exception of genuine emergencies, work should not intrude into days off or family time unless decided by 'two votes', i.e. with my spouse's agreement.

m) **Use gaps profitably** When odd gaps occur in working time, e.g. someone arriving late for an appointment, it is useful to have on hand a pile of straight-forward tasks to fill the time profitably.

l) **The 'one-in-four' rule** If a bishop has no children of school age at home, keep one Sunday in four free from preaching and public engagements, and spend the day quietly at home. If the family is geared to school holidays, adapt this ideal to the dates of terms and half-terms.

m) **Do not publish your diary engagements** For reasons of security and confidentiality it is not appropriate to publicise full details of one's schedule. This makes for greater flexibility, and reduces the need to explain late alterations or changed priorities.

These are small points in themselves, but their combined effect can improve time use significantly. Michael Whinney has a useful section on *'Priorities and Use of Time'* in his booklet *'Episcopacy Today and Tomorrow'* (pages 8-9). Management literature abounds in practical tips, and some helpful writers will be mentioned in the next chapter.

Punctuality

The pressure and public profile of a bishop's ministry make punctuality an indispensible virtue. My normal target is to reach any church where I am officiating at least a quarter of an hour before the service is due to start, or longer if there are books to be autographed and certificates to be signed. In addition, I build ten spare minutes into my travel schedule to allow for changing a tyre, traffic diversions or unforeseen delays.

Recognizing God's moment

The most important point of all is to be ready to change one's plan, or even set it aside temporarily, in response to the Spirit's promptings and to unexpected opportunities that crop up. From time to time God *'puts into our minds good desires'* (Collect for Easter Day, BCP) or suddenly brings to our attention some person or situation, apparently out of the blue. It requires spiritual sensitivity to discern whether this is a mere distraction or a nudge from the Holy Spirit!

The Greek language distinguishes between 'chronos' (time according to the clock) and 'kairos' (the ripe moment of opportunity). Paul exhorts the Colossians to *'make good use of every opportunity you have'* (Col 4, 5 TEV; cf. Eph 5, 16). I have often been surprised to find that following a momentary 'hunch' has led me to follow a better course than I originally had in mind. On several occasions news of some crisis has arrived just when I could actually do something about it. Our human designs must always be subject to a higher providence, though this is no excuse for failing to plan.

If a senior church leader changes plans that are publicly known, there is always a danger of misunderstanding, as the apostle Paul found in his dealings with the church at Corinth. He had originally planned to visit Corinth twice, but changed his mind and failed to carry out the second visit. We can deduce from 2 Cor 1, 15 – 2, 4 what criticism was being levelled against him. The Corinthian Christians had formed the impression that Paul could not make his mind up. At first he had said one thing, but then done another. This set them wondering whether he had changed his mind to suit himself. Was he just thinking about his own convenience, and not really concerned about them? Could they depend on him, or take him seriously?

Paul countered this strongly. He reminded them it was *he* who had taught them the Christian faith. He did not *need* to come to Corinth again, since he was actually on his way to somewhere else. It was precisely out of pastoral concern that he had intended give them the benefit of a double visit, but had then realised that it would be more prudent *not* to come again if was only going to stir up unpleasantness. So his true motive for not coming back was consideration for them, though this had been misinterpreted as lack of concern and fickleness. Paul makes an important theological point by asking:

'Do I, when I frame my plans, frame them as a worldly man might, so that it should rest with me to say, "Yes, yes" or "No, no"?

(2 Cor 1, 17 NEB)

He implies that worldly people plans things just to suit themselves, and give no thought to what God might want. What matters is the underlying purpose or motive. Our human plans must be kept under constant scrutiny, and we should be ready to adapt them, if necessary, to God's purpose. A similar point is made in the letter of James:

'You do not know what tomorrow will bring ... You ought to say, "If the Lord wishes, we will do this or that".

(James 4, verses 13-15)

The value of developing a well-made plan lies not in following it blindly or rigidly, but in being able to adjust it responsively without going overboard and falling into chaos. The trick is to be both methodical and flexible. Sometimes we get it wrong. When this happens, we must simply apologise, seek forgiveness from God and those concerned, make amends and try to do better next time.

'For everything there is a season, and a time for every matter under heaven ...' (Ecclesiastes 3, 1-8). To get the balance right in a bishop's ministry requires space for discerning God's purposes and promptings: prayer time, desk time, interview and meeting time, thinking and preparation time, travel time, family and leisure time, etc.. There must be room for all these, as well as the obvious and publicly visible activities.

CHAPTER 10

Working Together As A Team

SHARING THE TASKS

Vital though personal qualities are to bishops' ministry, the episcopal office has an essentially corporate dimension. However skilled bishops may be as pastors, teachers or leaders, it is impossible to fulfil these roles single-handedly without the co-operation of others. At the consecration service the archbishop reminds the candidates that bishops are *'chief pastors'* and that *'it is their duty to share with their fellows presbyters the oversight of the church'.* Similarly, in the ninth question at the ordination vows he asks the candidates: *'Will you work with your fellow servants in the gospel for the sake of the kingdom of God?'* Collaborative ministry is diametrically opposed to an individualistic or arbitrary style of operating. It demands a competence no less than is expected of other professionals in such spheres as teaching, human relations, finance or public administration, and calls for not just the desire to engage with other people's efforts but an actual ability to do so.

Moreover, leading and sustaining the whole life of the diocese requires sound structures to bring those with complementary roles together effectively. It presupposes a commitment to consult in a genuinely open way before reaching policy decisions. Bishops have to win trust by proving themselves utterly trustworthy. They tread on dangerous ground if they arouse unrealistic expectations, or if they give informal undertakings which they fail to deliver. They have to exemplify good practice, and not make do with sloppy or amateurish ways.

Bishops occupy a key position in stimulating the fullness of ministries – not just ministries within the church, but those reaching out into the community. Bishop John Robinson made the crucial point that:

> *'... the episcopé of the church cannot be confined to one man. Episcopé, like priesthood and ministry, is a function of the whole church ... An episcopal church is not merely a church that "has bishops". It is a church that takes episcopé – the episcopé of Christ – seriously at every level.'*
>
> (quoted by E. James, *'The Life of Bishop J.A.T. Robinson',* Collins 1987, p 85)

It is not the case that all ministry belongs in essence to the bishops, who then graciously let others share bits of it. Rather, the bishops carry out in person a range of ministerial functions, whilst at the same time sharing many tasks without offloading them entirely. As Kenneth Stevenson pointed out:

> *'they need to take the breadth of their priestly and diaconal ministries into their episcopate ... but not interfere with colleagues and others in an unhelpful way'*
> (Final presidential address to Portsmouth Diocesan Synod, June 2009)

Suffragans

Some people regard suffragan bishops as a theological anomaly, and argue for monarchical episcopacy as the universal standard. However, at many points in the church's history it has become apparent that the episcopal workload exceeds what one person can accomplish (see the Cameron Report entitled *'Episcopal Ministry'*, CHP 1990 – especially chapter 11). The pragmatic development of suffragan or auxiliary bishops is a phenomenon to be seen in the Anglican, Lutheran, Roman Catholic, Orthodox and Oriental Orthodox traditions. The need for other patterns of episcopal ministry in the Church of England was recognised (paragraph 433), though little evidence was offered about the merits or demerits of the various models quoted. Emphasis was laid on the communion of the Holy Trinity, and the importance of this model for the life of the church (chapter 2). Curiously, though, this approach was then side-lined in favour of a largely monarchical view of the episcopate, modified only slightly by describing suffragans as 'episcopal vicars'.

Bill Ind, in a paper discussing Christology, made this comment:

> *'From my experience of Lincoln [diocese] there is one episcopate which we all share, and that sharing is not all one way. It is not that the Bishop of Lincoln, out of his kindness, gives something to me and to the Bishop of Grimsby. It is that we share with each other, and there are some occasions, indeed – though it may sound odd to say so – in which the Bishop of Lincoln might be my agent, or the agent of the Bishop of Grimsby. That may sound like undermining the diocesan bishop's authority but, if we take the trinitarian model seriously, that is far from the case. If we look carefully as Rublev's icon of the Trinity, and then ask one another which one is the Father in that icon, almost always people assume that it is the figure in the centre. Yet our knowledge of iconography makes it clear that the Father is, in fact, the figure on the left, but somehow the pattern is such that they all seem to be paying attention to each other. It is difficult to see at any one time where ultimate authority comes from, because it is so fully and completely shared.'*
> (From an unpublished talk to a clergy cell, 1991)

Ways of working vary from one diocese to another. A few dioceses have formal area schemes for the suffragans, and several have informal ones. Difficulties sometimes arise where there is only one suffragan, especially if the diocesan bishop is reluctant to share or shunts the suffragan into looking after sector ministries. In some dioceses the archdeacons largely handle appointments, whilst in others this process is handled in a collegial manner.

Would it have been better if Lincoln diocese, the largest by area in this country, had been chopped up into three separate mono-episcopal units? I doubt it. If team ministry is valid at incumbent level, the same ought to be true at bishop level. The way in which responsibilities were shared between the three bishops, with the diocesan in ultimate charge and keeping direct touch with the diocese as a whole, was well understood by clergy and people. It had worked well since the 1960's, and made for flexibility. During a vacancy in see, or in the absence of any of the bishops in sickness or on sabbatical leave, or when national or international responsibilities fell heavily on any of them, they could re-distribute tasks amongst themselves seamlessly as long as they worked as a team.

In a parochial team daily face-to-face contact is possible, but at diocesan level links with colleagues must be sustained by different means. Though it can be difficult to join an established team, the Bishops of Lincoln and Grantham (Simon Phipps and Dennis Hawker) welcomed me very generously. It was a major adjustment for them to accept a new colleague fourteen years their junior, who had not shared their experience as army officers in World War II. I belonged to a different generation and culture, and it took me a while to grasp what was going on. Yet they never made me feel an outsider. It is always a delicate matter to appoint a new member to an existing team, since the newcomer is bound to have some impact on how it operates. It is mutual trust and respect, rather than role or seniority, and attending sensitively to one another's insights and concerns that make for a true team.

It was always regarded as axiomatic that the diocesan bishop had the right of first refusal for any episcopal engagement. Ordinations, confirmations, institutions, licensings and other public functions were divided between us on a roughly equal basis. Simon spread himself thinly over the whole territory, whilst Dennis and I normally stayed within our own halves of the diocese. Area boundaries were porous rather than water-tight, and we were free to stand in for one another or accept occasional engagements in the other half of the diocese without any sense of trespassing. For a few special diocesan occasions such as St Hugh's Day, the annual Renewal of Vows or the triennial Mothers' Union Festival all three of us would appear together, but as a rule only one bishop attended any event. Any parish, or group of parishes, could expect an average ratio of one visit by the diocesan to two visits by the area suffragan. In this way we built up a thorough acquaintance with the clergy and parishes, and tried always to pay regard to the needs of the whole diocese rather than simply ploughing our own furrow.

When Simon and Dennis retired, their places were taken in 1987 by Bob Hardy and Bill Ind. As the three of us were of similar age and had all been parish priests, we found it natural to share a common perspective. This trio continued without interruption for the next ten years until Bill's translation to Truro, and the pattern of staff work remained broadly similar. Our sense of collegiality was reinforced by the consultancy that the Grubb Institute conducted with us in 1989, to be described later. We became more aware of our responsibility to help our people face the need for change, and to work out its implications. Above all, we did our best to 'hold' the diocese, both in our prayers and in our public ministry.

When Bill moved on to Truro he was succeeded as Bishop of Grantham by Alastair Redfern, with whom I had worked at Tettenhall in the late 1970's. He brought his own distinctive contribution, and he, Bob and I operated on a similar pattern for my last four years up to retirement – another happy trio who complemented each other, as before. We saw the distinctive thrust of our episcopate as *apostolic* – bringing alive the contemporary relevance of the Gospel message, leading the mission of the whole people of God, affirming lay Christians in their witness and service in the world, developing a range of diverse ministries, and standing often at the edge of the church to 'build bridges' with all in the community who strive for the values of the Kingdom of God. This apostolic emphasis worked hand-in-glove with the distinctively *diaconal* role of the archdeacons, who stood in the midst of church life and were key figures in managing the day-to-day affairs of the diocese.

ARCHDEACONS

We held a 'high doctrine' of the archdeacon. None of the Lincoln bishops in my time had ever been archdeacons, or wished to encroach on their domain. We relied on their skill and efficiency in keeping the ecclesiastical machinery in running order. They carried an immense workload: dealing with faculties for over 600 churches and churchyards, as well as housing provision for some 250 stipendiary clergy; keeping a close watch on finance, especially the payment of quota and working expenses; negotiating over pastoral re-organisation, redundant buildings and the closure of churchyards; swearing in churchwardens and monitoring the quinquennial inspection of church buildings; liaising with the rural deans and lay chairmen of 23 deanery synods; attending to problem parishes, emergency PCC meetings and occasional disciplinary proceedings; and so on. It was they, together with the diocesan secretary, registrar and their small staffs, who really ran the diocese. However, they did not spend all their time 'in the engine room'. As senior and experienced priests they were integrally involved in the pastoral care of the clergy, the process of parochial appointments and the corporate policy-making of diocesan boards and councils.

Bernard gave shrewd advice to Pope Eugenius about the importance of appointing suitable people to his staff:

'Let us come to your colleagues and helpers. They are busy on your behalf. They form the inner circle of your friends. It follows that, if they are good, you more than anyone else reap the benefit. If they are bad, you more than anyone else suffer the harm ... Do not say that you are good if you are relying on bad people. What profit does your individual virtue bring to the churches of God when the views that prevail are those of people of an opposite tendency? ... On the other hand, if you have good people around you, the more often they assist you the better. It is your duty to summon – wherever they may come from – and admit to office not young people but those who are mature; old, I mean, not so much in years as in behaviour'

('*On Consideration*' IV, 9)

We Lincoln bishops were fortunate to have around us able, mature and dedicated archdeacons. In the south of the diocese the Archdeaconry of Lincoln was held successively by Michael Adie, Ronald Milner, Michael Brackenbury and Arthur Hawes. The north of the diocese was divided into two archdeaconries, Stow and Lindsey, which until 1994 were held in conjunction with other responsibilities – Stow with a small rural incumbency and Lindsey with a residentiary canonry at the cathedral. After that they were combined into one full-time post. In my time Bill Dudman, David Scott, Christopher Laurence and Roderick Wells were those with whom I had the privilege of working in tandem, and I owed a great deal to their friendship and practical wisdom.

It would be hard to exaggerate the importance of a close partnership between the archdeacon and the area suffragan. Every month I spent a couple of hours with each archdeacon, catching up on our personal agenda, reviewing cases of sickness or difficulty, preparing our suggestions for appointments to vacant posts, and keeping a watchful eye on everybody in our patch. We would feed any major concerns into the next meeting of the whole staff. In our latter years Roderick and I got into the habit of 'trawling' systematically through a couple of deaneries each time we met, so that no priest or parish in our territory should be lost from view. We tried to keep an up-to-date picture of how they were doing and where they might be heading. I wish that I had thought of doing this in a sustained and systematic way many years sooner!

The Bishop's Staff

The three bishops met rarely as a distinct sub-group – usually just once each September to plan the following year's confirmations services, though we often rang each other up. Every fortnight we joined with the whole Bishop's Staff, which normally included the dean, the three archdeacons, the diocesan secretary, the bishop's PA and sometimes another consultant. The diocesan bishop was firmly in the driving seat, and rightly so. Alternate meetings dealt with appointments – a heavy load of up to 40 vacant posts at once – a process to be more fully described in my chapter on *'Sending New Ministers'.* The intervening 'think' meetings were devoted to broader policy questions. We also met residentially away from the diocese for three days a year, assisted on occasions by a group process facilitator. This overall pattern made for a strong, flexible and supportive team life, of which I believe the benefits were felt throughout our widely dispersed diocese. The danger in all this was collusion, and it was salutary when a dissentient voice made us face awkward questions. Much of our time at staff meetings was spent on the problems of 10% of our clergy, but in a caring church this cannot be avoided.

Co-ordination

In areas of overlap it is particular important to have a clear agreement about 'who does what'. The most obvious examples of this are: sickness, emergencies and vacancies. When a priest or a member of a clergy family was ill, we generally arranged at staff meeting whether the diocesan, the area suffragan or the archdeacon would pay the next visit, so that we did not all turn up on the doorstep or in the hospital ward. Often the visit would be paid by whichever bishop or archdeacon would next be in that locality, since distance and time were major factors in such a large diocese. In particular cases a special trip might be necessary – e.g. to hospitals as far afield as Nottingham or Hull. Afterwards colleagues needed to be kept informed and, in protracted cases, a decision made about who should keep up the main ongoing connection.

There needs to be a clear strategy for handling issues that are of interest to the media, and a key role in this is played by the communications officer, where one exists. To cope with pastoral emergencies a plan must always be in place. For example, if a clergy marriage breaks down, it has to be agreed what should be announced in the parish, what cover can be arranged for parochial life to continue, what can be said to the press, what help the priest may need, who will look after the needs of the spouse and family (housing may be required at short notice), etc. This requires careful co-ordination. Vital roles are played by the diocesan secretary, the registrar, the chancellor, the communications officer and the bishop's chaplain – not just in an emergency but in the smooth running of diocesan life at many points where legal, financial and pastoral concerns intersect. Ultimately the diocesan bishop must see that it all holds together, and be able to rely on these helpers' integrity and sound judgement.

Operation 'Patchwork'

In November 1985 colleagues on the Bishop's Staff gave their backing to an operation that became known as the 'patchwork scheme'. We tackled it first in my area in the north of the diocese, later in the south too, and sustained it with some modifications for about fifteen years. The broad purpose was to develop a greater sense of confidence and responsibility at deanery level through four specific aims:

    a) to foster the partnership between rural deans and deanery lay chairmen as a vital element in enhancing the role of the 23 deaneries;
    b) to encourage area identity and cohesion as a counterbalance to the vastness and diversity of the diocese;
    c) to help deanery leaders (both lay and ordained) to encourage one another by sharing ideas and experiences between neighbouring deaneries; and
    d) to strengthen the personal links between deanery leaders and the Bishop's Staff.

This operation was designed to be workable with the existing set-up of area suffragans, archdeacons and deaneries, without first having to redraw the map. It complemented any formal devolution of responsibilities to deanery synods by diocesan bodies such as the Board of Finance or the Pastoral Committee. There was to be no extra cost to the diocese and no increase in the total number of meetings. The new 'patchwork meetings' were offset by pruning certain existing meetings. Separate gatherings of rural deans in the north and south were discontinued; diocesan boards and councils met every four months instead of three months; and archdiaconal Pastoral Sub-Committees either met less often or transferred discussion of some issues to 'patchwork meetings'.

This new style of meeting had the following characteristics:

- informal home setting over a light meal
- away from Lincoln, where most diocesan meetings were held
- three components – fellowship / worship / the church's mission in that patch
- agenda 'bottom up', not 'top down'
- no paperwork
- attended by rural deans and lay chairmen, usually from three adjacent deaneries, plus the archdeacon and area suffragan

This involved an average of eight people: 3 rural deans, 3 lay chairmen, the archdeacon and the area bishop. I had four such 'patches', each holding about three meetings a year. The mutual hospitality we enjoyed was a good catalyst. The quality of interaction was usually excellent, and we managed to cope with one over-talkative rural dean and draw out several rather shy lay chairmen. The archdeacon and I engaged with whatever agenda arose naturally, and avoided bringing up issues from 'them at Lincoln'. He and I intended that deanery leaders should feel that we were available to them on their patch and on their terms, so that they could square up to the challenges of their own area with whatever assistance they might request from the diocese.

The lay chairmen were drawn into a more corporate involvement than had previously been the case, and out of this came a pattern of regular meetings between lay chairmen, rural deans, archdeacons and bishops. These informal meetings were a barometer of local opinion across the diocese, as well as a sounding-board for the differences of mood between deaneries. It enabled us all to recognise that strategy in such a far-flung diocese had to be flexible, and to honour the different character of various deaneries.

INITIATING POLICY

Diocesan policy is not made solely by the bishop. A significant new emphasis was introduced by the Synodical Government Measure 1969 which stated that:

> *'It shall be the duty of the bishop to consult with the diocesan synod on matters of general concern and importance to the diocese'* (s 4 (3)).

Conversely, the diocesan synod has a duty *'to advise the bishop on any matters on which he may consult the synod'*. Moreover, it

> *'shall keep the deanery synods of the diocese informed of the policies and problems of the diocese, ... and shall keep themselves informed of events and opinion in the parishes, and shall give opportunities for discussing at meetings of the diocesan synod matters raised by deanery synods and parochial church councils'*
>
> (s 4 (2b) and (5))

This paints the picture of ideas and opinions flowing dynamically in all directions. The basic principles of synodical government are helpfully summarised by Colin Podmore in *'Aspects of Anglican Identity'* (CHP, 2005 – chapter 7), and pages 115-116 are specially relevant to bishops. Policy should be able to arise from any quarter. It is not for the bishop or his staff to dictate policy, yet their broad acquaintance with issues across the diocese does place an onus on them to initiate a good deal of policy. They should be neither too dominant nor too diffident. Whatever proposals they feed into the Bishop's Council or Diocesan Synod need to be tested in debate. As consensus emerges, the bishops and archdeacons play a key role in articulating it and encouraging its implementation. Hence the dictum that the church is 'episcopally led and synodically governed'.

At first I was surprised to discover how much longer a time-scale this process required at diocesan level than at parochial level. The Bishop's Staff generally needed to be thinking at least two or three years ahead, and had to show a good deal of patience and perseverance until the effectiveness or otherwise of any specific policy became apparent. It generally took about four or five years before a new idea reached the grassroots, and then not always successfully!

The bishop – whether diocesan or suffragan – should not, in my view, be too closely involved with specific proposals for pastoral re-reorganisation until the process of public debate is well advanced, and the extent of local support or opposition has begun to emerge. By holding back initially the bishop may be able to resolve contentious cases by conciliatory intervention later. Only once did I attend a meeting of an Archidiaconal Pastoral Sub-Committee at the archdeacon's request, but in general I held back from such discussions until the proposals had been clarified and tested. I would sometimes give the secretary of the Pastoral Committee guidance over the precise wording of the draft scheme immediately prior to its circulation to interested parties. The more the bishop can act as a neutral advisor the less it is likely that proposals will be contested by appeal to the Church Commissioners or Privy Council.

SIMON PHIPPS' APPROACH

Simon Phipps was aware that he did not excel at committee work, and developed his own way of relating to diocesan boards and councils. He did not usually attend in person, though his presence counted for all the more when he did. A day or two before each board meeting he would get its principal officer to take him through the agenda, so that he was forewarned what issues were likely to arise and could feed in his own ideas and suggestions. If there was something urgent or critically important, he still had the chance to attend, or to brief someone else to advocate his views. This saved him many hours, yet he knew what was going on, and we knew his mind which was often visionary. The principal officers kept in direct touch with him, and felt supported and understood in the responsibilities they bore.

He chaired the Bishop's Council, and sometimes we had good meetings that engaged positively with a number of his forward-looking ideas (see my essay in *'Simon Phipps – a portrait'*, published by Continuum 2003, pages 96-99). However, some of the problems it tackled – especially in the realms of manpower and finance – were never quite resolved and kept recurring. He experimented briefly with a new structure that brought together the chairmen and principal officers of the major boards, in the hope that their officers would work together more collaboratively, and integrate the range of their concerns. However, this was not effective, partly because the separate boards had too much institutional momentum and partly because their officers, who were mostly very talented, were heavily involved in their own programmes of work.

BOB HARDY'S APPROACH

In Bob Hardy's early years at Lincoln there was a growing feeling that the diocese was top-heavy with boards and specialist advisers who did not work together sufficiently, and that resources could be better shared for the benefit of the deaneries and parishes. In 1992 Bob grasped this nettle by setting up a small Structures Review Group, consisting of Ray Furnell, Ray Snell and myself. Our task was:

'to produce a committee structure and a method of tasking non-parochial diocesan stipendiary ministers and salaried or honorary staff which most efficiently facilitates the mission of the Church in this diocese'.

After wide consultation we recommended some streamlining of budgets and committee structures. More importantly, we put forward measures that would foster a greater sense that policy and finance were owned by the deaneries and parishes. The underlying philosophy was that diocesan resources should be geared in a way that enabled the Local Church in its tasks of worship, mission, evangelism and nurture.

A key element in transforming the culture of the diocese was to make the Bishop's Council a more effective 'super-board' that could co-ordinate other structures, together with officers and advisers, and resolve conflicts of sectional interest. David King has wisely pointed out:

'For policy to resolve conflicts, opportunity must be given for all parties to review and revise their needs. In other words, agreement on policy is essential for the resolution of conflict... Policy also enables persons to solve day-to-day difficulties by relating short-term situations to long-term aims and effects.'

(S.D.M. King, *'Training within the Organisation'*, Tavistock 1964, page 141)

Sound policy is as much about process as content, and Bob kept a firm grip on the separate boards by getting them to report regularly to the Bishop's Council and become more accountable. Board chairmen were expected to table an executive summary, rather than full minutes, of their last board meeting – each board on paper of a different colour. This résumé was to fit on one side of A4 paper, and to distinguish between decisions, information about ongoing work, recommendations and issues for debate. This gave a clearer sense of the overall picture. Bob put his weight behind a series of policy developments, such as *'New Times, New Ways'* (1991), *'A Manifesto – Developing a new Initiative'* (1994), *'Forwards in Mission and Ministry'* (1998) and *'Moving towards Total Ministry'* (2000). He successfully communicated throughout the diocese one simple aim, which most people got to know by heart: **'to secure a growing, worshipping, celebrating, proclaiming and caring Christian presence in each community of our diocese'.** This appeared on every agenda of the Bishop's Council, and was supported by strategic objectives – an approach that generated a sense of continuity, coherence and forward movement. People were helped to see where their individual contributions fitted into the bigger picture.

The bishop as manager

Some of these measures were largely a question of good management. No human organisation can do without management, and what matters is its quality. To some extent the bishop's role is comparable to that of a senior manager in many organisations, though that is only part of the picture. My own preferred definition of management is that of Sir Charles Reynold:

'Management is the process of getting things done through a community of people.'

The main functions of leadership are typically described in terms such as these:

i.   *to promote insight into the common aims of the group;*
ii. *to identify and harness the resources of the group, and co-ordinate effort;*
iii. *to help decisions to be made and carried out;*
iv. *to maintain cohesion and harmony;*
v.   *to represent the group to the outside world.*

Self-evidently these functions are closely relevant to the ministry of the bishop, who is the 'link person', 'coherence person' and 'identity person' of the diocese (to borrow useful phrases from *'Ordained Ministry Today'*, CACTM 1969, page 37). A proper emphasis on collaborative working does not, however, abrogate the responsibility of a leader to speak out and sometimes to stand alone. For bishops this is part of the cost of their own discipleship.

A theological understanding of Church & Kingdom

Whilst secular concepts of management can illuminate some aspects of the bishop's role and work, they cannot fully do justice to a theological understanding of the Church's purpose. As we have already seen, the notion of servant leadership has a strong biblical basis and Christological reference. A significant element in recent ecumenical dialogue has been to spell out a more explicit understanding of the nature and purpose of the Church, its mission and its ministry. At world-wide level this can be seen especially in the Anglican-Lutheran *'Niagara Report'* (1987), and in Anglican-Roman Catholic documents such as *'Church as Communion'* (1991) and *'The Gift of Authority'* (1999). At regional level in Northern Europe agreed statements on this theme have also emerged from the Meissen, Porvoo and Reuilly Conversations, notably "Porvoo" (1993), chapters 2 and 4. My own understanding of ecclesiology is along these lines, which is hardly surprising in view of my deep involvement in this work for many years. The General Synod has endorsed these reports as a fair reflection of current Anglican thinking.

This approach stresses that God's ultimate purpose is to restore all that he has made, and bring the whole of creation into unity with himself. The Church does not exist for its own sake, but is meant to be an instrument of that broader purpose by embodying a new quality of humanity in Christ. Life in communion with God and one another points to God's kingdom as a 'sign, instrument and foretaste of a reality that comes from beyond history'. The diverse and complementary gifts of the Holy Spirit are for the common good of all. The church itself is a divine and transcendental reality, yet at the same time a human institution marked by ambiguity and frailty, and needing to live by God's forgiveness. It is in constant need of repentance and renewal. Its visible unity is sustained by various 'bonds of communion', and faithfulness to its apostolic mission is carried forward by diverse forms of ministry, including the episcopate. This full-blooded portrait of the Church's nature that has been highlighted by many years' patient ecumenical dialogue cannot adequately be summarised in just a few lines, but is worth studying in detail. At its best the Church should, in all humility, portray a quality of life that has something of value to offer to all humanity.

Resources for new bishops

New bishops would do well to attend to the ecclesiological insights offered in "Porvoo", especially chapters II & IV. They also require a working knowledge of the Synodical Government Measure 1969, the Church Representation Rules, the Mission and Pastoral Measure 2011 and its Code of Practice. On management topics such writers as John Adair, Stephen Covey, Peter Drucker, Charles Handy, Patrick Lencioni, Peter Senge and Rosemary Stewart may prove helpful. Sociological research and contemporary novels can also yield valuable insights. Chapter 17 will deal separately with training courses for bishops.

Making the Connections

The *'Reuilly Declaration'* (1999) contained a significant clause, adapted from the *'Meissen Declaration'*:

> 'We acknowledge that personal, collegial and communal oversight (episcopé) is embodied and exercised in all our churches in a variety of forms, as a visible sign of the Church's unity and continuity in apostolic life, mission and ministry'.
>
> (paragraph 47 A (vi))

This ties in with John Robinson's point that episcopé in various forms is a function of the whole church, and has to be taken seriously at every level. There are many structures and groupings that sustain diocesan life, and the bishops need to be in touch with them all. To offer a simple analogy, a map of the London underground shows several 'lines' (e.g. Bakerloo, Central, Jubilee, Circle, etc) criss-crossing the capital. Each line is distinct, with a life of its own, yet they interconnect and at some points even run side by side. Together they service the whole community. Similar systems of communication exist across a diocese, serving different facets of the church's mission in society. Since episcopé is a function of the whole church, it follows that the episcopate must be integrally linked with these systems.

Here and in the next few chapters I shall pick out those particular 'lines' or networks that are of special significance for bishops' ministry. The two most obvious are the *episcopal* and *synodical* networks. The first one dates back many centuries, and especially in the more rural parts of Lincolnshire a strong rudimentary feeling persists that ultimately the diocese is simply the bishop and the parishes. Churchwardens, as the bishop's officers in the parish, are a fundamental link in that chain. Indeed, without them the local church would collapse in some communities. On occasions we made a point of getting churchwardens together to ensure that they were not overshadowed or marginalised by the synodical system. Much routine business of the parochial system passes up and down this episcopal network, in which churchwardens, parish priests, rural deans and archdeacons all have their place. Deanery clergy chapters engage most clergy, but not the laity. Although the Convocations of bishops and clergy still exist and can exercise residual rights, in practice they are largely submerged in the General Synod.

Parallel to the episcopal network is the synodical one, expressing the basic partnership and interdependence of laity, clergy and bishops. This 'line' stretches from the annual meeting of parishioners, through the Parochial Church Council to the three levels of Deanery, Diocesan and General Synod. It also embraces other statutory bodies created in the 20th century, such as the diocesan boards of Finance and Education and the Mission and Pastoral Committee. All of them in different ways express mutual obligations.

Bishops, on account of their essentially corporate role, are inescapably connected to both systems. Part of their job is to see that the two parallel networks interconnect as much as possible. Normally I aimed to visit 80-100 parishes a year. I have already described how, in partnership with the archdeacon, I tried to relate constructively to the twelve rural deans and twelve lay chairmen of my territory by means of 'patchwork meetings'. As regards deanery synods and clergy chapters, I aimed to pay an annual visit to each deanery – usually the synod in one year and the chapter in the next – though this did not always pan out neatly. Putting these occasions to their fullest use did, I discovered, require me to plan carefully the nature of my intervention, and not just leave my participation to chance. As regards diocesan bodies, it was not usual or desirable for all three bishops and all three archdeacons to attend those committees of which they were members 'ex officio'. It would have made the Bishop's Staff unduly dominant, and wasted a lot of time. Instead we shared out the coverage between us, and encouraged the streamlining of structures where possible.

Whether the episcopate is exercised by one bishop or more, the fundamental requirement is to operate in a corporate and participative manner. The loyalty that we show to one another as colleagues should provide a model that others can follow in sharing their tasks at all levels of church life. I would, therefore, describe the following aspects as integral to episcopé:

> **It is corporate** – not individualistic, but skilled in and committed to collaborative leadership; delegating, sharing in corporate consultation, and administering the Church's human and material resources professionally and competently.
>
> **It is accountable** – to God for living up to one's calling and the vows of consecration; to the Church for obeying and upholding its discipline and canon law; and to all those with whom we are bound by a common purpose.

CHAPTER 11

Caring for People Within & Beyond the Church

CHIEF PASTORS

In describing the ministry of a bishop the liturgy of ordination draws heavily on pastoral imagery derived from the Bible. The archbishop before administering the vows addresses the congregation in these terms:

> *'Bishops are called to serve and care for the flock of Christ. Mindful of the Good Shepherd, who laid down his life for his sheep, they are to love and pray for those committed to their charge, knowing their people and being known by them ... As chief pastors, it is their duty to share with their fellow presbyters the oversight of the Church ... With the shepherd's love, they are to be merciful, but with firmness; to minister discipline, but with compassion. They are to have a special care for the poor, the outcast and those in need. They are to seek out those who are lost and lead them home with rejoicing, declaring the absolution and forgiveness of sins to those who turn to Christ ... They are to confront injustice and work for righteousness and peace in all the world.'*

The same focus is evident in the seventh and tenth vows that a new bishop takes before being consecrated:

> *'Will you be gentle and merciful for Christ's sake to those who are in need, and speak for those who have no other to speak for them?'*

> *'Will you accept the discipline of this Church, exercising authority with justice, courtesy and love, and always holding before you the example of Christ?'*

Then in the ordination prayer the Archbishop prays:

> *'that as true shepherds they may feed and govern your flock ... Give them humility, that they may use their authority to heal, not to hurt; to build up, not to destroy ...'*

This is powerfully symbolised at the end of the service when the Archbishop hands a pastoral staff to the newly ordained bishop with the words:

> *'Keep watch over the whole flock in which the Holy Spirit has appointed you shepherd. Encourage the faithful, restore the lost, build up the Body of Christ.'*

In this chapter I first pick out some examples of how bishops' pastoral responsibilities have been understood and practised at various points in the church's history. Secondly, I describe my own approach to the care of clergy, church workers and their families, and some methods for putting this into practice. Thirdly, I look at caring for people in a corporate setting: the visitation of parishes, the review of ministry teams, engaging with other groups beyond church circles, and showing concern for other social realities that affect many people's daily lives.

Selected comments on Pastoral Matters

a) Pastoral imagery in Scripture

A rich seam of pastoral imagery, describing an intimate personal relationship, runs through the Old and New Testaments. The Lord himself is seen as the ultimate Shepherd of the flock: *'For he is our God; we are the people of his pasture and the sheep of his hand'* (Ps 95, 7). His care and protection are not merely generalised, but are felt individually: *'The Lord is my shepherd ... He makes me lie down in green pastures ... your rod and your staff, they comfort me ... Surely goodness and loving mercy shall follow me all the days of my life ...'* (Ps 23).

Over time various human roles develop within the Old Testament for mediating God's rule and care, such as the Lord's anointed king, the shepherd leader and the prophets whose task is to speak God's warnings and judgements. From this tradition Jesus emerges. In his person and ministry the zenith of pastoral ministry is reached: *'I am the door of the sheepfold ... I am the good shepherd ... I know my own sheep and they hear my voice'* (John 10). Already within the pages of the New Testament we can see this Christocentric concept of shepherding being consciously handed on in the apostolic church: e.g. Jesus' words to Peter, *'Feed my sheep'* (John 21) – the gospel passage most frequently read at consecrations; Paul's parting message to the elders at Ephesus, *'Keep watch over all the flock of which the Holy Spirit has made you overseers'* (Acts 20, 28-29); and Peter's charge to elders of the diaspora in Asia Minor, *'Tend the flock of God that is in your charge'* (1 Pet 5, 1-4).

b) The darker side of this analogy

The pastoral image, noble and inspiring though this ideal may be, can have its darker side. People have minds and consciences of their own, and do not want to be treated like sheep. It is unhealthy if pastors keep their flock in a dependent relationship, or fail to encourage growth towards responsibility and maturity. We have to beware of a "nanny church" and of overbearing priests or prelates.

Alec Graham (formerly Bishop of Newcastle) sounded this caveat:

'What is conventionally meant by pastoral ministry is one which perpetuates and thus reinforces highly dependent attitudes on one who is father and pastor, and as bishop you are both. Those who clamour for pastoral care ... often do not want to be led anywhere, rather to be assured and affirmed. They want in their parish priest a chaplain to a religious club, and in their bishop a sort of chaplain-general who keeps the offshoots of the club in touch with one another.

In the tenth chapter of St John's gospel the sacrificial note is clear and strong enough. Why do people keep sheep? Not as pets to be cosseted and fattened and endlessly provided for. If Jesus is the Good Shepherd and we his sheep, then he looks to us – as any shepherd looks to his sheep – for meat and for wool, to be fleeced and to be killed. In money and in living and dying the note of sacrifice is quite unambiguous. Sacrificial obedience then is what the Lord requires from his pastors, who are also his sheep. Sacrificial obedience is what the Lord seeks through his pastors to elicit from his people. That, I fancy, is a far cry from the pastoral model as generally understood ... The sacrificial implications ought to be made more explicit.'

(from an unpublished paper)

c) Gregory's approach

Gregory the Great's *'Pastoral Rule'* addressed social conditions very different from our own. His insight and practical wisdom have, though, an enduring interest and relevance not only for bishops in the exercise their pastoral office, but also for those occupying supervisory or tutorial roles in various professional settings. His observations were expressed as guidance to bishops, but are more widely applicable in the realm of spiritual direction. As a former abbot, he well understood the inevitable tension between pastoral and disciplinary roles.

In Part II of his handbook Gregory warned of the need for humility, particularly when exercising discipline:

'When bishops correct those under them who are at fault they must be careful, whilst punishing faults with due discipline by virtue of their authority, to acknowledge humbly that they themselves are only equal to the brothers whom they correct. The greater their power is demonstrated externally, the more it needs to be kept in check internally. The bishop's mind must not be carried away or elated by the enjoyment of power.'

(from Pt II, ch 6)

He also urged that the bishop should be judicious in applying severity or gentleness:

'The bishop requires prudence over whether to apply correction or whether to turn a

blind eye – i.e. whether he should be strict or gentle. There are times when people's faults should be prudently overlooked, though they must be given to understand that they are, in fact, being overlooked. Sometimes even what is openly known should be tolerated discreetly, whilst in other cases even hidden faults must be subjected to close scrutiny. Depending on the circumstances, they should either be taken to task gently or reprimanded sharply.'

(Part II, ch 10)

Gregory prudently advised bishops to mind their language when full of righteous indignation:

'When the bishop's mind is provoked to reprimand someone, it is very hard for him not to break out sometimes into words that would be better avoided. It usually happens that, when someone's fault is corrected with a harsh telling off, his superior is driven to use extreme language. When reproof blazes forth without moderation, the hearts of those that have offended can sink into dejection and despair ... To speak rudely kills the spirit of love in the hearer ...'

(Part II, ch 10)

In Part III of the *'Pastoral Rule'* Gregory underlined the bishop's need for the emotional intelligence to recognise what kind of person he was dealing with, and the flexibility to adapt his approach accordingly. He began with some simple analogies:

'The identical method of instruction does not suit everyone since all people are not endowed by the same type of character. Often, for example, what is beneficial to some is harmful to others. Vegetation that nourishes some animals kills others. The gentle murmuring that calms horses excites young puppies. Medicine that alleviates one disease aggravates another. Food that sustains a grown man would ruin the digestion of an infant.

The bishop needs, therefore, to adapt the way he gives spiritual instruction to the character of his hearers so as to suit the individual's particular need, though without deviating from the general art of sound education. The minds of attentive hearers can be likened to the taut strings of a harp. The skilful harpist plays by means of a variety of strokes ... The strings produce a harmonious sound since they are not all plucked with the same kind of stroke, even though they are played with one plectrum. For this reason every teacher, in edifying all people in the one virtue of love, must touch the hearts of his hearers using the same doctrine but not the same method of instruction for everyone.'

(Part III, prologue)

Gregory showed considerable insight into the contrast between the behaviour of people who are modest and those who are bad-tempered:

> 'Sometimes unassuming people in positions of authority fail to take action, which is the next thing to laziness. Their gentleness makes them too laid back, and their reproofs are less severe than they should be. By contrast, when bad-tempered people assume authority their irascibility brings them down in a frenzy, and throws the lives of those under them into confusion by driving away their tranquillity. When people are driven along by bad temper, they realise neither what they are doing in their anger nor what trouble they are making for themselves. Sometimes – and this is a more serious matter – they mistake their anger for righteous zeal. When they think their vice is a virtue, they have no conception of how much they are at fault ...
>
> Modest people have to exert themselves deliberately to be ardent, whereas bad-tempered people have to set aside their turbulence ... The Holy Spirit is shown to us under the symbols of a dove and of fire. All those whom He fills He makes both gentle with the simplicity of a dove and ardent with the fire of zeal. A person certainly cannot be said to the filled with the Holy Spirit if in his modesty he abandons his ardour, or if in his zeal he loses the virtue of modesty.
>
> We may perhaps explain this better if we appeal to the way Paul recommended different styles of preaching to two of his disciples ... When instructing Timothy he said: 'Convince, rebuke and encourage with utmost patience in teaching' (2 Tim 4, 2), yet when advising Titus he said: 'Declare these things; exhort and reprove with all authority' (Tit 2, 15). Why was it that this great master of the art of teaching suggested to one the exercise of authority and to the other the exercise of patience? Surely, was it not because he saw that Titus was endowed with too meek a spirit and Timothy too zealous a one? ... The one he urged on with a spur; the other he checked with a bridle!
>
> When we correct bad-tempered people it is better to steer clear of them while they are in a towering rage since, when their anger is aroused, they are insensitive to what is being said to them. But when they have been restored to their senses, they are more willing to accept advice'.
>
> (from Pt III, ch 16)

These few examples from the *'Pastoral Rule'* give the flavour of Gregory's approach to offering spiritual guidance and exercising discipline. In general, he advised bishops to be discerning and flexible in such pastoral work as they undertook in person, which is reminiscent of the apostle Paul's efforts to be 'all things to all people' so that by some means he might save some (1 Cor 9, 22). However, Gregory was not implying that bishops could realistically act as spiritual directors of all the clergy under their care.

d) Bernard's advice on the exercise of authority

Bernard made an apt observation when advising Archbishop Henry of Sens *'On the Lifestyle and Duties of Bishops'*. He commented on the exercise of authority as follows:

> *'Do not be ashamed to be subject to someone else if necessary. To sneer at submitting yourself makes you unworthy of promotion ...*
>
> *How beautifully that blessed centurion spoke, whose faith had no equal in Israel. 'I am a man set under authority, with soldiers under me', he said (Lk 7, 8). He did not boast of his authority ... He was not ashamed of the power that was over him, and for that reason was worthy to have soldiers under him ... He gave honour first to those placed above him, in order he might then rightly receive it from those set under him. He knew that what he received from his superiors he would pass on to his inferiors. From his own experience of subjection he learned how to moderate his own orders.'*
>
> (from ch 7, paragraphs 31 & 32)

Perhaps the wise young abbot had some inkling that Archbishop Henry, a zealous and strong-willed reformer, might need such advice. Ironically, some ten years later the Archbishop was temporarily suspended as a result of complaints that he had acted high-handedly in summarily dismissing an archdeacon without due process!

e) Second Vatican Council

The teaching of Vatican II about the bishop's ministry is expressed in general terms in *'Lumen Gentium'*. The bishop's pastoral obligations are summarised in paragraphs 27-28 under three categories:

- to cherish his subjects as true sons, and listen to them;
- to regard his priests as 'sons and friends, just as Christ called his disciples no longer servants but friends';
- to have compassion on the ignorant and erring.

This is amplified in the decree on *'The Bishops' Pastoral Office in the Church'*. Paragraph 16 speaks first of his office as father and pastor of the whole flock, who knows his sheep and whose sheep know him. He is to 'excel in a spirit of love and solicitude for all'.

Secondly, it describes the bishop's role in relation to his priests. He is to welcome them with a special love, to regard them as sons and friends, and to be concerned about their 'spiritual, intellectual and material condition'. This should involve holding special gatherings for them, e.g. for spiritual renewal, theological study and training in new pastoral methods. He is to treat as a priority those clergy who are in any sort of danger, or have failed in some respect, and to show them 'active mercy'.

As regards his care for lay people the bishop is urged to become acquainted with their social circumstances, especially through sociological research, whatever their 'age, condition or nationality'. Three categories are singled out for his attention: 'separated brethren' with whom ecumenical relations should be fostered; all who are unbaptised, whose welfare he should bear in mind; and marginalised groups such as refugees, seafarers, gypsies, tourists, etc for whom he should show special concern. The bishop should appoint others to share these responsibilities in his name. He is also to pay regard to people's 'social and civil progress and prosperity', and collaborate with those who hold public office.

This framework comes across as a church-centred view of the world, but is intended to have an outward-looking and inclusive emphasis. It describes a ministry orientated toward the whole human community and its common good – an approach similar to that advocated by the 1988 Lambeth Conference (paragraph 151), quoted earlier on pages 54-55.

f) The significance of the shepherd's crook

The significance of the shepherd's crook was drawn out by Kenneth Stevenson in this way:

*'There are two particular ministries that the pastoral staff expresses, which could be described as **nourishment** and **cautioning**. One of the greatest privileges of episcopal office is to encourage people and motivate them, and that can sometimes mean prodding them, with the end of that staff. The crook on the staff, however, is about cautioning, and sometimes exercising discipline over some of the flock, which in an age naturally suspicious of authority can be a difficult exercise.*

Both these aspects depend on persuasion and example ... Not everyone is straight forwardly strong or straight forwardly weak. We are all a glorious mixture. There will be times when space needs to be made for those who are strong in order for them to strive further, and for those who are weak or in difficulty to be given sustenance and care. The Rule of St Benedict says: 'The abbot must so arrange everything that the strong have something to yearn for, and the weak nothing to run from' (RB 64.19). Just as an abbot uses the prior and other senior monks in a large community, so a bishop relies on his colleagues – who themselves will require encouragement and (occasionally) being drawn back into line. It is impossible to do the job on one's own.'

(Final presidential address to Portsmouth Diocesan Synod, June 2009)

Symbolically the crook is an instrument, too, for supporting the injured and retrieving them from danger.

My own approach and methods

a) Four direct influences on me

The strongest influence on my own ideas of what it means to be a pastoral bishop has been that of the four diocesan bishops under whom I served, as incumbent and suffragan, in dioceses of Lichfield and Lincoln.

Stretton Reeve (Bishop of Lichfield 1953-74) became legendary for his knowledge of the 500 clergy who served under him. He could, when chairing a clergy conference, address every priest by surname and parish without forewarning. Though his style was formal, he was readily accessible. A letter from even the most junior curate requesting to see him would generally produce a telephone response at 9 a.m. next morning offering an interview within a couple of days – a remarkable achievement. He would listen carefully, with the ear of an experienced parish priest. His response would be fair-minded and forthright. You knew exactly where you stood with him. I appreciated his decisive style and clear manner of delegation, but he could be rather overpowering.

His successor, Kenneth Skelton (Bishop of Lichfield 1975-84), was smaller in physique and much less formal in style. You could have a levelling discussion with him, and explore a matter tentatively together. He did not mind being rung up for a chat in the late evening, and was ready to share his thinking in an open way. He brought his wide experience as a bishop in Central Africa and in the industrial North-East of England to bear on people and issues, and was a creative lateral thinker.

Simon Phipps (Bishop of Lincoln (1975-86) was an acute observer of human behaviour, as his gift of mimicry revealed. Though conscious of his lack of parochial experience, he had a sensitive and kindly pastoral awareness, and brought experience as a chaplain amongst university students and industrial workers. It was characteristic of him that he spent three months' sabbatical leave honing his skills in ministry to the sick under the supervision of a hospital chaplain. Throughout his time at Lincoln he would normally set aside one or two whole days a month for visiting clergy and families in their own homes. Four or five such visits would often take up a whole day on account of the distances, but he was glad to spend time in getting to know people in their own setting. A regular stream of individuals also came to see him in Lincoln, including his own senior staff at six monthly intervals. One of his main contributions was to set up a network for Pastoral Care and Counselling – a panel of qualified counsellors, doctors and psychotherapists to whom clergy in serious personal difficulty could be referred. He also created a panel of trained reviewers to assist clergy with voluntary appraisal – some 25 years ahead of the arrangements for Ministerial Development Review approved by the Archbishops' Council in 2010.

When Bob Hardy (Bishop of Lincoln 1987-2001) arrived, he quickly became known as a down-to-earth and warm-hearted pastor. He brought a great depth of experience as parish priest, university teacher and clergy trainer. He and his wife, Isobel, were immensely hospitable. He made himself very accessible, both out and about in the diocese and by telephone. He channelled a lot of energy into clergy reviews, and sustained a heavy rolling programme of interviews that trawled through the diocese deanery by deanery on a four-yearly basis. His preparatory letter to each priest would set out the issues to be explored. After each interview he would draft a written summary, which the priest concerned could amend and which remained confidential between them. He pinpointed what professional development might help him or her, and how that person's ministry might move forward. His encouragement of regular review did much to strengthen clergy morale, and he set up a panel of trained reviewers to help clergy to appraise their ministry. He was also enormously steadfast and patient, at great personal cost, in dealing with internal difficulties at his cathedral.

From each of these diocesan bishops I have taken on board different points that have contributed to my own view and practice of pastoral ministry.

b) Responding to the needs of clergy and licensed lay workers

To be effective pastors to those under their care bishops must have sensitive antennae, perpetually on the alert for signals and clues about the actual concerns of their clergy and lay workers. This entails the ability not just to hear what they are saying, but to elicit what is not being said and pick up its emotional flavour. People do not always feel what they "ought" to feel, and their attitudes may at times seem unreasonable. It is of little use to be irritated by this, and far better to discover what they are really saying and how they see their own needs. What is upsetting them? What are the nuances of their message? They deserve the right to express how they actually feel, and to know that they are regarded as worth listening to.

In most organisations upward communication tends to be patchy or haphazard, and needs to be actively fostered. For every member of the diocesan work-force who initiates direct contact with the bishop there are usually several others who thought of doing so, but never got that far. This is why bishops should let it be widely known that they are willing to arrange visits or interviews on request, ready to offer advice on specific matters (e.g. by letter, e-mail or telephone), and glad to meet clergy, lay workers and their spouses socially or informally from time to time. There is a particular need for bishops to make time to meet clergy in full-time secular employment, whose main ministry is through their paid job beyond church circles but who can rarely participate in clergy meetings or training held during the working day; those in this minority category should be supported in their often taxing frontier work.

Sometimes I used chapter meetings as an opportunity to put over a carefully balanced, two-pronged message. On the one hand, I would explain, the bishops of the diocese normally worked on the assumption that our clergy could be relied on to do their own job in their own way. It was **not** a dependent relationship, and for most of the time we would not be troubling them, nor vice versa! We wanted them to use their discretion, take their own initiative, and show courage and imagination in what they did. Our aim, as their bishops, was to affirm, encourage, advise and occasionally warn. Yet at the same time, just because we cared about them and were constantly praying for them, we wished to keep abreast of their family circumstances. If a new baby arrived, or their child had an accident or gained some prestigious award, or a parent died, etc., we liked to know. Wherever there was sickness, or a problem with debt, or strain within their marriage, we preferred to be aware of it sooner rather than later. We were always interested to hear how their work was progressing. If they wanted to chew over some new development in the parish or get a second opinion on some local problem, we would gladly talk such matters through with them. In the event of complaints being levelled against them, we would let them know what allegations had been made and give them a fair chance to put their side of the story (this was in the days before the Clergy Discipline Measure 2003 and its formal procedures). If they wished to weigh up seeking pastures new as against remaining in their present post, the message was: *'You know where we are, and the door is open.'* They should let us know whenever they wanted contact, and indicate how urgent it was. I promised that we would respond promptly and, in emergency, as quickly as possible – if necessary by cancelling something else.

It was noticeable that, when clergy were feeling hard-pressed or undervalued in their ministry, their frame of mind was often – though not always – exacerbated by three particular factors: shortage of money, having to live in tied housing, and being surrounded by unreasonable expectations. Were they having problems with particular individuals? Why were those around them not supportive? What specific problems needed to be addressed? How far were they caring for themselves – e.g. by setting sensible limits, creating space, praying, planning, taking time off, etc. – or were they were their own worst enemy? Such matters were unlikely to emerge from aggressive interrogation, but only from gentle exploration. No less important than the mode of listening is the mode of responding. If bishops seem to be threatening or moralising, belittling or humouring, distracting from the real issues or merely overwhelming with logical arguments, no trust is built up and nothing creative or therapeutic is likely to result.

It is worth adding that Lincoln's remarkable Diocesan Surveyor, the late Keith Nelmes, played a valuable role in sorting out practical issues to do with the housing of clergy and lay workers, but also in listening as a layman to their spouses. They found him a wise and caring ally, who exercised a unique pastoral ministry in his own right.

c) Some methods of systematic pastoral care

How is it humanly possible to care for large numbers of people, spread over considerable distances? Basically, there are three things that bishops can do:

- make themselves approachable and available;
- engage pastorally with as many people as they realistically can;
- lead a whole network that makes available others' pastoral skills as well as their own.

Here are some of the ways in which I tried to sustain pastoral care:

1. *Time-slots were earmarked* for home visits, interviews and hospitality. This had to be done well ahead, before allocating a slot to anyone in particular. Otherwise, I found that my best intentions of being accessible, available and hospitable were doomed to fail for lack of time. If a slot was planned, it was more likely to happen.

2. *Regular intercession and rolling review* – these were the matrix of pastoral strategy. The Good Shepherd 'calls his own sheep by name' and keeps a constantly watchful eye on the flock. Considerable effort was required to keep the ever-changing list of clergy, lay workers, spouses and children completely up to date – over a thousand names. I prayed for them often, by name and place. With the archdeacon's help I maintained a rolling review of everyone's progress, so that nobody dropped 'off the radar' and we kept in mind the majority doing a steady job as well as the minority in difficulties.

3. Keeping a *balance between proactive and reactive* – beside reacting to requests I needed to plan which contacts to initiate. Names often jumped out of the prayer list.

4. I needed to be clear in my own mind about the range of *different ways to engage* with people and the various expectations they might have. Was this to be a general social call for contact with the whole family? Would the focus be mainly on sickness, breakdown or other difficulty? Was the interview for job appraisal, work consultancy or career development? Or was it for spiritual direction, confession & absolution, or personal counselling. The focus might be more on

the parish: checking general progress, solving a problem, resolving a conflict, exploring a complaint, giving guidance or formal permission, laying down the law, etc.. Which mode was I in? To use Gregory's analogy, what stroke of the plectrum was called for? Or to use Kenneth Stevenson's analogy, was the crook supporting, prodding or retrieving? In each case I had to pause to consider: was I the right person to handle this and, if not, who would be?

5. Depending on the answers, my next step was to *pick the best medium*: a phone call, a letter, an interview, a meal together, a home visit, etc.. Distance and time entered into the equation, and so did the vital distinction between 'urgent' and 'important'. A quick chat on that day might suffice. On the other hand, the matter might be so important that I should book now an unhurried session later, and give the time that this matter deserved.

6. To sort competing claims into *order of priority* I normally used these categories:
   - sickness, death or emergency (such as breakdown)
   - those who asked to see me
   - those whose names had been suggested for a visit (usually by the archdeacon or rural dean)
   - those who came for counselling, say fortnightly for a limited period
   - those who came regularly for confession or work review, usually twice a year
   - 'start-up' reviews, usually one year after starting a new job (sooner if requested, or after six months for a deacon). This required keeping a sequence of the dates on which each person took office. My 'start-up list' in some years contained over 30 fresh names, and rarely fell below 15 a year.
   - 'milestone' reviews, e.g. ten years in that job (again based on the 'start-up list') or one year before the end of a curacy or expiry of a licence, or aged nearly 60, or with children finishing 'A' levels. This involved checking whether someone wanted to move, or was happy to soldier on without feeling forgotten.
   - those I got a hunch about, or felt that I had not seen recently.

7. *Setting an horizon*: towards the end of a visit or interview it was often helpful to agree in how many months' time we should review the issues.

8. *Reflecting* on how the visit or interview felt, and what had come to light. How could any issues be taken forward, and by whom?
9. *Recording* the event: making notes, and passing on any information if appropriate. The exception to this was, of course, any matter revealed in sacramental confession.

(Interviews for prospective ordinands and clergy seeking appointments will be treated separately under chapter 14).

d) Pressure points

Apart from the pressure points already mentioned that arose from time, distance and work-load, others arose from the intrinsic nature of pastoral work, e.g.:

- assessing how clergy performed with little feedback other than their own view
- figuring out how to help a lonely priest who chose to be isolated from deanery colleagues
- spending a disproportionate amount of time with a handful of needy clergy
- having to stand back when disciplinary procedures came into play
- occasional role-conflict between being confessor and bishop
- agonising whether a priest with serious personal and domestic difficulties should be offered another post and, if so, where
- sharing other people's burdens and dilemmas

When I first arrived in the diocese there was a dearth of spiritual directors. Initially I was drawn into more of this work than would have been possible later alongside increasing national and international commitments. This pressure was much eased when the Franciscans set up a community of four friars in a disused vicarage. Where there is only one bishop, it is doubtful whether he or she should act in the role of confessor to clergy of that diocese. Where there is an episcopal team, or retired bishops are available, greater flexibility is possible as long as clear boundaries of confidentiality are drawn. In my experience the main role-conflict lay in relation not to the client, but to dealings among the senior staff with whom I was not at liberty to share all I knew. New bishops must decide how much counselling, spiritual direction or ministerial review to undertake in person.

e) The pastoral network

The bishop needs to lead a whole network of skilled people with whom to share the tasks of pastoral care. This implies identifying and fostering such expertise within the diocese, and being willing to refer and delegate when appropriate.

Archdeacons, rural deans and team rectors are an obvious 'front line'; their pastoral aptitude should be amongst the qualities for which they were appointed in the first place. Some clergy have formal qualifications as counsellors or an established reputation as wise confessors, and can be recommended to those seeking such help. Hospital and mental health chaplains can often make a valuable contribution, as can any members of Religious Orders who may be available locally. For questions of exorcism or deliverance the bishop nominates an adviser, to whom all cases are referred in the first instance. Various other diocesan personnel can also play a part, e.g. the adviser for Continuing Ministerial Education, officers for widows and retired clergy, etc.

In Lincoln diocese we developed a system whereby the bishop's discretionary fund bore any professional costs incurred by clergy seeing a psychiatrist, psychotherapist or external counsellor. These consultations remained confidential. The bishops did not enquire who used them, but checked whether these outside consultants were in fact being used. For casework supervision we sometimes used student counsellors from local universities and colleges or 'Relate' tutors. In cases of debt the Diocesan Secretary would liaise with national charities for assisting clergy families, and provided sound advice and monthly monitoring until a priest's personal finances were back on an even keel. A few years ago John Saxbee (Bishop of Lincoln 2002-11) set up an advisory group on Spirituality, and brought together a team of 'Companions on the Way' – clergy and lay people trained to provide spiritual counsel in a variety of styles across the diocese. In retirement I became convenor of the supervision group for spiritual directors in the North of the diocese.

All this expertise is what I call the pastoral network. The combined effect of these provisions is to reduce the occurrence of crises, increase the overall sense of ongoing oversight, and create the confidence that releases people's full potential. Occasional crises can never be totally eliminated, but the level of pastoral awareness can be gradually raised, particularly amongst rural deans and team leaders, as they become better at picking up the warning signs of difficulty and taking preventive action. This is how it should be in a caring church, and bishops can make a difference by setting that ethos as well as by what they undertake in person. With the passage of time and the constant change of personnel the level of pastoral awareness always requires further attention. It can never be taken for granted, but needs to be fostered deliberately.

CARING IN A CORPORATE SETTING

a) The laity's bishop

To be not just *pastor pastorum* or the clergy's bishop, but also the laity's bishop

– this, too, is an essential dimension of episcopé. The bishop's concern is for the entire flock, both those who occupy the pews whether regularly or occasionally and the community as whole.

This understanding of the bishop's role in public life is expressed in Canon C.18:

> 'Every bishop is the chief pastor of all that are within his diocese, as well laity as clergy, and their father in God ... it is his duty to set forward and maintain quietness, love and peace among all men.'

The corporate setting of episcopé matters for another reason as well. Pastoral care cannot adequately be exercised solely in terms of individuals, or even families, and their personal agenda. It must take account of people's social circumstances, and of the structures and communal influences that bear upon their lives. Each city, town or village has its own identity and sense of place. Each congregation has its own 'culture' and ethos, its own particular way of doing things. What can be done in one place may be impossible in another because of local perceptions and attitudes. No parish priest can afford to ignore this, nor can the bishop.

b) Visitation

One of the main arms of episcopal ministry is 'visitation', an ancient biblical term with a somewhat ominous ring. It sounds like the next thing to catching the plague – a judgement from the Almighty! Yet a visitation is as much an opportunity to affirm and praise what is good in a given place as to find fault. Only by coming in person to the parish can the bishop gain an immediate sense of how things are. It is not enough to hover in the stratosphere. If bishops really care, they must experience how things really are at ground level. Above all, their ministry should be one of encouragement, best communicated face to face.

When writing to the congregation at Corinth about his coming visit, Paul pointed out that it was largely up to them what kind of an experience it would turn out to be:

> 'Everything we do, beloved, is for the sake of building you up. I fear that when I come I may find you not as I wish, and that you may find me not as you wish ... Examine yourselves to see whether you are living in the faith. Test yourselves ... We cannot do anything against the truth, but only for the truth ... I write these things while I am away from you, so that when I come I may not have to be severe in using the authority that the Lord has given me for building up and not for tearing down.'
>
> (selected verses from 2 Cor, 12 and 13)

c) Lutheran practice

Lutherans, though emphasising that all ministries of word and sacrament are basically one, clearly acknowledge that bishops carry out certain distinct tasks that are not shared by local pastors. One of these is:

'to give guidance to the common life of the congregations in the region under their care, especially through visitation, and to support their life together.'

(*'Episcopal Ministry within the Apostolicity of the Church'*, LWF 2007, para 45-46)

An earlier LWF study document listed as the first amongst a bishop's duties:

'advising and supporting congregations in their life of worship, witness and service, by visiting them, listening to their needs, responding to their questions and helping to solve their problems.'

(*'The Lutheran Understanding of the Episcopal Office'* 1983, para 17)

Since confirmation is normally administered by the local pastor and not an episcopal event, visitation is the main instrument by which Lutheran bishops relate to their congregations. It is generally taken very seriously, and is a more searching process than the bishop simply coming to preach occasionally and visit a few people. Dr Robert J. Marshall, an American Lutheran leader, described visitation as the bishop's best opportunity to encourage an outward-looking sense of mission, and to re-invigorate the congregation's concern for serving its neighbourhood and giving a Christian witness on issues of social justice. He pointed out that the bishop is particularly well placed to 'develop links between congregations in different situations, so that they learn from each other and support each other' (see his paper on *'Episcopé and the Mission of the Church in the 21st Century'* in the report of the Niagara Consultation 1987, page 108).

Tord Harlin (Bishop of Uppsala, 1990-2000) told me how in his Swedish diocese he would regularly spend a whole week in a parish, taking part not only in worship but in every activity and organisation that happened. He would usually be assisted by one or two 'assessors', i.e. skilled advisers (once I sent an archdeacon to accompany him, and on a different occasion the senior industrial chaplain from Grimsby assisted another Swedish bishop). It was not so much an inspection as a mission audit. At the end of the week the bishop would address a public gathering, attended by the mayor, the chief of police and other local dignitaries, to sum up his findings and make recommendations for the well-being of the community and the future development of congregational life.

In Germany the United Evangelical Lutheran Church (the VELKD, consisting of eight regional churches with about 10 million members) recently conducted a thorough re-evaluation of the meaning and practice of visitation. The report of its study commission was adopted by the Bishops' Conference in 2009, and is now available in English (*'Visitation – a study by the Theological Committee of the VELKD'*, edited by M. Lasogga and U. Hahn, Hanover 2011). It takes the view that visitation is not just one amongst various possible instruments of pastoral oversight and spiritual leadership, but has a unique value in expressing the nature of the church. Whilst local congregations are *ekklesia* in a full sense, none of them constitute the church on their own. They form part of a wider ecclesiastical whole, with which they need to cooperate and to whom they must give an account. Visitation introduces a dynamic of creative interchange, which integrates them into a wider dimension that transcends the local congregation. It relates not just to the clergy, but to the life and witness of the entire congregation in relation to its social and cultural setting.

d) Anglican practice

In the canon law of the Church of England the bishop is the principal minister within his diocese, and to him belongs the right to hold visitation 'to the end that he may get some good knowledge of the state, sufficiency and ability of the clergy and other persons whom he is to visit' (Canon C.18). Normally, however, this function remains delegated to the archdeacon who 'shall bring to the bishop's attention what calls for correction or merits praise' (Canon C.22). He or she holds annual visitations to admit churchwardens to office, and 'shall survey in person or by deputy all churches, chancels and churchyards and give direction for the amendment of all defects in the walls, fabric, ornaments and furniture of the same ...'

It makes good sense for the routine supervision of parochial fabric, finance and administration to be delegated in this way. It leaves bishops free to focus on broader issues of discipleship, spirituality, mission and ministry when carrying out their pastoral visits.

e) Bill Ind's approach

In his essay on *'Episcopal Ministry in Rural Areas',* written in 1992 for the guidance of new bishops, Bill Ind points out that the bishop enjoys a different status in rural areas than urban ones. He is felt to be part of the local scene, and his visits are widely known and commented on. The following is an edited extract:

> *'The bishop can affect morale by sharing an informed and sympathetic awareness of some of the special features that the parish clergy have to contend with, e.g. small congregations, rushing around several churches, too many PCC's and AGM's, having to live at close quarters with their failures, isolation, not enough people to make viable age groups, etc. This is especially important if, as is often the case, the priest or deacon comes from an urban or suburban background, where the shape of church life ... has been associational rather than communal. In village life people belong to the church by virtue of living in the village – it is there for everyone. In*

an associational church you have to express your membership by coming on a more or less regular basis. The shape of church life is very different.

The bishop will want to show in his own ministry how to live with paradox and ambiguity. Medieval churches dotted round the landscape are a millstone round the neck of a small local community, yet at the same time it is the only public building and space in the village still left functioning. It embodies the life of the village. Often maintenance of the building drives people to do things for the whole village. In other words, maintenance is the first inadequate stumbling towards a sense of mission.'

This well conveys the style that Bill developed in Lincolnshire, and that later reached a wider public through the television series on *'The Seaside Parish'* from Boscastle and the Isles of Scilly in Truro diocese. All bishops need to develop a distinctive style that corresponds to their own personality and approach, and frees them to engage creatively with the particular circumstances of their people.

He had this to say about the sense in which the bishop and the parish priest share the cure of souls:

'When we think about the [bishop's] words, "Receive this cure of souls, which is both yours and mine, in the name of the Father and of the Son and of the Holy Spirit", perhaps we can come to see that the invocation of the Trinity is not just a form of words. It tells us that the way we are to share ministry is the way that the life of the Trinity is shared. The pattern is one of 'koinonia', the sharing of common life.

In other words, the parish priest shares his ministry with the bishop, and the bishop shares his ministry with the parish priest. It would be easy to see this as hierarchical – the bishop giving to the priest something which is his. But in fact, in many situations, the reality is that the parish priest shares the ministry which is his with the bishop. He allows the bishop the benefit of his pastoral experience and pastoral care. So, for instance, to go on a day-visit to a parish is to share ministry in that place mutually.'

(From an unpublished talk to a clergy cell, 1991)

f) My own approach

My own pastoral efforts at corporate level were channelled on three main lines – deanery days, ministry reviews, and responsibilities in the community – which I will briefly describe.

From time to time I would set aside a *deanery day*, to be spent largely in a deanery or part of it. I would ask the rural dean to put together a mixed programme striking a balance between worship, church contacts and community contacts; between meeting prominent people and those less prominent or in social need; between education, industry, local government and the voluntary sector; and between laity and clergy. The day would often begin with a school visit or weekday Mattins in church with a handful of parishioners. After a couple of sick visits or a mid-morning discussion group in someone's home I would move on, for example, to call formally on the mayor and chief executive of the district council, or to drop in at some local group helping those in need, or to visit one of the main places of employment. Over lunch or during the afternoon there was often a chance to meet clergy spouses or ecumenical colleagues. After further tours or visits I would generally wind up by early evening, and get home for supper. Alternatively, the programme would begin at 2 p.m. and, after high tea in someone's home, I would take part in a full evening session – either worship or a public gathering of some kind. I found that I could cope with about an eight-hour programme, plus travel. If it involved both an early start and a late finish, it left me exhausted next day. Bishops have to be realistic about their own stamina! The value of these deanery days tended to be in proportion to the rural dean's vision and creativity in planning them and setting up local contacts. Whatever took me beyond my comfort zone taught me the most. I wish that I had spent more time in this way, and that I had given a stronger brief to those rural deans who had little imagination as to what the bishop's visitation might achieve in the public sphere.

Ministry reviews used a different method, designed to find out how far local ministry teams were developing effectively. My target was to review every team's progress after its initial three years, and then every six years – a schedule hard to maintain. I would be accompanied by two assessors, one man and one woman, of whom one was ordained and the other lay (these people were also part of the pastoral network). It was useful to include their differing perceptions within our panel. Prior to the review evening one assessor would sit in at a normal meeting of the team. Some written information was gathered in advance: team members filled in a questionnaire, and the parish priest sent me a confidential report on each member. The review evening in the parish would be attended by the clergy, readers and all other team members, as well as by the churchwardens and a few representatives of the congregation who did not belong to the team. The evening session would begin with a brief act of worship, locally led, followed by personal introductions all round. Each reviewer would then conduct two or three separate half-hour interviews e.g. one with the churchwardens and lay representatives together, to get feed-back from the congregation's point of view; others singly with the parish priest and each team member. The review panel re-convened a couple of days later, usually at my house, to share our impressions and make sense of what we had seen. I would draft a report of our observations and recommendations.

When this had been checked by the parish priest for factual accuracy and agreed with my fellow assessors it was circulated to all interested parties and the bishop's staff. It was brought to the next PCC meeting of the parish concerned, which I sometimes attended.

This process generally succeeded in identifying the main issues as openly as possible. The reviewers did not pretend to extraordinary wisdom. We simply said what we thought we had observed, and tried to say something encouraging and something challenging. This rarely contained surprises, but served the purpose of bringing matters into the public domain. I wish that I had given more attention to following up the implementation of our recommendations, but my focus moved all too quickly to the next review elsewhere. These reviews were intended to complement Bob Hardy's rolling programme of clergy appraisal, and to a large extent they did. However, they resulted in the bishop's staff giving more attention to parishes with local ministry teams and less to the general run of other parishes.

Beside these church-based visitations I devoted some time to taking on a few responsibilities in the wider community as opportunity arose, but selectively and for limited periods. In 1979 I became chairman of St Andrew's Hospice, Grimsby when the project started from scratch, and continued in this role for ten years until the work of the hospice expanded to a point where more 'hands on' management was needed than I could offer. In the other large urban centre, Scunthorpe, I presided over the local branch of Marriage Guidance (now 'Relate') for a three-year cycle. For 15 years I was a governor of St James' School, Grimsby – a Woodard School with choral foundation. From 1989 I served for seven years on the governing body of Grimsby College, a large Further Education institute, and took a particular interest in special educational needs and community issues. In the mid-80's I was an active member of the local consortium which set up an independent local radio station (now 'Viking Radio'). From 1992 for five years I belonged to the Humberside Training and Enterprise Council, which tried to stimulate the economic growth of the sub-region and raise its skills' base. In these ways I endeavoured, however imperfectly, to show care and concern for particular needs in society and to become better briefed about them, especially in the fields of terminal illness, marriage breakdown, remedial education and unemployment. There were severe limits on what I could realistically undertake, but at least my presence in these spheres expressed solidarity with the issues in question and local efforts to tackle them. From time to time the chance arose to contribute a Christian viewpoint, but this had to be done sensitively in genuine partnership with those of other outlooks who worked for the common good.

New bishops should be on the look-out for suitable openings, and seek to achieve some measure of strategic and geographical spread in their community involvement. They must make up their own minds as to how, in their particular social setting, they can best show a *'special care for the poor, the outcast and those in need',* and identify appropriate ways *'to confront injustice and work for righteousness and peace in all the world'* (from the Ordinal). These high ideals are not easily fulfilled. Moreover, openings often arise at inconveniently short notice, and can be acted on only if there is leeway in the diary to switch some previous commitment into an emergency slot. Kenneth Stevenson warned his Portsmouth clergy:

> *'We ignore the world's concerns and its pain at our peril ... [but] we cannot afford to become a church burnt up by a pragmatic activism wholly lacking in an underlying vision and theology of where and how the Kingdom of God is leading us'.*
>
> Ad Clerum, August 2009

g) Further pressure points

In addition to the pressures mentioned earlier, there were others that arose from the nature of exercising pastoral care in a corporate setting, e.g.

- needing to give feed-back promptly after a review;
- challenging the authoritarian attitudes of many clergy towards their laity;
- puzzling out how to help a parish where the congregation itself is the block to creative developments;
- overcoming inter-group suspicions, and resolving inter-personal clashes or conflicts of interest;
- getting acquainted with technical jargon and sets of initials in different spheres;
- mastering mountains of agendas, minutes and policy papers.

PASTORAL EXPECTATIONS

Anglicans have high expectations that their bishops will be approachable and act with pastoral sensitivity. If any bishop is less than outstanding as a preacher, scholar or administrator, this may often be forgiven, but to fail as a pastor is generally regarded as a very serious shortcoming. Small practical points can make a big difference, such as greeting people at the door, remembering their names, taking a real interest in what they wish to tell you, showing appreciation, staying for most of the 'bunfight', answering letters, etc.

One important way of caring is to deal conscientiously with complaints. Bishops never know what problems may land on their plate, and new bishops must be particularly aware that certain types of situation, at the serious end of scale, are regulated by statutory codes that must be followed. These are issues such as clergy discipline, the protection of children and vulnerable adults, major breakdown of the pastoral relationship between priest and people, grievance proceedings, allegations of serious professional inadequacy, criminal charges, etc. Such instances tend to attract media interest, and this can be daunting for the bishop particularly if they are drawn out over a lengthy period. At the opposite end of the scale are frivolous, petty-fogging, anonymous or unsubstantiated complaints, which should be treated with no more importance than they deserve. In the middle ground, however, every effort should be made to explore and resolve complaints, and to get to the bottom of misunderstandings that have arisen. During Bob Hardy's sabbatical, when I was acting diocesan bishop, more complaints came my way than usual. In order to keep track of such matters and not let them stagnate I kept a written record of each complaint in three parts:

- who complained about whom, or what
- what line of resolution to pursue, including my next intended step
- a note of every episode (e.g. letter, phone call, interview) with dates and times

By consulting this dossier on two particular days each week I could quickly check the progress of each matter, and see what called for further action on my part.

Summary

All that I have written in this chapter leads me to sum up the pastoral dimension that is integral to episcopé in these terms:

> **It cares systematically** for people within and beyond the church, in partnership with others, on a continuing basis and in crisis.
>
> **It encourages**, affirms, inspires, builds trust, floats ideas; equips and enables the ministry of others; and exemplifies by one's own ministry.

CHAPTER 12

Leading Worship

PRESIDING OVER PUBLIC WORSHIP

Public worship lies right at the heart of the bishop's ministry. Indeed, it is in this context that people in the pew most often see their bishop, i.e. when baptising or confirming new Christians and when ordaining or licensing new ministers. To lead the rites of Christian initiation and to ordain or license clergy is a major element in the bishop's public role. A fuller picture is given in the 'job description' paragraph at the service of consecration, when the archbishop uses these words:

As principal ministers of word and sacrament, stewards of the mysteries of God, (bishops) are to preside at the Lord's table and lead the offering of prayer and praise. They are to feed God's pilgrim people, and so build up the Body of Christ. They are to baptise and confirm, nurturing God's people in the life of the Spirit and leading them in the way of holiness ... They are to preside over the ordination of deacons and priests, and join together in the ordination of bishops ... They are to seek out those who are lost and lead them home rejoicing, declaring the absolution and forgiveness of sins to those who turn to Christ ...'

Immediately after the laying on of hands the archbishop prays:

'Make them steadfast as guardians of the faith and sacraments ... and faithful in presiding at the worship of your people.'

Reflecting on the nature of the episcopate, the 1968 Lambeth Conference stated this plainly:

'The service of the bishop has its centre in the liturgical and sacramental life of the Church, in his celebration of the Eucharist and in ordination and confirmation'

(Resolutions and Reports, page 108)

THE IGNATIAN MODEL

This role as liturgical presider can be traced right back to Ignatius, the second bishop of Antioch (approx 69-107 AD), one of the principal models of episcopacy in the Early Church. At that time there was one bishop and one eucharistic assembly in a city, and when the entire Christian flock met together 'the local bishop presided in a way which marked him out as the symbolic person in whom the identity of the community is focused and represented' (*Niagara Report*, CHP 1988, § 47). A Lutheran document summarised the point in this way:

> *'For Ignatius of Antioch the bishop is primarily the one who presides at the eucharist. The church, in his view, is essentially eucharistic by its nature: there is an organic relation between the Body of Christ understood as community, and the Body of Christ understood as sacrament. The theme of unity and interdependent relationship between one bishop, the one eucharistic body, and the one church is common in his writings.'*
>
> (*'Lund Statement'*, LWF 2007, paragraph 12)

Despite the 4th century shift from a local episcopate to a regional one, this Ignatian ideal has exercised a lasting influence. A convenient summary of later historical developments can be found in the report *'Episcopal Ministry'* (CHP, 1990) – especially chapters 4 and following.

Promoting holiness

Through the growing influence of the 20th century liturgical movement parallel emphases are evident in the documents of the Second Vatican Council and the 1978 Lambeth Conference. In both cases the bishop is portrayed as the focus of the eucharistic community, and as exercising a key role in regulating public worship and nurturing the sanctification of all God's people.

The Second Vatican Council's decree on the *'Bishops' Pastoral Office'* states that:

> *'In fulfilling their duty to sanctify ... bishops are the principal dispensers of the mysteries of God, just as they are the governors, promoters and guardians of the entire liturgical life in the church committed to them. Hence they should constantly exert themselves to have the faithful know and live the paschal mystery more deeply through the Eucharist and thus become a firmly knit body in the solidarity of Christ's love ... Bishops should be diligent in fostering holiness ... according to the vocation of each'.*
>
> (paragraph 15)

This tallies with Vatican II's picture of a bishop's ministry in *'Lumen Gentium'* (paragraph 26), as well as with the practical injunctions in the Constitution on the *'Sacred Liturgy'* (paragraphs 41-46) for bishops to foster liturgical renewal in their cathedrals and parishes.

The approach of the 1978 Lambeth Conference to this issue, though less 'top down', was expressed in almost identical terms:

> *'Christian worship is always the action of the ascended Christ, in which he offers himself and his whole Body to the Father in the power of the Holy Spirit. The Eucharist is the heart of Christian worship because it is the showing forth of his death and resurrection until his coming again ...*
>
> *There has been a welcome growth in the understanding that worship is a corporate activity in which all members of the Body of Christ have their proper share ...*
>
> *The bishop's office is to be the chief liturgical minister in his diocese, and from that comes his general responsibility for the oversight of worship within his jurisdiction. Liturgy is a living thing which grows with the life of the Church. Growth in both individual and corporate prayer is essential and is the work of the Holy Spirit (Rom 8, 26). We encourage Christians to engage in worship of different kinds in groups of different sizes, e.g. in the intimacy of the small group and in the occasional large or festival gathering. Both of these can complement the regular worship of the congregation.'*
>
> (Report of the Lambeth Conference 1978, pages 94-95)

AIMS IN WORSHIP

When bishops are conducting the Church's public liturgy, they – like any worship leaders – need to be constantly looking in two directions at once. Their attention should mainly be directed towards God in the offering of prayer and praise. The primary aim, therefore, is doxological. At the same time they should be drawing in the participation of others, so as to enable the corporate priesthood of the whole people of God. Canon B.1 (2) puts it neatly: '(The minister) shall endeavour to ensure that the worship offered glorifies God and edifies the people'.

To keep these twin aims in balance is not always easy, especially under the pressure of a major public occasion. Within the outward rites and ceremonies must burn the living flame of worship 'in spirit and in truth' (John 4, 24). Every element that contributes to the offering of praise should be well prepared to a standard that is fit for the Almighty, and also uplifting and edifying to those who take part. What so often makes a great occasion is the expectation that people bring to it, every bit as much as what the bishop may do or say. As chief liturgical minister, the bishop has to set the mood, facilitate other people's contributions, heighten their attention or release tension as appropriate, and hold the parts together. This calls for professional skill.

On some occasions there will be a palpable sense that 'the Lord is here'. The heart of some visitor may be touched in the way that Paul envisaged:

> *'If some ordinary person comes in, he will be convinced by what he hears. His secret*

thoughts will be brought into the open, and he will bow down and worship God confessing, "Truly God is here among you" (1 Cor 14, 24-25 TEV).

Many pastoral opportunities arise from an experience of meaningful worship. The person who sees a relative or friend being baptised, confirmed or ordained may be moved to take the same step later. The bishop's aims in leading worship must be not only doxological, but pastoral and evangelical as well. The French have a term for it: *'la pastorale liturgique'* – an approach to worship that is sensitive to and expressive of human needs, concerns and aspirations.

SOME CHALLENGING QUESTIONS FROM NIAGARA

When bishops continue in office for some years, they gain in experience but need also to be open to renewing the manner in which they exercise their ministry. With the intention of helping them to examine themselves the Anglican-Lutheran *'Niagara Report'* posed a number of challenging questions (see paragraphs 99-110). The following six questions related to the area of liturgy:

- *Do those who exercise episcopé understand their liturgical role to be central to their responsibilities, and do they carry it out in a creative way?*
- *Do they lead the offering of prayer and praise with a sense of awe and reverence, inspiring clergy and congregations to offer well prepared and heart-felt worship to God?*
- *Do they maintain a proper balance between word and sacrament in their programme of public worship events?*
- *Do they encourage the renewal of liturgy, and hold together diverse styles of worship within the Church's life?*
- *Do they take care to retain those skills which they now exercise less often than they did at an earlier phase in their ministries?*
- *Do they perform their liturgical tasks in a manner which symbolizes that all ministry is shared with others?*

(*'The Niagara Report'*, CHP 1988, paragraph 107)

All these questions are meant to evoke a positive answer. It seems to me that there are broadly three ways in which bishops can and should act on these matters:

a) by setting a good example in the services that they conduct in person;
b) by nurturing the whole network of worship leaders; and
c) by encouraging and regulating public worship wisely.

It is time to explore the practical implications in each of these areas.

Good practice in the bishop's own liturgical ministry

a) General approach

Since bishops are representative and focal persons, they should be exemplary in observing the Declaration of Assent that is required of all clergy at their licensing:

> 'In public prayer and administration of the sacraments I will use only the forms of service which are authorised or allowed by Canon'
>
> (Canon C.15)

This is not the straight-jacket that it may sound. A wide range of liturgical resources is currently available, and is meant to be used creatively. The preface to *Common Worship* (2000) draws attention to:

> '... the multiplicity of contexts in which worship is offered today. They encourage an imaginative engagement in worship, opening the way for people in the varied circumstances of their lives to experience the love of God in Jesus Christ ... Worship is for the whole people of God, who are fellow pilgrims on a journey of faith, and those who attend services are all at different stages on that journey.'

Canon B.5 permits variations, as long as they are not of substantial importance and do not depart from the doctrine of the Church of England, and this leaves room for pastoral discretion and flexibility. There is also scope for special events and ecumenical occasions reaching beyond the basic provisions for Anglican public worship.

Bishops minister on behalf of the whole church, and should rise above sectional interests. Regardless of personal preference, they should rejoice in being equally competent and at ease in a range of worship styles. They should not be idiosyncratic, but operate within the normal spectrum of what is recognisably Anglican. When the bishop comes to lead a service, people rightly expect a good style and quality. This means being loyal not just to the letter but to the spirit of the Church of England's general custom and practice, as well as that of their own diocese. It also involves being sensitive to the particular tradition of the parish in which they are ministering, and respecting its 'locally established custom' (Canon B.9 (2)).

b) Preparation before the day

Those fortunate enough to have served their title under a good training incumbent know how much depends on carefully planning and preparing the details of a service. At St Mary's, Stafford Dudley Hodges trained us curates to cathedral standards, based on his own early days at Southwark Cathedral under

Provost Haldane. As bishop I soon discovered that a few clergy had had only a minimal grounding in the practicalities of liturgy; consequently they had poor standards and needed help. Once, in my first year, I was amazed to find out just before a Confirmation service that the vicar had given no thought to which hymns or readings would be used! Subsequently I made a point of consulting well in advance, by telephone or more recently by e-mail. Typically the parish priest either rang for guidance, or sent a draft order of service for approval, often based on a similar previous occasion. Most clergy were conscientious in this regard. At my desk I kept a supply of handy slips listing the options at various points in the service (e.g. would there be an Old Testament reading, who would read the Gospel, was 'The Peace' normally shared, would the Sursum Corda and Proper Preface be said or sung, did the Dismissal normally precede or follow the recessional hymn, etc). I would fill this in whilst talking on the telephone, and tuck it in my loose-leaf note-book on the day.

Six main issues needed to be clarified in discussion with the person locally responsible:

- *What items are to be included in the service?* This was particularly important as regards adult baptisms, those to be received into the Church of England, those already confirmed who wished to re-affirm their commitment, the giving of testimony, the use of chrism, etc. At a licensing there might be an ecumenical element to be included. One occupational hazard was the request, "While you're here, Bishop, would you please bless the kneelers / restored roof / scout pennant, etc?" I recall one incumbent telling me on arrival that, in view of his lighting the Advent ring and distributing Sunday School prizes during the first part of the Confirmation service, there would not be enough time for me to preach a sermon! Preach it I most certainly did. Draft services generally needed to be pruned, and not weighed down with extra items or too many long hymns.

- *What is to be the thematic thread?* Often this was predetermined by the liturgical calendar or nature of the occasion. Would the normal Sunday readings be suitable for this occasion? Were three readings necessary, or would two suffice? I generally specified what reading(s) would fit in with the sermon, and asked the parish priest to choose the hymns in consultation with colleagues and candidates. The liturgical colour needed to be agreed, and visiting clergy informed in order to bring a stole of the right colour. I still cringe to think about the occasion when I turned up to preach at Sunday Evensong in the cathedral, having prepared an exegetical sermon on the Old Testament reading of the day. "Oh, by the way", said one of the canons shortly beforehand, "did I tell you this will be a special service for the International Year of the Child?" (No, he didn't). It would have been nice to know in time to prepare something suitable!

- *What roles in the service can be shared?* The bishop should not just sweep in and take over the whole service, at the risk of making the parish priest and others feel superfluous in their own church. It is the opportunity to model shared ministry, and to foster active roles for ecumenical representatives, for any deacon or reader serving in that parish and for other lay participants. The rubric entitled 'Ministries' on page 158 of the *Common Worship* core book sets out some of the possibilities.

- *What books or service papers will be in the hands of the congregation?* If a special leaflet is to be produced, a copy should be sent in advance so that the bishop can become familiar with the page lay-out, and come armed with the full text where it simply says: 'Now the bishop blesses the water ...' !

- *Do any special needs to be anticipated?* The age of confirmation candidates makes a big difference, and it is helpful for the bishop to know if they are all adults, or if they include some who are very young. When a confirmation is a joint ecumenical occasion several special factors apply, as explained in Bishop David Hawtin's helpful booklet *'Bishops Behaving Ecumenically'* (page 23). If a candidate is disabled or has learning difficulties or is exceptionally nervous, these factors must be accommodated, e.g. how will a deaf-and-dumb candidate signal consent? Once I had to negotiate some way of helping a woman candidate recovering from a violent sexual assault. We mutually agreed that I would leave the bishop's chair, and we would stand together on the same level. We would quietly pause until she felt ready to initiate the next move. She would reach out, take my hand, place it on her own head and, after the Confirmation prayer, lay it aside again. This made her feel in charge of what was happening to her, and resolved her deep apprehension about this strange man laying hands on her – an occasion when a woman bishop would have been more suitable.

- *What arrangements are envisaged before and after the service?* Car parking; toilet facilities; signing registers, certificates and gift books; photographs; parish 'bun-fight', etc. Such points may require clarification.

If all these points were resolved in advance, I found that anxieties could be minimised all round and details affecting other people could be ironed out at rehearsal. Sorting out this agenda for 100 or so events a year was quite time-consuming, but it was time well spent. Where a good chaplain or personal assistant is available, they can be of real assistance in saving the bishop's time, though I still think that a first-hand conversation between the bishop and parish priest is the best option.

Occasionally a candidate wishes to change his or her Christian name at confirmation, as provided by Canon B.27 (6). The bishop may create a certificate to the effect that the new name is thereafter deemed lawful, and the diocesan registrar can give guidance on the correct wording and format, including details of the date of birth and of the date and place of baptism.

c) Rehearsal

Though most episcopal occasions require a rehearsal, this can generally be delegated. A confirmation rehearsal is best conducted by the priest locally responsible, who knows the building and most of the candidates. Similarly, the rehearsal for an institution and induction or licensing is generally conducted by the rural dean who has overseen the vacancy or, within a team ministry, by the (acting) team rector. It generally works best if the rural dean is firmly in charge, and knows that the bishop will stick by whatever choreography is agreed at the rehearsal. When an ecumenical partnership is involved, extra elements need to be accommodated in the service, such as the role of ecumenical representatives or the new minister signing up to an existing local covenant. If this is not worked out in advance, it can easily be overlooked and the standard Anglican pattern followed by default.

For an ordination, however, the ordaining bishop always has to be directly involved, not least because of adapting to that building and its customs. At Lincoln cathedral this was usually a joint operation with the canon precentor. When I ordained in a parish church, the rehearsal was a joint operation with the parish priest, for whom it was usually not a frequent occurrence. At least an hour was generally needed for going through the practical details.

d) Vesture

In its wisdom Canon B.8 lays down only broad and simple guidelines for liturgical vesture, and says nothing about the 'other customary vestments'. My own custom was to follow Michael Ramsey's example of wearing a plain alb and mitre with chasuble or cope for sacramental occasions. In most Lincolnshire churches eucharistic vestments are the norm, and only a handful of evangelical parishes expect Convocation robes. If the parish priest expressed a preference, I was content to go along with this. Best practice, in my view, is to wear the mitre only for processing in and out and at the time of receiving oaths, laying on hands, or giving a blessing. Too much 'hats on, hats off' can get fussy and unedifying. I generally took off the mitre to greet people at the church door afterwards, unless photo-shoots were in progress. Roman accoutrements were definitely not my style!

For choir offices and special occasions, such as a High Sheriff's service, rochet and red chimere was generally the most appropriate attire. For funerals and consecrating churchyards I generally wore 'magpie' – i.e. rochet and black chimere. However, when a burial ground was not adjacent to a convenient building, it was not very practical to don this gear in some windswept hedgerow. A simpler option was cassock and gown (or cloak, if wet). In rural Lincolnshire a bishop must always be prepared to get mud on his cassock!

The ecumenical cassock-alb and stole are becoming more usual episcopal attire, and for many non-sacramental occasions and outdoor events just a cassock is quite adequate.

e) *Personal preparation on the day*

In addition to the bishop's own devotional prayers, time and space are needed, before setting out, to run over the sermon (especially if it is to be preached without notes), and to recollect the names of clergy, spouses, children, churchwardens, lay ministers, ecumenical colleagues, etc whom the bishop will meet. If these people are already being remembered regularly in prayer, the bishop is already half-way to being attuned to the situation.

It makes a huge difference if the bishop can arrive in good time – composed and without any sense of rush. This sets an example, and is conducive to a mood of reverence and attentiveness to God. On arrival it is important to be sensitive to the ethos of that place, and to adapt oneself to its style and set-up. It is a very different experience from arriving simply as a stranger or visiting preacher, since a special bond of relatedness builds up between the parish and its bishop, who knows many of its key personalities.

It is helpful to tackle immediate tasks in a clear sequence. The first job is to 'inspect the pitch before play commences' – checking the lay-out in church, pages in the altar book, microphone switches, musical cues, etc. It is best to get this pottering about done before the church fills up.

Next comes the chance to meet key people informally, in particular those to be baptised, confirmed, received or ordained. This helps breaks the ice, and put them at ease. Then signing registers, certificates and gift books can be done behind the scenes in the vestry, before getting robed and wired up with the portable microphone. I usually invited the local clergy to lead the vestry prayer.

f) *During and after the service*

Rather than simply ploughing through the set order of service, it is important for the bishop to be sensitive to the tempo of the occasion. When people's attention is rapt, some point in the sermon may be slightly extended or the devotional atmosphere savoured in an extra moment of silence. At evening services with a largely adult congregation there is often more concentrated attention. At confirmations it is noticeable how the congregation 'perks up' if the candidates are introduced to them interestingly, and if those giving personal testimony are encouraged to speak briefly and from the heart. When people get restless or the service seems to drag, it may be necessary to quicken the pace or even cut something out (e.g. superfluous hymns at the administration of Holy Communion).

There were usually two or three items of feed-back worth paying attention to. After each occasion I gathered my own impressions whilst driving home. How was that? What was going on there? Were there any points to note for next time? This conscious de-briefing, sometimes assisted by my wife, helped me to learn lessons and follow up pastoral pointers.

g) *Adapting to a wide range of situations*

One of the joys of a bishop's ministry is to lead other special occasions of worship, such as the blessing of oils, the renewal of ministerial vows, the consecration of a new church building, a service of healing or corporate penitence, or an open-air gathering. These events, out of the ordinary run of parochial life, are opportunities to offer people new insights. A few random examples spring to mind. Sometimes the setting may be less formal. I recall, for example, a simple but very moving confirmation in the home of a very sick man who could not manage without his oxygen cylinder. One Easter morning, two former drug addicts came to the swimming pool at Cleethorpes leisure centre for baptism by immersion, witnessed by their local congregation, and straight afterwards I administered confirmation and first communion in their church. On another unforgettable occasion I was in Grimsby hospital at the bedside of a seriously ill patient who wanted to be baptised, confirmed, anointed and given Holy Communion shortly before death. Having been brought up a Baptist though never actually baptised, he requested me: "Please, Bishop, make sure you put on plenty of water" (in bed!). Another day, I had the unusual experience of blessing a new dredger on the Humber estuary! Assemblies in a wide range of schools were something I found quite challenging, but always enlivening and refreshing. Conducting the occasional wedding or funeral, usually for clergy families, was the chance not to lose touch with my former skills as a parish priest. In whatever setting, bishops as *'principal ministers of word and sacrament'* should try to set a good example in all worship they lead or in which they participate.

NURTURING THE WHOLE NETWORK OF WORSHIP LEADERS

a) *The worship network*

There is a whole army of people with whom the episcopate share the tasks of leading the offering of prayer and praise, and making public worship available in each locality. This includes the clergy, accredited lay workers, licensed readers, local lay ministers, those who assist with the distribution of communion in church and in the homes of the sick and house-bound, and those who lead all-age family worship. All these people form what I call the worship network.

The crucial question is: how well do they carry out their activities? The cathedral is a show-case of high standards in worship, such as to inspire all who come to the Mother Church of the diocese on various occasions. Lincoln diocese is fortunate in also having a chain of large parish churches with a good quality of music and liturgy (e.g. Barton-on-Humber, Boston, Gainsborough, Grantham, Grimsby, Holbeach, Louth, Sleaford, Spalding, etc). The resources available at the cathedral and these 'minster' churches outstrip those of most ordinary parishes, yet high standards are achievable anywhere if worship is offered simply and well. Bishops have the overall responsibility of seeing that effective systems are in place to train and sustain *all* ministers forming part of the network that leads public worship appropriately and competently throughout the whole range of parishes.

b) Sharing out the work

The major burden of providing both initial training and continuing education for worship leaders falls on the training team in any diocese. The names and structures vary from one diocese to another, but similar functions are carried out everywhere.

In many cases a useful supporting role is played by a Diocesan Liturgical Committee, whose members are conversant with new materials generated by the national Liturgical Commission, authorised by the General Synod or commended by the House of Bishops. Such local liturgical experts can play proactive role in organising study days to bring new resources to the notice of ministers trained in an earlier era, and can help bishops in preparing services for diocesan use under the provisions of Canon B.4 (3).

Local representatives of the Royal School of Church Music also have a valuable part to play in raising the musical standards of organists and choirs – work that is reinforced and extended by a Diocesan Music Adviser, where one exists.

An important area of ecumenical co-operation lies in combining the resources of Anglican readers and Methodist local preachers, and in the joint training of worship-leaders with a more limited brief (usually undertaken at deanery / circuit level). Though stipendiary clergy are in short supply, there is no dearth of local talent for the range of ministries comprised within the worship network. At their consecration bishops are charged *'to discern and foster the gifts of the Spirit in all who follow Christ'.*

Encouraging and regulating public worship

There is a delicate balance between three elements in the Church of England's way of regulating public worship, in which national, diocesan and local factors all carry their own due weight. The House of Bishops controls the final format in which liturgy is authorised by the General Synod. In each diocese the bishops exercise general oversight over the ordering of worship, authorising local arrangements and resolving disputes. At local level the incumbent and parochial church council make joint decisions about the pattern of worship in their parish. Let us look more closely at the interplay of these elements and the different ways in which bishops are involved.

a) *What the House of Bishops does*

The House of Bishops examines every proposal emanating from the Liturgical Commission before sending it on for wider debate. During my ten years as an elected member of the House I found liturgical business to be some of the most interesting, especially the extensive materials for *'Common Worship'* – the core book, the initiation services and the pastoral services. Sometimes the House refers specific theological issues to its Theological Group for detailed analysis and comment. For six years I belonged to this group, and benefited a good deal from others' scholarship and insights.

The synodical process of debating and revising liturgy is a very open one in which bishops, clergy and laity all have a voice. In addition new forms of service are also 'road tested' for an experimental period, as allowed by Canon B.5A, before final approval. However, an important requirement is enshrined in Article 7 (1) of the General Synod's constitution:

> *'A provision touching doctrinal formulae or the services or ceremonies of the Church of England or the administration of the Sacraments or sacred rites thereof shall, before it is finally approved by the General Synod, be referred to the House of Bishops, and shall be submitted for such final approval in terms proposed by the House of Bishops and not otherwise.'*

Each House has its own voting rights in giving final approval, but the House of Bishops also has the ultimate say over the terms in which final approval is given. The reason underlying this entrenched power is the ancient principle *'lex orandi, lex credendi'*: the way in which people worship affects their understanding of the Christian faith. Good liturgy and hymns foster sound doctrine. Bishops corporately have a duty to promote this, and guard against the opposite effect.

b) What the bishops do in the diocese

Bishops oversee the right ordering of worship throughout their own diocese. As 'Ordinary' – i.e. the one exercising ordinary jurisdiction – the diocesan bishop has certain powers in relation to the conduct of public worship, generally known as the *ius liturgicum*. The historical background and current position are briefly set out by Chancellor R.D.H. Bursell in the festschrift for Bishop Eric Kemp entitled *'English Canon Law'* (University of Wales Press, 1998) on pages 76-81. Nowadays the diocesan bishop normally shares this function with suffragan colleagues. In practice it boils down to four functions:

- *Giving pastoral guidance and directions* – e.g. advising clergy about liturgical experiments, and about the discretion they may exercise under Canon B.5 regarding special services or variations to authorised services. Bishops sometimes need to discourage unsuitable practices. I recall one parish priest who inherited from his predecessor the confusing practice of distributing unconsecrated wafers to children not yet confirmed; I had to ask him to stop doing this.
- *Giving approval* – e.g. for diocesan forms of service under Canon B.4 (3) such as celebrating a new ministry, consecrating a churchyard, or commemorating local saints on Holy Days observed locally under Canon B.6. Where bishops are satisfied that the right criteria are in place, they may allow admission to Communion before Confirmation in accordance with the House of Bishops' guide-line (GS Misc 488). From time to time acts of worship are requested in buildings closed for regular public worship, and bishops may authorise these after the consultation required by Part 6 of the Mission and Pastoral Measure 2011, Sections 57 (9) and 61 (2)(c).
- *Giving various people permission to carry out liturgical functions* – e.g. to permit an Anglican priest to officiate in a non-Anglican church, or to invite a minister of another church to officiate during an Anglican service, as provided by Canons B.43 and B.44. In many parishes the bishop authorises lay people to assist with administering Holy Communion, as provided by Canon B.12 (3) and the regulations approved in 1969. It is the bishop who ultimately controls who may preach – see Canon B.18 (2).
- *Resolving disputes* – e.g. where there is a disagreement between the incumbent and PCC over proposed changes of liturgical vesture (Canon B.8) or the frequency of services (Canon B.14A); or over the form of service to be used for occasional offices, where the persons concerned object beforehand (Canon B.3 (4)); or admission to Communion where grave scandal has been alleged (Canon B.16).

When the bishop's formal permission is required, it is important to check that the incumbent and PCC have already backed the proposal. Most cases are uncontroversial, but unforeseen difficulties sometimes arise. I recall two congregations where there was bitter division about who was an appropriate lay person to administer communion. Deeper pastoral issues were at stake, and had to be thoroughly explored. Sometimes the bishop may withhold permission for good reason.

c)   *What the local clergy and lay representatives do*

Although appeals can be made to the bishop, in my experience this is rare. A healthy feature of parochial life is the degree of devolved responsibility which incumbents and PCCs jointly exercise in regard to the public worship. They recognise their obligation to resolve matters at local level as far as possible, and to consult and decide in a collaborative manner. In general canon law, liturgical rubrics and diocesan guide-lines are well respected, and the whole system of regulating public worship is not experienced as being a heavily 'top down'. There is a strong feeling of local autonomy in the parishes, but the bishop is there in the background as a friend, adviser or referee – roles to be used wisely, as need arises.

RESOURCES FOR NEW BISHOPS

New bishops are likely to be already familiar with current liturgical practice, but it is important to keep up to date with the explosion of new hymnody and fresh materials which can be variable in quality. A working knowledge is required of those points of canon law mentioned above, of the Church of England (Worship and Doctrine) Measure 1974, and of the Code of Practice attached to the Ecumenical Canons.

SUMMARY

I would summarise this aspect of episcopal ministry as follows:

> **It leads** the offering of prayer and praise, including the sacraments.

In this chapter I have tried to show how bishops can do this partly through their own example of good practice, partly through nurturing the whole network of worship leaders with adequate training resources, and partly through using wisely the many opportunities that occur for them to encourage and regulate the Church's public worship. Above all, a firm theological and practical basis needs to underlie all that they undertake in this regard.

CHAPTER 13

Spreading the Christian Message

CHIEF TEACHERS

The bishop's role as chief teacher is made abundantly clear in the service of consecration. In the introduction the archbishop explains that:

'Bishops are ordained to be ... guardians of the faith of the apostles, proclaiming the gospel of God's kingdom and leading his people in mission'.

This is spelt out in the questions that precede the third and fourth vows:

'Will you lead your people in proclaiming the glorious gospel of Christ, so that the good news of salvation may be heard in every place?'

'Will you teach the doctrine of Christ as the Church of England has received it, will you refute error, and will you hand on entire the faith that is entrusted to you?'

The same emphasis is borne out by Canon C.18 (1) which states that:

'It appertains to [the bishop's] office to teach and to uphold sound and wholesome doctrine, and to banish and drive away all erroneous and strange opinions ...'

Precisely because the principal church in which a diocesan bishop is enthroned contains the *cathedra* or symbolic episcopal seat, the building is called a 'cathedral'. In the Jewish synagogue the scribes and Pharisees sat *'on Moses' seat'* (Matt. 23, 2). When Jesus read from the prophet Isaiah in the synagogue at Nazareth, he handed back the scroll and – significantly – sat to address the congregation (Lk 4, 20). He assumed the posture of a teacher. In the early Church it was quite usual for the bishop to preach from his throne whilst remaining seated.

In those days of a local episcopate the bishop often exercised a powerful preaching ministry within the liturgy at his cathedral, expounding the scriptures exegetically week by week. Ironically, bishops today have less opportunity for this than most parish priests. The need to address many different congregations in their pastoral area, perhaps 80 to 100 each year, often on special occasions, offers little scope for continuity of teaching. This difficulty is compounded when the bishop's visit occurs, as it often does, at the same season year by year. Hard though it is to be an effective 'chief teacher' at diocesan level, this role must be attempted.

TEACHING AT THE CORE OF CHURCH LIFE

Jesus was an outstanding and memorable teacher, who cast himself in a similar role to the Jewish prophets of old. Not only was teaching one of the main planks of his own ministry. He also charged his apostles to make disciples of all nations and teach them to obey everything that he had commanded them (Matt 28, 19-20). The tasks of handing on the gospel, building up believers in their faith and spreading the Christian message were central to the Church's mission, and have always been a major responsibility of its leaders. We can see this starting to happen within the pages of the New Testament. Indeed, the main motive for compiling such a collection of documents was to act as a tool for teaching. It became important to have as leaders those capable of interpreting the scriptures, and the office of bishop soon became a focus for the teaching function in church life.

SOME EXAMPLES FROM CHURCH HISTORY

a) The Irenaean model

In the sub-apostolic period the Church increasingly needed to give its attention to sound doctrine, and to differentiate itself from Judaism, from various mystery religions and from Greco-Roman society in general. In contrast to the Gnostics who shared their ideas within a closed circle of their own, the mainstream Christian tradition was handed on by an open tradition of teaching – a point strongly made by Irenaeus in emphasising the bishop's role as teacher of the faith. Since his ministry spanned East and West, he has been called the first great Catholic theologian. For him 'apostolic succession' was primarily about faithfulness to a publicly known series of teachers, traceable back to the first apostles.

> *'For Irenaeus, the bishop is above all the one who preserves the continuity of apostolic teaching in succession from the apostles. It is through the bishop's faithful proclamation of the gospel in each local church that unity and continuity in the apostolic tradition is preserved in the church'*
>
> ('*Lund statement*', LWF 2007, paragraph 13)

b) Early Fathers

Unsurprisingly, many of the published theological writings of the early Fathers were produced by bishops. They exercised their teaching ministry directly and personally in four main ways: preparing converts for baptism, preaching to the faithful, publicly expounding the Scriptures, and writing theological treatises. The preaching of such bishops as Cyril of Jerusalem and John Chrysostom in the East, or Ambrose and Augustine in the West, was enormously influential. After Christianity gained the support of the Emperor Constantine the episcopate gained a higher profile in public life. Its focus shifted from the town or city to the wider region. Since the bishop's role as teacher *par excellence* within the community was already firmly established, he could delegate responsibility for teaching to others who derived their authority from him. This led to a new emphasis on the bishop's responsibility for the formation of the clergy as preachers, teachers and spiritual guides. Parish schools were encouraged, and some clergy were commissioned for educational work.

c) Gregory's advice

Although much of Part III of the *'Pastoral Rule'* concentrates on how bishops should address individuals according to their circumstances and types of personality, Gregory gives some general guidance on public speaking. He stresses the need for careful preparation, especially when speaking out challengingly:

> *'When the bishop prepares to speak out, he must see that he chooses his language with great care. If his address is delivered hastily or put together in a slipshod way, the hearts of his hearers may be harmed by error. Though he wishes to appear wise, he may through lack of wisdom fail to take his hearers with him. He should be careful that his words do not divide his audience. Bishops should take great care not only that nothing evil passes their lips, but that even what is appropriate is neither exaggerated nor loosely expressed. The force of what is said can often be wasted when a careless or offensive torrent of words turns his hearers off.'*
>
> (from *'Pastoral Rule'* Pt II, ch 4)

Gregory also warns that 'the man is the message', i.e. that the sort of person he is speaks more loudly than words:

> *'What the bishop says will enter his hearers' hearts all the more effectively if it is borne out by the way he lives. Whatever words of advice he may give, it is his personal example that will most help people to carry them out.'*
>
> (ibid Pt II, ch 3)

> *'Every bishop in his teaching ministry should make himself heard more by deeds than by words. By the righteous way he lives his life he should leave footprints for others to tread in, rather than simply showing them the way to go by word alone.'*
>
> (ibid Pt III, ch 40)

d) Medieval period

In later centuries several factors combined to undermine bishops' effectiveness as preachers of the apostolic faith and exponents of Holy Scripture. Literacy declined during the Dark Ages. Ignorance and superstition became widespread. Most people had no direct access to the Bible, and the few who did relied increasingly on exegesis that was allegorical and speculative. The initiative in nurturing sound learning passed to monasteries and universities, and much preaching was undertaken by Dominican and Franciscan friars. Bishops for their part had to struggle with the practicalities of running huge dioceses, in which travel was fraught with difficulty and danger. Some of them were also secular princes, holding prominent positions in public life and exercising their power in questionable ways. The energies of the episcopate tended to be directed towards political, administrative and disciplinary tasks rather than to theology. Some bishops allowed themselves to be drawn into worldliness, corruption and intrigue, and lacked credibility as spiritual leaders. None the less, church leaders were obliged to engage with broad issues affecting church and society.

e) *Reformation and Counter-Reformation*

Amongst many strands that brought about the upheaval and renewal of Western Christendom in the 16th century was a driving impulse to reclaim the importance of sound teaching and preaching, and to put more resources into this ministry. The Augsburg Confession of 1530, which became a touchstone of Lutheran orthodoxy, defined the church as *'the assembly of saints in which the gospel is taught purely and the sacraments administered rightly'* (CA 7). This description was closely echoed in the Church of England's XXXIX Articles (Art. 19). The Augsburg Confession confirmed the office of bishops in the church, and emphasized that their primary duty was to see that people learned about the gospel and the love of Christ (CA 28). Bishops were to care for the church's apostolic faithfulness, and congregations were bound to obey bishops provided their teaching was in accord with the gospel. All members of the church, whether ordained or lay, were understood to be subject to the Word of God. Congregations were expected to be capable of identifying the voice of the Good Shepherd and distinguishing true teaching from false – a very different understanding of the church from the traditional distinction between those who teach (clergy) and those who are taught (laity). Martin Luther's shorter and longer catechisms of 1529 are testimony to his zeal to raise the laity's level of doctrinal knowledge and their maturity in the faith.

In the Church of England the questions to a new bishop, defining his role as a teacher in the church, were first introduced into the 1550 ordinal. A growing number of bishops amongst 16th and 17th century divines made substantial theological contributions to emerging Anglican theology, e.g. Thomas Cranmer, Nicholas Ridley, John Jewel, Lancelot Andrewes, William Laud and Jeremy Taylor. The Bible also became increasingly available in the language of the people, and the Prayer Book catechism exercised a wide influence on clergy and laity.

In the Roman Catholic Church the Council of Trent decreed in 1546 that the bishop's primary responsibility was to preach the word. This understanding was clearly reflected two centuries later in William Ullathorne's tract on *'The Office of Bishop'* (1850), published when the hierarchy was restored in this country – two decades before the First Vatican Council. His mature reflections on the priorities of the episcopate were expressed in his sermon at Henry Vaughan's consecration in 1872:

> *'The bishop is the ruler of the churches, the guardian of the revealed truth, the witness and the judge of faith, the custodian of God's law, the enforcer of the Church's canons, the father of his clergy and their judge, the pastor of his people, the chief preacher of the Word of God to the flock and the guide of souls.'*

In his latter years Ullathorne developed an outward looking sense of the Church, and laid stress on the bishop's prophetic task of engaging with contemporary society and challenging the ways of the world (see J. Champ, *'William Bernard Ullathorne – a different kind of monk'* (pages 381-383).

f) Second Vatican Council

Similar points were developed more fully by the Second Vatican Council: briefly in *'Lumen Gentium',* 1964 (paragraph 25) and more fully in the *'Decree on the Bishops' Pastoral Office in the Church'* 1965 (paragraphs 12 and 13). Mention is made not only of proclaiming the gospel, but also of taking seriously the world's current problems. Bishops have to strike a balance between guarding Christian doctrine and entering into dialogue with human society. They are urged to do so with clarity of speech, humility, gentleness and love. They are reminded that various methods of communication are available – preaching, conferences, public statements, use of the media, catechesis appropriate to different age groups, etc. Bishops are charged to see that all those exercising a teaching function within the church are properly trained, thoroughly grounded in Christian doctrine and equipped with a good grasp of psychology and teaching methods.

g) Anglican insights into the bishop's teaching role

Important though bishops' role as chief teachers may be, Alec Graham (Bishop of Newcastle, 1981-97) sounded a salutary warning against any presumption that they could do this on their own:

> *'I am suspicious of the model which places the transmission of the authentic tradition solely in the bishop. He is a representative figure. He does not do it as a lone individual, nor in any sense apart from the Church ... It is the whole Church which believes, which hands on its faith, its scriptures and its very life (which is not its own but that of Christ) to the next generation. The bishop, unworthy heir of the*

apostles, is but an agent in this process. He acts, properly speaking, neither apart from Christ nor apart from the Church, but as Christ's agent within the Church and as the Church's agent in the name of Christ. If he acts as the Church's agent, then he acts on behalf of the believing people, in so far as they know and in so far as they seek to know. He acts in the name of the barely literate as much as in the name of the theological professor. He needs to listen to, and learn from, both.

Why do I labour this? Because of siren voices which put the weight on you and you alone, as if you and I [bishops] are the only links in the golden chain of authentic teachers. ... We make any sense only as figures representative of Christ and of his Church, and of Christ in his Church. Often enough, that cuts us down to size. The whole Church has a share in the transmission of the tradition. We are but articulators of what we and countless others have received.'

(from an unpublished paper)

A similar concern was also voiced by Prof John Macquarrie (Oxford University, 1970-86) in a valuable article entitled *'The bishop and theologians'*, in which he urged the need for partnership between bishops, theologians and the laity:

'Theology is a responsibility of the whole Church, and can only rightly be done if the whole Church participates ... [There is a special responsibility for bishops] to encourage enquiry ... get such thinking going ...and enable and guide the dialogue'.

(From *'Today's Church and Today's World'*, CIO 1977, pages 252-253)

h) Lambeth Conference 1978

Attention has already been briefly drawn to the report of Section 2 of the 1978 Conference, which stressed that the bishop's teaching function should be exercised not only within the church, but also prophetically towards the world:

'It is [the bishop's] function to teach, in fulfilling which it is his responsibility to organise the teaching of the faith effectively for the life and witness of his people ... Again, it is [his] responsibility to exercise a prophetic ministry toward the world. To do so requires consultation about the situation and about the most effective method of doing so.'

This statement was expanded in Resolution 18:

'The Conference affirms that a bishop is called to be one with the apostles in proclaiming Christ's resurrection and interpreting the Gospel, and to testify to Christ's sovereignty as Lord of lords and King of kings. In order to do this effectively, he will give major attention to his public ministry. Reflecting the ministry of the prophets, he will have a concern for the well-being of the whole community (especially of those at a disadvantage) not primarily the advantage or protection of the Church community. The bishop should be ready to be present in

secular situations, to give time to the necessary study, to find skilled advisers and to take sides publicly if necessary (in ecumenical partnership if at all possible) about issues which concern justice, mercy and truth. Members of the Church should be prepared to see that the bishop is supported in such a ministry.'

i)   'The Nature of Christian Belief' (1986)

In the mid-1980's a lively public debate was sparked off by some comments of David Jenkins, who became Bishop of Durham in 1984. In the preceding years a number of major works by liberal and modernist theologians had gained prominence (see Adrian Hastings, *'History of English Christianity 1920-1985'*, chapter 41), and the conservative backlash focussed on the question how far bishops ought publicly to question traditional formulations of orthodox belief. In response to a General Synod debate in February 1985 the House of Bishops produced a brief statement, backed up by a fuller and immensely constructive exposition on *'The Nature of Christian Belief'* (CHP 1986). The corporate elaboration of this material was a sign of the House of Bishops growing into a new role of issuing occasional teaching documents, of which several others soon followed.

The statement affirmed the House's adherence to the apostolic faith, and the assured place of the Holy Scriptures, the catholic creeds and the official formularies of the Church of England. After four brief doctrinal clauses dealing with the Resurrection of Christ, the Empty Tomb, the Trinity and Incarnation, and the Virginal Conception of Christ, the statement went on to speak of the need to 'proclaim the faith afresh in each generation'. There must always, it was argued, be a place in the Church's life for tradition and enquiry, and bishops had a responsibility to distinguish in their own teaching between the ideas of theological exploration and the corporate teaching of the Church. This approach is worked out in detail in Section E entitled *'The Individual and Collegial Responsibility of Bishops for the Faith of the Church'*. This provides an Anglican counter-balance to the heavily papal emphasis of Vatican II's ecclesiology (especially in *'Lumen Gentium'*, chapter 25). The stress on mutual responsibility within the Body of Christ has close parallels with the LWF *'Lund Statement'* of 2007, quoted earlier.

There is much wisdom in Section E of *'The Nature of Christian Belief'*. It makes clear, for example, that bishops have a duty to listen to the whole people of God, and to keep various points of view open to each other. They are to work for a common mind (paragraphs 64 and 65). They have a twofold task: to *'guard, expound and teach'* but also to be *'apostolic pioneers'* (paragraph 67). In leading mission towards those who are not church members they need to search for idioms that will touch and persuade different audiences (paragraph 68). They should help the

Church to benefit from the work of professional scholars, and help to integrate their insights into the Christian community (paragraph 69). They should foster the continuing process of theological education for all ministers, clerical and lay (paragraph 73), and be aware of the mind of the wider Church (paragraph 76).

On this last point bishops need to be alert to the opportunities for sharing with their ecumenical counterparts in speaking with a single voice. If they are to make a common proclamation, this requires time for prior consultation.

j) Some challenging questions from Niagara

With the aim of helping bishops to be constructively self-critical the Anglican-Lutheran 'Niagara Report' (1988) posed the following challenging questions in this sphere of ministry:

- *Do these exercising episcopé in the Church expound and commend the Christian faith in a sustained way, not just preaching on special occasions or during isolated visits to congregation?*
- *Do they take real care to enlist the advice and help of those skilled in communications in the modern world, and to address those issues which are of urgent concern to people?*
- *Do they make the most of their corporate teaching role as a conference of bishops, and provide collegial support to one another in the exercise of their teaching responsibilities?*

('The Niagara Report', CHPP 1988, paragraph 106)

THE BISHOP'S OWN TEACHING MINISTRY

Against the backdrop of these ideals and expectations, bishops have to engage with a range of ways to teach. What is appropriate and sustainable differs according to circumstances and from person to person. It will be influenced by three main factors:

- the bishop's own gifts, experience and limitations
- strategic choices about which opportunities and methods to take up
- keeping oneself resourced for this work

a) Gifts, experience and limitations

Candidates come to episcopal office from various backgrounds. Those who were previously theological teachers are likely to bring a well-stocked brain, a breadth and depth of learning, and some skill at engaging with enquiring minds. Those whose previous experience was mainly in parochial ministry are likely to be familiar with catering for a wide range of age-groups and levels of education, and in touch with views and prejudices 'in the pew' that often cannot be tackled at an intellectual level. Those who are already 'media savvy' are likely to be sensitive to the needs of the wider public, and to have some proven ability in putting across a Christian viewpoint to a non-church audience. Those already versed in experiential methods of adult education will find this background highly relevant to enabling people to mature, to modify their own behaviour and to resolve conflict. Those knowledgeable on issues of urban industrial society may have little experience of rural affairs, and vice versa.

It goes without saying that any bishop should be capable of preaching well, and members of the Crown Nominations Commission now hear short-listed candidates preach to them – what in Free Church terminology is known as 'preaching with a view' (i.e. to appointment). Whilst all candidates are expected to bring appropriate gifts and experience to their new role, they also have some gaps and inadequacies that need to be addressed in further training. Bishops need to be realistic about their own strengths and weaknesses as teachers and communicators, and get what help they need to match up to the whole range of the duties that belong to this aspect of their calling.

b) *Opportunities and methods*

Bishops have to cope with a heavy programme of preaching engagements throughout the year, a plethora of other speaking invitations from within and beyond the church, an expectation of producing regular articles or statements through diocesan channels, and an unrelenting barrage of media requests for instant comment on current affairs. Owing to the constraints of time and energy many invitations have to be declined. The critical issue is to identify what simply *has* to be done, what room there is for manoeuvre and what areas of strategic choice remain.

- The major portion of the bishop's teaching ministry is *preaching in the parishes*, perhaps 80 to 100 times a year. This is an important opportunity of face-to-face contact with the whole spectrum of ordinary parishioners, and requires sensitivity to each local situation. The substance of the sermon needs, of course, to be carefully worked out, but there is a danger of being over-prepared. The manner of delivery must be adapted flexibly to the actual situation. For the congregation the bishop's visit is a change from their normal preacher but, because there is not the same bond as the people have with their own parish priest, bishops often have to preach to the unknown – which can mean a difficult adjustment from their earlier ministry. This adaptation takes some time, and can only be achieved by closer acquaintance with the new situation. The bishop's sermon should exemplify a good standard of preaching, but parochial occasions suffer from certain limitations. Sadly, many Parish Communion congregations are not used to substantial sermons, and have a fairly limited attention span. A short 'one-off' sermon offers little scope for developing connected teaching, though making the most of seasonal themes and the biblical passages provided by the lectionary can lend greater coherence. Even though the bishop does not usually get the chance to preach a series of addresses to the same congregation, it is possible to reinforce the normal teaching they receive and arouse not only their attention but also their sense of commitment. It is the bishop's prime opportunity to deepen the Christian understanding of those who do come to church, and to raise their spiritual sights.

- Many of these parochial occasions will be for the sacrament of *confirmation,* sometimes with *baptism* too. When the full initiation rite is used, it is best to keep the address short and let the symbolism of the liturgy speak for itself. The address needs to be vivid, simple and memorable for the candidates and their families. Over the years I developed a number of different types of confirmation addresses: those with a seasonal focus, general sermons on Christian commitment suitable for all ages, and deeper talks for older or more thoughtful candidates. I found that a longer attention span was often sustainable at an evening service or with older candidates. A good confirmation sermon can be re-used in another parish or deanery, but I tried – by recording where and when each address was given – to avoid repeating it to the same hearers.

- The *institution or licensing* of a new priest tends to be a well attended occasion with a great sense of expectancy. For the sermon I tended to follow a standard pattern, touching on three distinct themes: something to *introduce* the new priest to parishioners and colleagues in the deanery; something biblically based on the theme of *ministry* (linked with suitable readings); and something from the 'statement of needs' about the *coming phase of work* and its challenges. In general, I preferred the ministry section of the sermon to be more dominant, but sometimes the local situation required more comment, especially when a new grouping or structure was being introduced.

- Bishops are often invited to preach on *special occasions,* such as the completion of a building project or the dedication of new church furnishings. After checking with the archdeacon that this work has been authorised by faculty, the bishop needs to get a clear briefing in advance: How much did it cost? Where did the money come from? Was it given in someone's memory? Will the architect, builder or artist be present? Who should be publicly thanked? etc.. The parish priest may need to look up some of these facts, and cannot be expected to produce them on the spur of the moment. Armed with this information the bishop can then try to lift up the occasion into some overarching Christian theme that can outshine the 'nuts and bolts'. Another example of the need for careful briefing is a *fund-raising campaign*. Expectations have to be clarified. Some clergy and congregations are scared of the full-blooded message of Christian stewardship – time, talents and money, including tithing – and this subject needs to be tackled sensitively, though without dumbing it down.

The fact remains that most of the population are not church-goers, and bishops cannot reach them by the parochial route. If the number of parochial speaking engagements is not limited, no leeway remains for wider communication. Quality time must be earmarked for some events that offer a larger time-slot, or the possibility of developing more connected teaching, or the chance to uphold in public life the standpoint of faith and the values of God's Kingdom. When budgeting the time and effort involved in preparation, it is worth considering how many people are likely to be reached. The spread of the media has opened up the opportunities enormously. Through the secular press or a well presented diocesan newspaper or local radio the bishop can reach a wide public. The new potentialities of web-sites and bishops' blogs are being utilised in many dioceses, and in the course of time the advantages and disadvantages of these new technologies will become apparent.

The range of possibilities includes:

- a radio or TV interview, or speaking in public debate (e.g. in the Lords or locally)
- a panel discussion
- a day conference or residential week-end
- a Lent course with sessions spread over several weeks
- a retreat, quiet day or devotional evening comprising two or three talks
- a course of lectures
- a workshop lasting several sessions
- a teach-in or training session – e.g. for clergy, readers or local ministers

- an educational item at a diocesan or deanery synod meeting
- an essay, article, report, or book

Careful choices have to be made about what to spend one's time on, and a sensible balance maintained. Under pressure of time I have often had to ask myself: if I spent twice as long in preparation, would it be twice as good?

Spoken utterances need not be confined to monologue, even if assisted by an overhead projector or power point presentation. A well-thought out educational design can encourage dialogue and interaction. Sometimes the terms of an invitation can be re-negotiated. For example, when asked to address a deanery synod about the Virgin Birth, I agreed to tackle this subject on the understanding that the meeting should be split into small groups and the time divided into three mini-sessions. Or again, when the headmaster of a grammar school invited me to speech day for the third time, I asked whether instead of giving a formal address I could have a wide-ranging discussion with the Sixth Form. He readily agreed to "throw me to the lions" for a whole afternoon which worked out fine (I suspect that they were on their best behaviour!).

From my time on Michael Ramsey's staff I remember what good use he made of the eagerly awaited annual visit of post-graduate American ordinands from the Roman Catholic University of Louvain, Belgium. He would receive this group of about 20 young men in his sitting room at Lambeth Palace, where they perched on the few available chairs or mostly sat on the carpet. From his armchair he would engage in lively dialogue, with no holds barred. He and his visitors stimulated one another and, as shyness melted away, this encounter brought out his gifts as a scholar and communicator.

c) *Keeping oneself resourced*

Mention has already been made of the need to keep up one's own studies, of drawing on previous work and current reading, and of being prepared to use skilled advisers. Many bishops do not have research assistants or speech writers, as many leading politicians do, but have to do the preparatory work themselves. They do have a wide circle of colleagues from whom they can, and perhaps on more occasions should, invite advice and help.

I wish I could say that I set aside regular and frequent times for study, but honesty compels me to admit that most of my study was orientated towards some forthcoming event. I blocked off half-days or three-hour sessions within my normal programme, and did some reading and planning during school holidays and half-terms. Many bishops use their sabbatical study leave to good advantage for studying and writing.

Some time for reverie is needed to get in touch with the existing knowledge stored within us. We need to brood and think, and have the confidence to realise that once upon a time we did actually know a thing or two. We must have the courage to be ourselves, and release the wisdom we already have. I found it helpful to note down my initial thoughts on a chosen subject at an early stage, and refine them later. Devising a clear outline structure made the task manageable, and showed me where more work was needed. I often took blocks of material prepared for one purpose, and adapted them for some other. I tried to keep up with new publications, and let wide reading feed lateral thinking. It was always an encouragement when I saw that Simon Phipps, Bob Hardy, Bill Ind and Kenneth Stevenson had their study-tables overflowing with piles of new books or journals to dip into, and I tried to follow their example.

When bishops work beyond their own specialist field, it is important to take soundings or request briefings from diocesan advisers, or the staff of General Synod boards and councils, or the 'lead bishop' on that subject. We should not try to beat the experts at their own game, but at least show an informed awareness of the issues they wrestle with. For example, when preparing an after-dinner speech for the annual bankers' or accountants' dinner – highlights of the business year in Grimsby – I took advice from a friend with relevant professional expertise in another part of the country. Before calling on the Docks Manager I sought a briefing from the senior industrial chaplain. When working pastorally with a trans-gender couple, I kept in close touch with the secretary with the Board of Social Responsibility who knew how this sensitive matter was being handled in other dioceses. As bishops endeavour to affirm and inspire people engaged in various walks of life, it is good to create dialogue between various specialisms, and act as a bridge for others' ideas as well as our own. We can but try to do this, but it does take some time to do the homework. After that, the rest – in Richard Holloway's phrase – is "a mixture of adrenalin and hope!"

Michael Mayne's sermon at my consecration drew out tellingly the connection between 'oversight' and 'insight'. He had this to say:

> *Jesus comes to open the eyes of the blind. That covers the whole spectrum from a blind man regaining his sight to the post-Easter vision of the world transfigured and redeemed. Like Paul, at first blinded and then with restored sight, in Christ we see the world and each other with new eyes.*
>
> *The oversight and insight we demand of our bishops is rooted in this vision of how things truly are. We need you to be a <u>seer</u> and an overseer: to look not just at the church but at the world: with one eye to see its disorder and confusion, and with the other to discern the glory and the activity of God within it. To speak of God*

and what He is doing in his world; to show people they are loved and valued and forgiven; and to do it in a language that relates to real life and in terms all can understand.

For some of us who speak and write and preach that will mean joining the human race again: seeking to discern in the world about us the hidden presence of God pervading the scene, and pointing it out. It will mean, in the words of Simon Barrington-Ward, 'scanning the broken surface of the world and discerning hidden connections like an artist, a scientist or a novelist'.

It will mean, above all, an attentiveness to what the world is saying. Therefore, I beg you, in ordering your life as a bishop, to make your first priority the creating of a proper space: time to be still, time to contemplate the world around you, time to look at – and listen to – your wife, your children and your neighbour. Time to read novels and poetry. Time to look at pictures, and listen to music. Time to watch television and listen to the radio. Time to think and to pray and to <u>see</u> ...'

These are some of the ways in which, as bishops, we may seek to resource ourselves.

Nurturing the whole teaching & learning network

Beside their individual ministry as teachers and communicators of the Christian faith, bishops need to put time and energy into fostering links with a range of other people engaged in these tasks. Broadly speaking, the episcopate should relate to and try to encourage two main groups:

    i) those providing general education through schools, colleges and universities
    ii) those enabling Christian discipleship and ministry.

The way in which bishops share out their direct involvement in this work varies from diocese to diocese.

Schools and colleges

For centuries the church has been a pioneer and provider of education. This includes not just religious knowledge or Christianity, but any learning or skill that helps human beings to reach their potential. The church is present in education neither to evangelise, nor simply to build up its own members and protect its own interests, but to contribute to the common good. It holds no monopoly in this sphere, but stands as a committed partner alongside other education providers.

Most bishops exercise an active role in the governance of some university, college or school – not just those of Christian foundation. In my own case, for example, I served for 15 years on the managing body of a Woodard School; for 7 years on the corporation of a Further Education college; and for 4 years as a governor of a C. of E. (Controlled) primary school in the village where I live in retirement. Such involvement inevitably takes up a good deal of time, but I believe that bishops have a duty to engage with others in serving these communities of learning and, as opportunity permits, to contribute whatever we can to their ideals and good practice.

Lincoln diocese's major stake in public education was through 150 church schools in which around 25,000 children were taught, and through Bishop Grosseteste College – now a university – with a fine reputation for training primary teachers. For many years the pattern was for the diocesan bishop to sustain the major link with the College and with the annual gathering of Bishop's Visitors to church schools, and for one suffragan and one archdeacon to participate actively in the Diocesan Board of Education. This body, which I chaired for ten years, worked in partnership with the counties of Lincolnshire and Humberside (the latter is now split into the unitary authorities of North Lincolnshire and North-East Lincolnshire) as well as with the Methodist Church in relation to five ecumenical primary schools. All three bishops played a role in the Church Schools' Festival which drew hundreds of school children to the cathedral each summer, and we visited schools and colleges of all types across the diocese when invited to do so. The diocesan bishop made a point of visiting church schools that had had a recent OFSTED inspection, in order to encourage and support them.

Training in discipleship and ministry

The episcopate sustains a major field force of clergy, accredited lay workers, licensed readers and local lay ministers, all of whom rightly see a teaching element in their ministry. As Simon Phipps put it to me in his original letter of invitation, a bishop should be someone who *'reads and thinks, and can help the clergy to do their theology'.* This obviously overlaps with the pastoral and worship networks already mentioned. Bishops need to ensure that, amongst the clergy of their diocese, there is a sufficient number whose level of theological training is above average. Key roles have to be played by the diocesan training team and all who serve as part-time tutors for various courses. During my Grimsby years I made a point of nominating one or two priests a year to attend summer schools in Strasbourg, to broaden their international awareness and experience a European style of theological engagement. Most dioceses now operate a rolling programme of sabbatical study leave for clergy. Much depends on the bishop to encourage applicants, to facilitate staff cover, and to plough back into the flow of diocesan life the enrichment gained by clergy during their sabbaticals. Without active episcopal support the potential benefits of sabbatical study can easily be dissipated.

It must always be remembered that the calling to be an adult disciple of Christ is more basic and wide-reaching than authorisation to exercise a public ministerial function within the congregation. Ministry can – in Helen Oppenheimer's phrase – be a very "hungry concept". Training people for jobs in the church (paid or unpaid) tends to claim more time, attention and resources than strengthening the general run of ordinary lay Christians for their daily work and witness in the world. Two useful reports published by the General Synod Board of Education – *'All are Called: towards a theology of the laity'* (1985) and *'Called to be Adult Disciples'* (1987) – aimed to encouraged a climate in which the laity's gifts and contributions are recognised, valued and developed. The latter report went so far as to say:

> *'The need to maintain church life, in terms of staffing, funding and resourcing with support and continuing training, poses a serious threat to the apostolic task of the bishop ...'*
>
> (paragraph 43)

It recommended that each bishop should appoint a senior staff member to share the responsibility for focusing and developing the role of the laity in the 'dispersed' church – a concern that is fundamental to the church's mission. Over the past three decades hundreds of lay people in Lincoln diocese have signed up for the Bishop's Certificate course. Some have done this to gain a qualification or take on public duties. Many others have not aspired to public ministry, but have been caused by some difficult life experience – e.g. bereavement, divorce or pressing ethical issues around work or family – to think more deeply about their faith. They want to clear their minds, do a refresher course, engage with current issues and simply become better Christians. This real intellectual engagement sometimes turns out to be a springboard to public ministry, though that may not have been the original aim in view. Bishops must play their part in raising the status of adult learning in church and community, and in promoting spirituality and retreats.

RESOURCES FOR NEW BISHOPS

As new bishops adjust to their role as chief teacher and take up their place within the collegiality of the episcopate, the slim document mentioned on page 152 – *'The Nature of Christian Belief'* – may be of use, especially Section E about engaging with a wide audience.

There are numerous books on preaching, amongst which we all tend to have our favourites. In re-assessing my own homiletical efforts I have found none more stimulating than the *'Lectures on Preaching'* by R.W. Dale (Hodder & Stoughton, 1877) who sustained such a remarkable ministry for over 45 years at Carr's Lane Congregational Church, Birmingham in the late Victorian era. These lectures to the students at Yale combine theological earnestness, humour, breadth of European culture, social engagement and pastoral wisdom. His comments in the sixth lecture on sermon preparation and delivery are invaluable, not least his discussion of extempory preaching and using old sermons.

On facilitating learning with adults I have particularly enjoyed the experiential approach of Carl R. Rogers in *'Freedom to Learn'* (1969) and *'Encounter Groups'* (1973). When bishops try to encourage self-motivated change in groups or individuals, it is of little avail to pose as authority figures or experts. Any attempt to bully or dominate people has the effect of intimidating them and stifling their personal growth. If, on the other hand, the bishop interacts as a 'real' and fully human person, this style of leadership can have quite the opposite effect. It enables people to become more self-aware, open up their feelings and respond creatively.

Summary

In the light of what I have written in this chapter, I would sum up the teaching function that is integral to episcopé in these terms:

> **It teaches**, proclaims, guards and interprets the Christian faith;
> it explores and makes sense of current issues in the light of that faith;
> it ensures that theological resources are available to laity & clergy sharing in ministry;
> it co-operates with those providing public education at all ages and levels.

CHAPTER 14

Sending New Ministers

At the service of consecration, just before the candidates make their consecration vows, the archbishop summarises the responsibilities of bishops in words that include the following:

'[Bishops] are to discern and foster the gifts of the Spirit in all who follow Christ, commissioning them to minister in his name ... As chief pastors, it is their duty to share with their fellows presbyters the oversight of the church ...'

The earlier version of the ordinal (ASB 1980) had expressed this in narrower terms:

'[The bishop] is to ordain and to send new ministers, guiding those who serve with him and enabling them to fulfil their ministry.'

The fifth vow of the current ordinal has been worded inclusively to cover all forms of public ministry, both ordained and lay:

'Will you be faithful in ordaining and commissioning ministers of the gospel?'

THE APOSTOLICITY OF THE CHURCH

A fundamental mark of the church is to be 'apostolic', meaning 'sent'. On Easter night the risen Christ said in the upper room to his apostles:

'As the Father sent me, so I send you' (John 20, 21)

He entrusted them not simply with the message that he was risen, but with the errand of spreading it and helping it to take root. In the writings of Matthew and Luke Jesus' final marching orders are also recorded in similar terms:

'Go and make disciples of all nations; baptise them in the name of the Father and of the Son and of the Holy Spirit; teach them to obey everything I have commanded you'

(Matthew 28, 19-20)

'When the Holy Spirit comes upon you, you shall be my witnesses in Jerusalem, in all Judaea and Samaria, and to the ends of the earth'

(Acts 1, 8)

The essence of being an apostle lay in being commissioned and sent out, as a witness of the risen Christ, to spread the good news, to baptise people into the life of the church, and to teach them to obey everything that Jesus taught. The expansion of the church and its rooting in different places and cultures did not just happen co-incidentally. It was a dynamic process, empowered by the Holy Spirit and requiring clear human intent, as Paul explained:

> *'If you confess with your lips that Jesus is Lord and believe in your heart that God has raised him from the dead, you will be saved ... 'Everyone who calls on the name of the Lord shall be saved'. But how are they to call on one in whom they have not believed? And how are they to believe in one of whom they have never heard? And how are they to hear without someone to proclaim him? And how are they to proclaim him **unless they are sent**? How welcome are the footsteps of those who bring good news!*
>
> (Romans 10, 8 ff.)

The process of sending has always been a vital element in the church's life. What the first apostles had received from Jesus they transmitted with his authority. It was vested in key persons and in the congregations that they founded, who in turn passed this treasure on to others. To be apostolic was both to be 'on message' – i.e. true to Christ's teaching – and to be in fellowship with the whole network of similar communities.

In drawing up the Porvoo Common Statement we (the Anglican and Lutheran delegates) took the trouble to spell out the short-hand phrase "apostolic succession", which is too often assumed to be simply a matter of ministerial pedigree:

> *'We set out at greater length an understanding of the apostolicity of the whole Church and within that the apostolic ministry, succession in the episcopal office and the historic succession as a sign. All of these are interrelated.'*
>
> (Porvoo, §35)

> *'... the primary manifestation of apostolic succession is to be found in the apostolic tradition of the Church as whole. The succession is an expression of the permanence and, therefore, of the continuity of Christ's own mission in which the Church participates.'*
>
> (Porvoo, §39)

The whole of chapter IV in "Porvoo" is a carefully balanced statement of where bishops fit into the bigger picture of what the whole Church is about. Like any visible society, the church needs signs and instruments of its identity and communal life. Carrying out its mission *'requires the coherence of its witness in every aspect of its life, and this coherence requires supervision'* – i.e. pastoral oversight or episcopé (see *'The Niagara Report',* §20).

Ways in which bishops 'send'

Against this theological background it is self-evident that bishops hold a key role in providing structure and support for the church's ongoing mission. Their particular contribution is to maintain an overall sense of purpose and direction in deploying the human and financial resources of their diocese wisely, as well as treasuring the seed-corn on which future growth depends and fostering new initiatives. In this chapter I shall explore what is involved in seven distinct processes that impel mission, and in ensuring that these are sustained on a sound footing:

- nurturing new life for all forms of ministry
- encouraging developments in shared ministry
- sponsoring and selecting candidates for ministerial training
- ordaining new deacons and priests to suitable curacies
- providing a range of ministerial posts to match changing pastoral demands
- co-operating with all who share in the process of clergy appointments
- enabling clergy to exercise satisfying responsibility throughout their ministry

Examining each aspect in turn, I shall discuss what measures may contribute to good practice in sending new ministers into the Lord's vineyard or transferring existing ones to new work within it. The right sort of episcopal lead can make all the difference, but none of this work can be done single-handedly. Here another of the bishop's strategic networks comes into view – the ministerial network.

Nurturing new life for all forms of ministry

When a benefice falls vacant, churchwardens often expect the bishop or patron simply to find a new priest from somewhere, anywhere. As an interregnum drags on, it becomes evident that there is no great pool of spare clergy 'out there', still less any queue of applicants for what is increasingly likely to be a multi-church benefice! Rarely does it occur to churchwardens to wonder where clergy are recruited, or to face the question whether their own parish has produced any ordinands over the last thirty years. The fact remains that all clergy emerge from one source – namely, the active lay membership of the church.

Most vocations flower in parishes and chaplaincies, though a few may come to light in less usual settings. The most effective seed-bed of vocation tends to be a lively congregation of definite churchmanship, where the notion of taking Christian ministry seriously is at least thinkable. If the local church is not a live option in the first place, it is little wonder if it generates few lay leaders or ordinands. I had the great blessing of growing up in the vibrant parish of Solihull, which in the 1950s produced about ten priests and two women church workers in as many years. The possibility of devoting one's life to such work was in the very air we breathed there. The clergy fostered this ideal. The stream of new deacons coming from theological college to be trained in the realities of parochial life made the congregation aware that well-rounded and experienced priests do not simply drop down from heaven, ready-made. New blood always needs to be encouraged, and it certainly was in that parish. To become an ordinand was not such an oddity, and there were other people of my own age-group with whom to talk through the issues. Nor was it not just a question of ordained ministry. Over a dozen house-groups met each month under lay leadership, and the leaders also met monthly with Harry Hartley at his rectory to prepare their next session and to give corporate shape to the parish's whole mission strategy. It was a spiritually bracing environment that stimulated much growth for ministry in various ways.

This is the pattern I tried to emulate in my own years as a parish priest, sharing a large measure of responsibility with lay people as well as nurturing some vocations to the priesthood. The need to create a climate in which the laity's gifts are recognised, valued and developed has already been mentioned. This front-line work of awakening the sense of Christian vocation within parishes and chaplaincies has to be backed up by what the diocese can provide, especially through the bishop's training network.

As to the specific challenge of ordination, for several years at Tettenhall I used to hold informal evenings twice a year for those already in theological training to report how they were getting on, and for any others to explore what going down that track might mean. This informal group had a fluid membership of about a dozen, in those days exclusively male. Not all parishes have the critical mass of numbers to make this approach viable, and so diocesan and national structures have a vital part to play. From time to time the Church of England has held nation-wide campaigns to recruit more clergy, with varying degrees of success; that at Trinitytide 1951 probably had the most impact. Some residential conferences for those exploring the vocation to ordination should be available every year, as such events do much good. Most crucially of all, it falls to the bishops of each diocese to put in place their own pattern of continuing provision under the Diocesan Director of Ordinands (DDO). For example, in Lichfield diocese there was the Guild of St Stephen for all aspiring ordinands. A few incumbents assisted the DDO by serving as area wardens, and kept in regular and frequent touch with potential candidates. The whole Guild met annually for a eucharist and day conference on the theme of vocation, presided over by the bishop, which was a supportive and effective system.

In Lincoln diocese it was our custom for many years to hold an annual vocations' day at Edward King House, when all three bishops were present throughout. It was a good opportunity to meet potential ordinands and church workers informally, and for them to mingle with 'us three' at close quarters.

No word in English quite catches the same flavour as '*Nachwuchs*' ('new blood') in German. It is about giving birth to a new generation and actively looking out for those who are 'up and coming' – the recruits on whom the future will depend. This rising talent has to be spotted before it can be sent. Passively waiting for volunteers was not how Our Lord enlisted his first apostles. Bishops have a direct and personal role to play in watching out for promising candidates, putting the challenge on appropriate occasions, and giving a jog of encouragement where needed. They are responsible for keeping in place a back-up force of advisers throughout the diocese, and getting them to provide a range of opportunities for people to explore vocation in its broadest terms beyond the bounds of their own parish.

ENCOURAGING DEVELOPMENTS IN SHARED MINISTRY

It also falls to the bishops to guide the introduction of new patterns of clergy / lay co-operation, and keep an eye on how this is working. Here I draw on my experience of the Local Ministry scheme which Lincoln diocese pioneered during my years of office. Over the course of time that scheme evolved and changed, and has continued to do so. Indeed, the practice in regard to training and commissioning lay ministers varies a good deal from one diocese to another. Nevertheless, certain general principles hold good. When any parish begins exploring the implications of shared ministry, it is like planting a time-bomb. It may cause a creative revolution, or it may be a recipe for frustration, power struggles and disillusionment. A number of issues have to be faced. Have the clergy and PCC members taken a thorough look at the biblical material on Ministry in its broadest terms? Is the incumbent capable of changing gear into a collaborative style of ministry in which responsibility is truly shared? Is he or she committed to staying in post for several years to see these changes through? How whole-heartedly does the PCC support this approach? Is the congregation willing to accept some lay people ministering in a public role? Will this enhance the active ministry of all the baptised, or simply produce yet another layer of thinner cream that leaves most of the milk in the bottle unchanged? A major paradigm shift is involved. Such factors call for wise pastoral discernment by the bishop and by diocesan advisers and tutors. Local conditions may be ripe for training to go ahead, followed later by commissioning. If not, more cautious and gradual steps may need to be encouraged.

Letters appear in the press from time to time, arguing that fewer stipendiary clergy should require fewer bishops. I totally disagree. The explosion of lay ministry and the greater complexity of ordained ministries call for more supervision, not less. These developments make the demands on bishops' time all the greater.

SPONSORING AND SELECTING CANDIDATES
FOR MINISTERIAL TRAINING

Bishops have a double-edged responsibility in relation to those seeking ordination: to affirm those suitable for training, and to protect the church from those who are not. Less harm is done to the church at large by weeding out unsuitable candidates than by giving them the benefit of the doubt, ordaining them and courting public disaster later.

The early stages of discerning priestly vocation are handled by the Diocesan Director of Ordinands (DDO), assisted by vocations' advisers and members of the diocesan advisory panel. There may be obvious gaps in a candidate's qualifications, theological understanding, devotional discipline, experience of church life, or personal maturity that must first be addressed. This may take some time, and sheer time is always a factor in allowing for growth to occur. When the DDO thinks the moment ripe, he or she requests the bishop to offer the candidate a sponsoring interview.

My own practice was to ring up the candidate straight away to fix a mutually convenient time, usually within the next week or two, and to explain that his or her spouse would be welcome to come too, though this was not obligatory. All but a few married candidates chose to be accompanied by their spouse. In the rare case of my having a conflict of personal interest, I would refer the candidate to the Bishop of Lincoln instead.

I would normally conduct this interview in my study at home, allowing about an hour, and end by telling candidates whether or not I was willing to sponsor them for a 'Bishops' Advisory Panel' (BAP) at national level. My rule of thumb was to sponsor candidates only if it seemed at least 51% likely that the BAP would recommend them for training. I took the view that it would be irresponsible to expect national selectors to do the weeding out for me, and that I should have the courage to say 'No' there and then if need be. Leading a candidate 'up the garden path' creates greater disappointment than necessary, and wastes the Church's central resources. My motto was: *'If in doubt, OUT'*. When I declined sponsorship, I would immediately alert the DDO and parish priest to the need for pastoral follow-up. However, I did sponsor about three-quarters of those sent to me, and would write back to the DDO with any comments to be added to their sponsoring papers. Where the candidate or spouse was re-married after divorce, but had a partner from a previous marriage who was still living, the DDO would then launch the procedure to seek an Archbishop's Faculty under Canon C.4 – an option available only since 1991. Nowadays all candidates also require vetting by the Disclosure and Barring Service (DBS, formerly Criminal Record Bureau), and are subject to 'enhanced disclosure'.

After candidates had attended the Advisory Panel they expected to hear the outcome soon. The selectors' report normally reached the bishop and DDO within the following week. I made a point of normally doing the de-briefing myself, again allowing about an hour. To minimise delay the DDO gave me advance notice of the date when I could expect the selectors' report, and I would book a slot for the next available day. If I was due to be away then, I would ask the DDO (or occasionally the Bishop of Lincoln) to act in my stead.

The Advisory Panel, as its name implies, offers *advice* to the bishop. Having carefully considered that advice, the sponsoring bishop then decides whether to accept it, or (in rare cases) to modify or even overturn it – a course not to be lightly taken. I found that in about two-thirds of the cases the panel's advice was exactly as expected: a positive recommendation to enter training. If so, the de-briefing was pretty straight-forward, and was a chance to build on what the candidate had learned from this experience. However, when the advice was *'not recommended'* this was a difficult and delicate task. The bishop, even if in no doubt about endorsing it, would look for every available clue to help interpret the result back to the unsuccessful candidate. By hearing a candidate's first-hand account of how he or she had got on during the BAP I could usually make sense of the panel's advice, and figure out what the various selectors' comments related to. The hard part was feeding back the negatives without making the person feel destroyed. If someone had a blind spot, it was often almost impossible to help them see it. My duty was to block their aspiration to be ordained, yet I had to try to avoid trampling on positive features of their current life and to steer their Christian discipleship into channels other than ordination. It could take quite some time for disappointed candidates to come to terms with not being recommended. How they coped with being turned down was generally a good measure of their calibre. Some learned from it, and either pursued some other path or came back later all the stronger. Others became defensive and resentful, and their unsuitability became all too apparent.

In the main I found selectors' reports wise and perceptive. In two of my cases they 'smelled a rat' without being able to pin down why the people concerned did not ring true, yet in both instances the candidates were arrested shortly afterwards on a serious charges – one for fraud and the other for incest. The selectors' instincts had been right. In another case they recommended a candidate for non-stipendiary ministry, but with the proviso *'as long as the bishop is satisfied that ...'.* They drew my attention to a local factor which they were in no position to evaluate, but that I was. Their comment alerted me to the risk of an unworkable situation, and I overturned their provisional 'Yes' to a 'No'.

In a handful of other cases I felt it right to overturn a 'No' to a provisional 'Yes', but only after very careful consideration and consultation. When I was deeply uneasy over a non-recommendation, my first step was to talk it through with the Bishop of Lincoln and the DDO; if they felt the advice should be accepted, I did so. If they shared my disquiet, I would contact the Staff Secretary who had sent the report, made our concerns known and invited further comments. Interestingly, these cases generally turned out to be on the border-line where the selectors had found it hard to agree. If I eventually overturned a non-recommendation, I built in a proviso that barred the candidate from extending training beyond the first year unless certain signs of promise were sustained or specific criteria were fulfilled. This was particularly relevant to older candidates for whom this was the last chance to attend a selection conference. However, I believe it is axiomatic that a bishop should not overturn a non-recommendation unless that diocese is prepared to live with the results – i.e. to provide a post for the candidate, subject to training being satisfactorily completed. The Ministry Division would rightly take issue with any bishop who exercised this right lightly or too often. The whole machinery of selection and training is undertaken on behalf of the House of Bishops, and the whole college of bishops has a corporate duty to respect the agreed norms. As a former chairman of selectors I would say that this task of discernment is undertaken with great thoroughness and integrity. We all make some mistakes and miss a few clues. No system is perfect, but this one is pretty good and all the better for greater freedom of information. It is crucial that bishops operate within such a framework responsibly, not arbitrarily.

ORDAINING NEW DEACONS AND PRIESTS TO SUITABLE CURACIES

No deacon or priest can be ordained without a 'title' – that is, a job to go (whether paid or unpaid) and a community of which to be part. This pre-requisite was laid down by the Council of Chalcedon in 451 (Canon 6) and enshrined in the Canon Law of the Church of England in 1604 (Canon 33). It follows that the bishop, before agreeing to ordain any candidate, has to line up a potential title or training curacy. In practice this needs to be under consideration at least a year in advance.

If a curacy is to be stipendiary, the bishop has to identify five factors: a suitable parish, a suitable training incumbent, a stipend, adequate housing and an assurance that working expenses will be properly reimbursed. If a curacy is to be non-stipendiary, stipend and housing are not involved, but the other three factors still apply. The House of Bishops' annual allocation of new stipendiary deacons for Lincoln diocese was around seven during most of my 'Grimsby' years. Since a curate normally served for at least three years and the next post could take a few months to become available, the bishop's staff assumed that the next title in any given parish could not follow until four years later. This meant working out a rolling programme of about 28 paid curacies, fairly spread across the diocese, over a four-year cycle, for which stipends were earmarked independently of each deanery's staffing establishment. Non-stipendiary curacies were additional to this, and we knew year by year how many home-grown candidates were in the pipe-line.

Paid and unpaid posts were equally important, and required the same care in preparation. The bishops kept two lists under constant review – suitable training parishes and suitable training incumbents. Only where these criteria coincided would a new deacon be placed. If an experienced curate trainer moved or retired, it interrupted the pattern and in any case new trainers needed to be brought on-stream. In May each year we updated the provisional schedule of 'titles' for the next four years. As soon as the coming year's schedule had been agreed, the area suffragan (usually in May or June) would request a draft profile of the training curacy from each incumbent. The DDO advised on the format, and circulated these parish profiles to the Principals of theological colleges and courses before the start of the students' final academic year.

We began matching prospective deacons and parishes by the late summer, beginning with our home-grown candidates, who were generally fewer than the allocation. If an exploratory visit worked out positively, the incumbent would get the suffragan bishop's permission to extend the formal offer of a title. We had a model letter for the incumbent to send, setting out terms and conditions. If the initial proposal did not work out, we would de-brief to learn any lessons and move on to 'round two', and so on. For ordinands and training incumbents alike the method of choice was 'one at a time ... yea or nay', *not* 'take your pick of the bunch'. Based on our knowledge of the broader picture we bishops proposed the most likely match, but did not ride roughshod over people's feelings. We were glad to welcome prospective curates from other parts of the country who could not be placed by their home dioceses; without them we were sometimes hard put to claim our full entitlement of new qualified stipendiary clergy, especially after Lincoln Theological College had closed.

The diocesan bishop made the formal decision to go ahead with ordination in the light of the Principal's final report. We three bishops took it in turns to conduct the main ordination in Lincoln cathedral at Petertide and Michaelmas, and these was complemented by other services held locally. Curates normally had at least one of their ordinations in the cathedral. Parishioners tended to feel more engaged in the priesting, by which time they were better acquainted with the candidate.

Providing a range of ministerial posts

As the clergy of any diocese comprise different levels of ability and experience, there needs to be a range of varied posts available. The Mission and Pastoral Committee has a duty to pay regard to two factors, amongst others, in reviewing the pastoral supervision of the diocese:

'the need to allocate appropriate spheres of work and to ensure that appropriate conditions of service are enjoyed by those employed or holding office in the diocese and, where relevant, that reasonable remuneration is provided for all those engaged in the cure of souls'

'the traditions, needs and characteristics of particular parishes'

(Mission and Pastoral Measure 2011, Section 3 (2))

The pattern of pastoral organisation across the diocese has to strike a balance between urban, suburban and rural needs as well as accommodating sector ministries and specialist advisers. It can make use of team and group ministries. Additionally, since 2008 'Bishops' Mission Orders' have become available as a means of authorising pioneer work beyond traditional parameters, as now provided by Part 7 of the above Measure.

Most curacies are urban, yet priests equipped for rural ministry are also needed. We arranged some rural placements during urban curates' third year. Conversely, the few curates who trained in rural situations sometimes needed more experience of conducting the occasional offices than was locally available, and this deficit was met in a nearby town. Bishops need to keep the whole picture in view, matching the pattern of posts to changing pastoral demands, such as shifts in population or clergy stress. It is counter-productive to create clergy posts that are impossible to discharge without causing a nervous break-down, or that nobody is prepared to tackle.

Sharing in the appointments' process

There is much wisdom in the fact that the right to appoint to benefices does not rest in too few hands, and that most clergy cannot be moved against their will. They are not employees but Office Holders, whether by freehold or under Common Tenure. Parishes have the right to be consulted during a vacancy, and their appointed lay representatives can veto the patron's nomination. Patronage rests in many hands, for historical reasons. Though the bishops have a good deal of influence over appointments, they have no monopoly of power. The bishop's staff cannot 'pull all the strings', and on balance it is to the church's general benefit that power is dispersed.

The appointments' process is a shared one, calling for good teamwork and co-ordination. As mentioned earlier (page 101), tasks need to be clearly allocated between the bishop, archdeacon and rural dean. The pattern varies from one diocese to another. The Lincoln practice in my time was that the *area suffragan* normally dealt with patrons of benefices and the national Clergy Appointments' Adviser; placed advertisements when needed; drew up short lists; and invited prospective candidates to pay an exploratory visit. Sometimes I would conduct my own separate interview. On receiving reactions to the visit I would feed the gist of this back to the candidate and, where positive, recommend the patron to extend a formal written offer. If so agreed, I would write on the patron's behalf. The *archdeacon*'s specific tasks were to debrief the previous incumbent, to see that statements of need were produced by the PCC's, and deal with any issues of finance, housing or pastoral re-organisation. He also kept the churchwardens periodically informed of progress in making the appointment. The *rural dean*'s tasks were to provide cover for Sunday services and occasional offices; make local arrangements for prospective candidates to meet parochial lay representatives (a complex matter in multi-church benefices) and ecumenical spokespersons (in Local Ecumenical Projects); feed the representatives' views back to the area suffragan; and eventually organise the service of institution or licensing, including a rehearsal beforehand and social gathering afterwards. The *diocesan bishop*, as well as chairing the appointments' meeting of his staff, sometimes chose to be directly involved in particular cases. At any given moment we were generally dealing with over 30 active vacancies, spread over a terrain of nearly 2,700 square miles.

The appointments' process also involved screening out unsuitable applicants. Bishops are responsible for implementing the policy that all clergy are vetted by the Disclosure and Barring Service (formerly CRB) to the level of 'enhanced disclosure' before taking up any new post. The paper-work for this is administered by a designated person, usually the bishop's chaplain or PA. In addition, bishops need to ensure that the names of all who apply for vacant posts, or are proposed by patrons, are checked against the Archbishops' List which names those clergy who are currently under discipline or temporarily barred from public ministry for various reasons (Clergy Discipline Measure 2003). The registered patron of a benefice cannot make a formal offer to any priest until the bishop has signified approval. The bishop, on being notified of a name, has up to four weeks in which to take up references and make enquiries about 'the sufficiency and qualities' of every minister. If the bishop refuses permission, he or she must notify the reasons in writing to the patron, who has a right of appeal to the archbishop [see Canons C.9 and 10, and the Patronage (Benefices) Measure 1986 section 13]. These safeguarding procedures are of utmost importance in maintaining public trust in the credibility of the Church's ordained ministry, and have to be strictly followed.

The outgoing incumbent and spouse are specifically excluded by the Patronage (Benefices) Measure 1986 from parochial consultations about appointing a successor. Nevertheless, we found it valuable for them to have a chance of telling the archdeacon their version of the parochial realities, and he normally paid them a pastoral visit of at least an hour to hear what they wished to say. He was also glad of the opportunity to express thanks on the bishop's behalf as responsibilities were handed back. We judged it to be psychologically important that such endings were properly done.

We fostered the notion that an interregnum should not be hurried, and this was in no way for the purpose of saving money. Building on the work of the Alban Institute in the USA, we believed it was the *'Prime Time for Renewal'* – to borrow the title of Bill Yon's booklet on creative vacancies. Parishioners needed space in which to disentangle themselves from the outgoing incumbent, to re-assess their current situation and to articulate their future aspirations. Sometimes our St Hugh's missioners acted as external consultants in these developmental tasks. We discouraged the needless holding of Section 12 meetings with bishop and patron where no exceptional issues had to be addressed, but encouraged great care in preparing a Statement of Needs – jointly wherever possible in multi-church benefices. If this statement was mere window-dressing, and less than honest or realistic, it risked arousing false expectations on both sides.

Every month we published a list of current and forthcoming vacancies in the diocesan bulletin, and clergy were encouraged to let the area suffragan know if they were interested in being considered for any post. This created greater openness, and made the bishops more aware of which clergy wanted to move and to what type of post. My regular practice was to ask patrons whether they would welcome possible names and, if so, I did my best to suggest one or two. For geographical reasons it was common in many walks of Lincolnshire life for national advertisements to produce little response. Since advertising was expensive and fairly unproductive, we 'headhunted' as far as possible. I aimed to put forward, jointly with the archdeacon, two or three names (in order of preference) for each vacancy in my area at the monthly staff meeting. If these names came to nothing, I would approach further candidates only if I had the interim backing of the diocesan bishop or the archdeacon. This 'two vote system' between meetings saved waiting another whole month, and kept things on the move. A few private patrons had a limited understanding of the issues, but most took their responsibilities seriously and had the parishioners' interests at heart. Those officers acting for The Crown, the Lord Chancellor, the Duchy of Lancaster and the major patronage trusts were well informed, and handled their duties with professionalism. Their contribution was of considerable benefit to the diocese. Patronage arrangements in multi-parish cures could be extraordinarily complex and time-consuming, often with several patrons operating jointly. The whole appointments' process has to be a co-operative one, and bishops should exercise their own rights fairly, responding to the concerns of all parties.

ENABLING CLERGY TO EXERCISE SATISFYING RESPONSIBILITY THROUGHOUT THEIR MINISTRY

Kenneth Stevenson pointed out in *'The Bishop and the Fathers'* (published in *'Theology'*, March 2011) that the bishop's role is analogous to that of the abbot in a monastery:

> *'He must so arrange everything that the strong have something to strive for and the weak nothing to run from'*
>
> (Rule of St Benedict, §64.17)

This analogy cannot be pressed too far. Clergy are not under monastic vows, but autonomous persons in charge of their own lives and families. They operate in a free market as far as jobs are concerned. Too much paternalism or dependency is unhealthy. Nevertheless, the bishop has the duty of overseeing the diocese's total resources, human and material, which involves providing the possibility of stepped responsibility throughout a priest's career. I have already mentioned the value of keeping a 'watchful eye' (page 100), of 'milestone reviews' (page 121) and of continuing pastoral care and spiritual counsel (page 123). Sometimes the shepherd must lead his sheep to new pastures, or at least urge them in the right direction! Some clergy need encouragement to broaden their experience. The bishop should try to see that priests do not get stuck or overwhelmed, nor let anyone's character be damaged by intolerable frustration or conflict. This can be hard to achieve, especially as some people are their own worst enemies. The bishop may need to bring matters to a head where a priest is struggling under the burden of deteriorating health or the collapse of his or her marriage.

A helpful tool is to keep a 'start-up list' in date order. This enables the bishop to be aware how long ministers have been in their current post, and to discuss it with them. I found it useful to think of clergy posts in categories: e.g. curacy, team vicar / standard urban, major urban, team rector, standard rural, major rural, market town, part-time (linked with specialism), etc. After a curacy the usual progression is to a first incumbency that is not too demanding, or a tough team vicar post with the support of colleagues. The next step may often be a major post of a similar kind, or a switch from rural to urban or vice versa. Sometimes a specialist task linked with a half-time cure is suitable for a few years, or work in a Local Ecumenical Partnership. A team rectorship or the incumbency of a large ancient church with a civic dimension is likely to be appropriate later in a priest's career. Some clergy in their late 50's are glad to move to a quieter post for their last stint before retirement, especially when there are health problems, and it is good that this can be achieved without loss of status or income. The bishop tries to bear these points in mind, whilst exercising discernment and discretion in handing out additional responsibilities, such as training incumbent or rural dean. Helping all clergy to have a realistic notion of their abilities is no less important than identifying a few high flyers for eventual senior appointments, as diocesan bishops do annually. None of this detracts from freedom of action on the part of clergy or patrons, which effectively rules out the orchestration of any centralised plan. Nothing can alter the fact that every appointment is a risk and that, once made, may last for years! Occasionally the bishop needs to persuade a priest to retire, but compulsory retirement at 70 has greatly reduced the need for this.

THE MINISTRY NETWORK

From what I have written above it is clear that another of the basic networks through which any bishop has to operate is that to do with recruiting, sending and deploying ministers. This ministry network has three major components:

- a) the Diocesan Director of Ordinands, vocations' advisers, those nominated to serve on selection panels, the staff of diocesan and regional training schemes, the secretaries of the Mission and Pastoral Committee and Stipends Committee and the safeguarding adviser;
- b) the officer for Continuing Ministerial Education, training incumbents, and all who assist in conducting clergy reviews;
- c) the Diocesan Board of Patronage, those who act as patrons or officers of patronage trusts, the 'designated officer' who notifies vacancies (usually the Diocesan Registrar), and any who exercise a consultative role during interregna.

Building up personal acquaintance, local knowledge and a degree of trust inevitably takes time. Towards in my latter 'Grimsby' years I was dealing with the four or fifth vacancy in some posts during my time. It is useful if the bishop's staff comprises a good deal of corporate memory.

Resources for New Bishops

As new bishops plunge into this bewildering scene and build up their working knowledge of the people and systems involved, the following documents (available on-line) provide basic information:

- Criteria for Selection (1993) Policy Paper 3B, Ministry Division
- Bishops' Regulations for Ordination Training
- Patronage (Benefices) Measure 1986
- Team and Group Ministries Measure 1995
- Dioceses Pastoral and Mission Measure 2007
- Ecclesiastical Offices (Terms of Service) Measure 2009
- Mission and Pastoral Measure 2011

The Codes of Practice linked with this legislation throw much light on the practicalities. It is essential to be thoroughly conversant with the current guidelines for the protection of children and vulnerable adults, and to adhere to this policy closely.

As regards the creative use of interregna I found a number of American publications helpful, such as:

> Loren B. Mead – *'The Developmental Tasks of the Congregation in search of a Pastor'* (The Alban Institute, Washington DC, 1977)
>
> W.A. Yon – *'Prime Time for Renewal'* (The Alban Institute, 1977)
>
> C. Hahn – *'The Minister is Leaving'* (Seabury Press, 1984)

Many more titles on congregational life have emerged from this fascinating scene. The website www.alban.org gives details of these, together with information about current seminars on such themes as *'Crunch Time in the Small Church'*, *'Stepping up to Staffing and Supervision'* and *'Finishing Strong, Ending Well'*.

Summary

This chapter has drawn together some of the strands that lead me to sum up the 'sending' function that is integral to episcopé in these terms:

> **It is corporate** – committed to collaborative leadership; delegating, sharing in corporate consultation, and administering the Church's human and material resources professionally and competently;
>
> **It promotes mission** and sends new ministers, wisely deploying those already available and nurturing new life for all forms of ministry.

CHAPTER 15

Building Bridges in Society & within the Church

Reconciliation in the church and the world

One question which the archbishop puts to candidates at the service of consecration has a direct bearing on unity. Before the sixth vow comes this question put uniquely to bishops:

'Will you promote peace and reconciliation in the Church and in the world; and will you strive for the visible unity of Christ's Church?'

This makes it clear that episcopal ministry is meant to have a distinctive thrust towards working for reconciliation and unity in the midst of diversity and division, which are continuing features of human life. This ministry of reconciliation is directed towards unity within society at large, and not simply within one's own church or between different Christian denominations. To focus solely on internal church concerns would fall short of this requirement, and it is an inescapable obligation to engage constructively in the tensions and divisions of broader society. Unity is a mark of the Church's very nature, and it follows that episcopal ministry has to be in the service of unity.

In this chapter I explore four aspects of the bishop's vocation to foster unity and to be its focus:

    a)   in society
    b)   within the diocese
    c)   within the Church of England
    d)   within the Anglican Communion

The next chapter will then be devoted to the ecumenical dimension – i.e. fostering visible unity with churches of other traditions at various levels.

Unity in society

Gregory's *'Pastoral Rule'* was influential not just within the church, but in setting a standard of governance throughout Western Europe just when the

Roman empire and its institutions had crumbled. It was not a tool of centralised ecclesiastical bureaucracy, but rather a contribution to the texture and moral quality of public life.

Any bishop has to be constantly reaching out beyond church circles into the wider world. For centuries the bishops of the Church of England, before and after the Reformation, took an integral role in national and local affairs, not least in pioneering educational and nursing provision for the population at large. In the latter half of the 19th century bishops like Samuel Wilberforce (Oxford 1845-69 and Winchester 1869-73) and Edward King (Lincoln 1885-1910) set a new standard of pastoral diligence in travelling tirelessly around all parts of their dioceses, becoming well known public figures to the wider community. The 1978 Lambeth Conference placed a renewed emphasis on the bishop's role beyond the ecclesiastical scene, and the 1988 Lambeth Conference used such phrases as 'leader in mission', 'initiator of outreach to the world', and 'a voice of conscience within society' (see references on pages 52 and 54-55). The revised ordinal of 2006 was accompanied by a House of Bishops' statement on ordained ministry that contained the phrase:

> *'Christ's ministry and mission turn the Church outwards towards the world that God so loved that he sent his only Son'.*
>
> ('Ordination Services', study edition 2007, p 5)

It is worth noting that in Homer's *'Odyssey'* the word 'episkopos' was used for a watchman or look-out. From time to time bishops get the opportunity to articulate the concerns of their region, and to focus public attention on issues affecting the common good. For example, the economic life of the area, or the job prospects of particular occupation groups, may be under serious threat and many families' standard of living adversely affected. In speaking out the bishop contributes to drawing the whole community together. Some major disaster or high-profile tragedy may occur, such as the loss of a lifeboat, the collapse of a public building, serious flooding or some horrendous crime. On such occasions the bishop is often expected to lead a public act of worship to express the feelings and reactions of wider society. Such activities claim the bishop's time and attention no less appropriately than internal church affairs. A greater onus falls on those diocesan bishops in the House of Lords who have few fellow peers from their region. Whilst James Jones was Bishop of Liverpool, he played a key conciliatory role in chairing the Hillsborough Independent Panel (2010-12) which disclosed the circumstances surrounding the UK's most serious sporting tragedy.

In my Grimsby years I set time aside for a steady trickle of secular events such as meeting civic leaders, helping to establish a local radio station, joining a public debate on safety in inner urban areas, making contacts with the voluntary sector, chairing a forum for parliamentary candidates prior to a General Election, etc.. My 'deanery days' included some space for secular contacts and meeting those in social need of various kinds, and I actively encouraged local training workshops for the unemployed. In retrospect I wish that I had devoted a larger proportion of time and effort to getting involved in public life, and that I could have received more training to help me develop surer instincts about when and how this was appropriate – an aspect of professional development taken up in a later chapter. This chimes in with my earlier comment about the bishop's place being at the edge of the church rather than its centre. William Countryman enlarged on this point in his paper at the Niagara consultation 1987 as follows:

> *'If we see the episcopate in terms of the gospel's reaching out to new groups along with us into a renewed and fuller community of faith, then we shall expect to find bishops on the peripheries, functioning as agents of mission and change .... We must find ways to re-envisage the bishop so that we think of this person no longer as the holy of holies at the heart of a temple, as remote as possible from outsiders, but as a host at the door of the house reaching out to bring strangers in as members of the growing family. As the family grows, the house will have to be rebuilt to accommodate it; but the bishop will remain at the perimeter of construction, on the look-out for others who have not yet been welcomed into it ... The apostolic task is to break down the exclusive boundaries around the holy community.'*

(*'Mission and the Reform of Episcopé'*, pages 6 and 10, published ACC/LWF 1988)

UNITY WITHIN THE DIOCESE

a)   *The basic concept of pastoral oversight*

The Cameron Report explains succinctly where the basic idea of *episcopé* comes from:

> *'The story of oversight in the Church begins with Jesus' own calling and sending out of his disciples. In the first generation the primary ministry was that of the Apostles themselves ... Local Christian communities were kept in touch with each other through those who, like Paul, were founders of the communities. These leaders continued to exercise oversight, to exchange greetings and news, to take collections for communities in need and to maintain a consistency in belief and practice between the scattered Christian Churches ...*
>
> *The ministry of oversight is not a human invention, but a gift of God to the Church. It is a gift of guardianship of faith and order, enabling the Church to carry on the ministry of Jesus and to become what God intends, in mission, unity and holiness. It is God's creative act to bring into being and sustain a pastoral office in which an*

image of his own nature can be seen, and in which and by which he points to the very nature of the Church itself... The ministry of oversight was thus first and foremost a ministry of unity and communion ... By visits and letters and meetings of leaders, those who exercised the ministry of oversight in the first generation in New Testament times were already beginning to act as ministers of unity in the maintenance of a single Church of Christ and to carry a responsibility for the handing on of tradition for the future ... A ministry of personal oversight clearly emerged as the young Church struggled to be missionary, spreading the good news, as well as to be faithful to the Gospel and to preserve internal coherence.'

('*Episcopal Ministry*', **CHP 1990 – GS 944, extracts from chapter 3**)

The senior leaders in any organisation set the whole tone of its life and 'culture'. They have the potential to be a unifying factor, and to raise or lower morale. What the episcopate in any diocese should be doing was admirably summed up in Bob Hardy's phrase '*holding the whole*'. Of course, the diocesan bishop is always pre-eminently the 'head' and the ultimate focus of diocesan unity, and the duty of the suffragans is to contribute to that and not detract from it in any way. In my Grimsby days we three Lincolnshire bishops endeavoured to act as one in our dealings with the diocese, and worked hard to achieve consistency of policy so that nobody could play one off against another. Whichever bishop anyone cared to approach, the response was meant to be broadly the same. This was not simply a matter of 'singing from the same hymn sheet', but a deeper issue of getting people to understand one another and work together with a sense of common purpose. Within our senior staff group we prayed together, planned together, enjoyed fellowship together, and did our best to operate as a real team in ways already described (see chapter 11), and I believe that this made a positive impact on the sense of our far-flung diocese being some kind of a family. When people felt they belonged together, it was noticeable that they were less self-preoccupied, more sympathetic to one another's needs, and all the readier to pull together in the mission of the church. The episcopate's task was to focus unity not just in the terms of management, but as an expression of the Church's sacramentality in gathering God's people to himself – an inclusive catholicity. Wherever bishops lead public worship, the manner in which they fit into the local style of churchmanship helps to affirm that congregation's valued place within the diocese.

The richness of a diocese's resource derives in large measure from the diversity of its people, places and institutions. Amongst them differences are bound to exist, but if these can be held together the Church's mission is strengthened. Sadly, polarities can develop all too easily. For example, rural parishes may resent suburban ones having access to more people and money. Parishes that carry the burden of an ancient building often feel that other parishes do not understand the constraints under which they have to work. Differences of churchmanship and theology co-exist peacefully in most cases, but can give rise to conflict or estrangement. Opinions are bound to vary over the fairest way to apportion quota payments or numbers of stipendiary clergy. Many congregations are slow to recognise the value of sector and specialist ministries. The workload of clergy varies greatly according to their social setting, and sympathy can be lacking between clergy about the different pressures involved, for example, in shouldering a heavy load of occasional offices or ministering to tiny numbers across scattered communities in all weathers. To a certain extent robust independence can be laudable, but every diocese has a few awkward individuals whose angularities are hard to reconcile. In certain pastoral and liturgical matters bishops have the power to settle local disputes.

The Second Vatican Council in its Decree on Bishops said:

'Let [the bishop] so gather and mould the whole family of his flock that everyone, conscious of his own duties, may live and work in the communion of love' (§16)

In similar vein Archbishop Michael Ramsey pointed out that a bishop, like any priest, has to be a reconciler in holding the life of the church together:

'As reconciler he will be perhaps less the absolver of individual penitents than the one who unites people and groups and conflicting tendencies in the common service of Christ.' (*'The Christian Priest Today'*, page 97)

Michael Mayne's sermon at my consecration touched on the same theme:

'More than anything else it is that serenity, that space at the heart of you, that will clear your vision and allow you to be an effective pastor to the many who look to you as a reconciler and interpreter: one who points men to Jesus as their true centre and to the Spirit of God active in their midst'.

The 1988 Lambeth Conference spoke of the bishop as 'head of the family in its wholeness, its misery and its joy' and as 'the family's centre of life and love'.

(*'The Truth shall make you free'*, page 61)

Reflecting on the church's exercise of authority in a post-modern world, Alastair Redfern (Canon Theologian of Bristol, subsequently Bishop of Grantham, then of Derby) pointed to episcopé as:

' ... a key resource in bridging the tension between radical pluriformity and radical oneness ... [Episcopé] is not submission to a rigid system, nor is it a one-way system. It is essentially fluid and dynamic – open to, and agent of, change and newness ... The gifts of grace, to Christians and non-Christians, will be so diverse that individuals and groups will inevitably have different and apparently contradictory callings and experiences. The prime function of episcopé is to facilitate

the comparing of these "independent testimonies" (Gore) for the mutual learning and up-building of the whole, and of each of the various parts.

This is a far cry from simply managing the Church as an institution, or from trying to be a nice pastor to everyone – which are two of the more recent models! A proper understanding and exercise of episcopé can embrace all the disparate variety so loudly trumpeted by post-modernism with confidence, not to solve tensions, but to witness to the oneness and greatness of the God who lives within, and yet beyond, everything given to us ... The system [of episcopé] is based upon collegiality, interaction, openness, exploration and development. There is room for individuals and particular groups to be taken seriously, but always as second to the whole corporation and the call to a more radical oneness.'

(From an unpublished paper for the General Synod Board of Education, 1994)

b) *The cathedral*

In any diocese the cathedral has the potential to foster a sense of diocesan unity and loyalty. Its purpose, according to the Cathedrals Measure 1999, is to be '*the seat of the bishop and a centre of worship and mission*', and its unique link with the diocesan bishop is defined by its constitution and statutes, whether or not he actually resides adjacent to it. Lincoln Cathedral includes amongst its aims to be '*a symbol of unity for the diocese as its Mother Church*' (from the Mission Statement). It is the obvious and natural venue for many important diocesan gatherings, such as ordinations, church schools' festivals, degree ceremonies, and civic occasions at county level, some of which the diocesan bishop attends in person. The suffragans also officiate there for some diocesan occasions, and in my case this was usually about six times a year. For many members of the broader public the only time they see a bishop is at a large diocesan event in the cathedral. This provides a valuable platform from which to welcome and address them, and often enables those who attend to feel part of something bigger than their local parish. The worship and witness of a lively cathedral community can, when it is functioning properly, set a fine example to inspire others.

c) *Transcending deanery boundaries*

Clergy are blinkered by deanery boundaries to a surprising extent, and have all too little contact with colleagues from other parts of the diocese. One of Simon Phipps's best initiatives in the closing months of his episcopate was to hold a series of consultations that drew together small groups of priests from similar situations spread across the diocese, e.g. rectors of major civic churches, those working in ecumenical partnerships, incumbents of rural multi-church cures, those in inner urban areas, etc. In hosting these gatherings he assisted mutual learning and appreciation amongst the clergy who took part, and helped to foster a deeper sense of unity. I have already described how in later years the 'patchwork' scheme, our corporate approach to clergy deployment and pastoral re-organisation, and various support networks all conspired to unify the diocese. This work never stayed done, and the bishops needed constantly to show people where they fitted into the bigger picture.

d)   Genuine consultation

Bishop John Baker (Bishop of Salisbury, 1982-93) drew attention in a valuable paper at St George's House, Windsor to the widespread suspicion and cynicism that many people have towards consultation. It can look like a façade – as if those in authority have already made their minds up, and want approval in order to feel good or 'cover their backs' if something goes wrong. He suggested certain basic rules, if consultation was to be a credible method and taken seriously by all concerned:

'(1) Begin as early as possible, while the maximum number of options is open.

(2) Supply all the relevant information you can, honestly.

(3) See that the process to be gone through is fully explained, and what other parties are involved, and at what stages decisions will be taken, and of what kind at each stage.

(4) When decisions are taken, inform and explain <u>fully</u> what they are, and why they were made, and what points which arose from the consultation have been incorporated – it will not always be obvious – and why others had to be turned down.

... The final result ought always to contain some useful features emerging from the consultation, even if these are not strictly necessary – not as window-dressing but to make the result genuinely participatory – because in human terms that is a better result ... Genuine consultation and communication actually makes us better people.'

(from an unpublished paper, Diocesan Staffs' Conference, October 1984)

A related point was made succinctly by Bob Hardy:

'Problems that are properly aired and dealt with lose their negative power'

(from an unpublished paper **'Episcopal Oversight its Cares and Concerns'**, November 1990)

UNITY WITHIN THE CHURCH OF ENGLAND

a) *Sharing out national responsibilities*

Bishops are not just for their own diocese, but for the whole church. It follows that every bishop has to be ready to take a proper share of the roles and responsibilities at national level that are spread across the whole college of bishops. Those who distribute these tasks (i.e. the Appointments' Committee of the General Synod and the Archbishops' staff) keep a note of the interests and qualifications of each bishop, and make every effort to allocate matching responsibilities. Whether or not bishops find congenial the jobs they are invited to undertake, they have to balance personal preference with a sense of corporate duty. The requirement in each case is to function on behalf of the whole English episcopate.

For example, Bob Hardy was appointed Bishop of Prisons concurrently with the suffragan see of Maidstone, and continued this national role after moving to Lincoln. In a period of unprecedented structural change in the Prison Service he engaged actively with a succession of Ministers and senior civil servants at the Home Office. For sixteen years he was involved not only in appointing chaplains, but also in conducting an energetic programme of visits to prisons and Young Offenders' institutions all over England. He became a leading spokesman on law and order issues in the Lords and the General Synod, and chaired the relevant committee of the Board for Social Responsibility. He initiated four international consultations that provided a valuable inter-disciplinary forum and contributed to public debate on justice issues.

In my own case the main area of wider responsibility allocated to me was in the field of ecumenical relations. This fitted well with my training as a linguist, my post-graduate studies in Athens and Geneva, and the experience gained in working at Lambeth Palace with the C. of E. Council for Foreign Relations. The ecumenical dimension of bishops' ministry will be explored in the next chapter.

Other tasks came my way which I might not have chosen, but in hindsight I recognise how much they helped my own ministry to develop. They lay in three areas:

> *Mission* In 1979-85 I was given the job of chairing the annual three-day training conference for Diocesan Missioners. This able and diverse group comprised a wide range of churchmanship and theological approach, and helped me to appreciate the breadth of the Church of England. In 1982-83 I also led a General Synod working party exploring the nature of the Church's mission.
>
> *Theological Education* In 1980-86 I chaired the assessment panel of the Aston Training Scheme, a national course for ordinands not yet ready to

enter Theological College. This involved attending summer schools and residential weekends with the students and their spouses – about 12 days a year. I learned a great deal from my fellow assessors about discerning vocation and tracking the progress of ministerial candidates towards maturity. Also in 1986-87 I served on the House of Bishops' working party on initial training and continuing development for bishops.

<u>House of Bishops</u>   For ten years (1990-2000) I served as an elected suffragan in the House of Bishops (HB) of the General Synod. Beside chairing the Council for Christian Unity for six years I served on three subsidiary groups. The HB Theological Group was like a post-graduate seminar, where I picked up a lot from some very learned colleagues. A Contingency Planning Group met from June 1992 under Archbishop Habgood to steer preparations for ordaining women to the priesthood. Later Archbishop Hope led another small group of bishops to explore how episcopal ministry could contribute more effectively to the church's synodical life. All this work I found interesting and creative.

Wider responsibilities of this kind give bishops a refreshing change from regular duties in their own diocese and access to a national scene. They bring an enriching breadth of experience, and are a stimulus for new learning. They take their toll in time, but provide beneficial spin-offs for discerning the local situation.

b)   The quality of corporate encounter

The fine principles of collegiality are not always matched by the actual quality of corporate process. Some bishops' gatherings are more effective than others. At the Lambeth Conference one has a palpable sense of belonging to a universal episcopate. However, when I first became a bishop in the late 1970s, most suffragans received no documentation about the proceedings of the General Synod or House of Bishops. Apart from snippets gleaned from the media or gossip, it was not easy to pick up the wave-length of debate, but people in the parishes still expected any bishop to be well informed. When changes have to be communicated within the church, it is essential for all those directly involved in implementing them to know why they have been made and how decisions have been reached. After pressure by the elected suffragans, the House of Bishops introduced better communications in the mid 80s, and this greatly improved the sense of belonging.

In the Midlands region all suffragans from Ludlow in the West to Grimsby in the East used to meet informally about twice a year, sometimes for a day-gathering with our wives and sometimes residentially. These meetings, generally of high quality, were a valued forum of discussion across diocesan boundaries. In the early

90s the Midlands suffragans agreed to discontinue this series to support a new pattern of regional meetings across the country for diocesan and suffragan bishops together. This was a step forward, though the quality and value of such meetings turned out to be variable. During the ten year span that I served on the House of Bishops much was done to improve its mode of operation, and greater care was taken over the educational design of annual sessions of the full college of bishops (which in every third year included our Irish, Scottish and Welsh colleagues). When the quality of experience was good, the sense of collegiality was edified.

Unity within the Anglican Communion

a) The Cyprianic model

In the early church it was the Donatist schism in North Africa that provoked Cyprian (Bishop of Carthage) to write about the unifying value of the corporate episcopate in his treatise 'On the Unity of the Catholic Church' in 251. His contribution has been well summarised in this way:

> 'For Cyprian of Carthage (d. 258) there is a clear emphasis on the bishop's ministry as the bond of unity amongst the local churches within the universal church. Here the collegial aspect of the bishop's role comes to the fore. The bishops are seen as belonging to a world-wide network. They meet in council and reach a common mind under the Spirit's guidance, and are in this way responsible together for maintaining the teaching and unity of the churches'
>
> (LWF Lund Statement 2007 on 'Episcopal Ministry')

b) Recent thinking

On this topic the documents of the Second Vatican Council show, as one might expect, a strongly Petrine emphasis, as can be seen from 'Lumen Gentium' §22 and the decree 'On Bishops' §4-7. Other episcopally ordered churches do not view the matter through Roman eyes, but can nevertheless affirm many of the points made there.

Anglican thinking was summarised by the Cameron Report, which explored the notion of the bishop as the point where three planes of the Church's life intersect – the local community, the universal church and the church continuous through time. Regarding the second of these planes the report builds on the Cyprianic model and points to the significance of conciliarity and collegiality (see §76-85), which have now become issues of great urgency within the Anglican Communion. Following the General Synod's debate on the Cameron Report in 1991 the Faith & Order Advisory Group and the House of Bishops gave further thought to the collegiality of bishops, and published in 2000 a valuable occasional paper entitled *'Bishops in Communion'* (GS Misc 580). This was a useful survey not only of the theological roots of this topic, but also of its practical outworking at various levels in church life, e.g. the Lambeth Conference, primates' meetings, the House of Bishops, regional meetings of diocesan and suffragan bishops, and the wider fellowship of episcopally ordered churches. The paper examined these issues from the perspective of how bishops could work together effectively in leading the Church, and how their corporate ministry could strengthen the mission and ministry of the whole Church. The personal qualities identified as necessary for bishops to be capable of functioning corporately were cited earlier (page 15-16).

Under the 'bonds of communion' that hold the Anglican Communion together the Windsor Report 2004 spells out the role of the episcopate in §63-66. In the proposed text of the *'Anglican Communion Covenant'* section 3 deals with *'Our unity and common life'*, and the role of the episcopate is specified in §3.1.3 of the Ridley Cambridge draft of April 2009, currently under debate throughout the Communion. Such is the importance of the corporate nature of the episcopate that the very idea of a schismatic bishop, or group of bishops, should be seen a contradiction in terms. It only compounds the fundamental anomaly of disunity within the one, holy, catholic and apostolic church.

Bishop Alec Graham, speaking about the implications of collegiality, commented:

> *'There is nothing comparable in Anglican structures to the magisterium of the papacy. All threads in the Roman Church eventually lead to Rome. Loyalty to Rome's teaching will determine the manner of life and the content of teaching of each individual bishop. That holds the show together. We have no such constraints. Therefore, it is all the more incumbent on us to exercise restraint, however strong our personal convictions, for the good of the wider Church in expressing views or performing actions at variance with Canons or formularies of one's Church, or at variance with policy commonly agreed on with and by one's episcopal colleagues. The exercise of this restraint can be a keen participation in sacrificial ministry.'*
>
> (from an unpublished paper)

This is not just an Anglican issue, but applies equally to all the world-wide families of non-papal episcopal churches who share a similar ecclesiology.

c) Holding an international focus

There is no substitute for bishops having some first-hand experience of church life outside the British Isles, both within the Anglican Communion and ecumenically. This equips them better than anything else to help the people of their own diocese to think globally. Some bishops have already benefitted from international experience before their consecration, and it is desirable that others should be given the opportunity, even though this costs money. There are various ways in which experiences of this kind may occur. Often a bishop is sent abroad to represent the Archbishop or his/her own diocese at some major event, which offers the chance to see something of church life in another country. Sometimes an overseas link is realised through a World Mission partnership with an Anglican diocese in the developing world.

Overseas visits are not mere 'gallivanting', but move beyond ecclesiastical tourism into real engagement with the Church's mission in some other setting. When bishops stand with one foot in their local scene and the other anchored in personal relations with episcopal and other colleagues abroad, they are well placed to be act as 'go-betweens'. Experience of the church at work in some other country or culture does not provide ready-made solutions to our own situation, but has an indirect value: it holds up a mirror to ourselves, and sends us home full of ideas and questions. It is a strong stimulus to intercessory prayer and to lateral thinking, and has a spin-off in our preaching, pastoral planning and understanding of global issues.

If such exchanges are to be reciprocal, bishops must be prepared to make time and money available to welcome foreign guests properly. Suitable arrangements need to be made for hospitality and local travel, and events carefully planned so as to facilitate mutual contact and learning. There is scope, too, for exchanges of clergy and church workers. For example, during my Grimsby years the diocese received the services of clergy from Zimbabwe and South India, not to mention those of other church traditions, as the next chapter will illustrate. When bishops appoint overseas clergy to permanent posts in the Church of England, whether from other Anglican provinces or from 'churches in communion', the provisions of the *Overseas and Other Clergy (Ministry and Ordination) Measure 1967* apply. On appointing clergy from 'Porvoo' churches the House of Bishops issued in 2000 detailed guidelines about the procedure to be followed, about which new bishops should become aware.

CHAPTER 16

Fostering Visible Christian Unity

STRIVING FOR VISIBLE UNITY

In the last chapter it was noted that the archbishop's question before the sixth consecration vow contains the phrase:

'Will you strive for the visible unity of Christ's Church?'

In addition, the ninth vow (which is identical with the wording of the seventh vow made by those to be ordained deacon and priest) deliberately includes working ecumenically:

'Will you work with your fellow servants in the gospel for the sake of the kingdom of God?'

This makes it clear that the peace and reconciliation towards which all bishops are supposed to be working cannot be confined to their own denomination. Ecumenism cannot be treated as an optional extra that can be left to experts or those with a special interest. A commitment to foster visible unity with churches of other traditions is integral to the vocation of every ordained minister. This chapter looks at ways in which bishops can do this at various levels.

A negative experience

In February 1958, when engaged in post-graduate research into the Orthodox Church, I visited a market town near the north-west coast of Greece. My main purpose was to interview two young Greeks who had applied for World Council of Churches' scholarships for study abroad, and to report to the Athens office of the WCC on their proficiency in English. I took the opportunity of calling on the local Greek Orthodox bishop to pay my respects and learn about a typical rural diocese. He extended the usual hospitality of Turkish coffee and sweet cherries in syrup, and we conversed for over an hour about a wide range of ecclesiastical topics. He told me how many churches, monasteries, priests and lay preachers he had in his diocese. He wanted to know whether I would recommend his two candidates for WCC scholarships. Towards the end of the interview came the moment I remember so vividly. I enquired whether he had any Greek Evangelicals,

Roman Catholics, or followers of the Zoe renewal movement in his diocese. There was a long pause. Then he peered forward, spread out his hands and swept them all around, as if to indicate the whole diocese. Pointing to himself he said *'episkopos'.* Then gazing over the imaginary diocese spread before him at the desk he uttered two separate words *'epi skopo'* – implying 'I keep a close watch over them all'. He emerged from his reverie, and with a clap of the hands announced triumphantly, *'The vineyard is clean. I know all my sheep, and they all know me'.* In other words, no heterodox Christians exist in this diocese!

Here was the picture of a monochrome, conservative diocese at unity with itself and traditional Eastern Orthodoxy, but wary of the rest of the Christian world. To the bishop's credit he was willing to sponsor ordinands for foreign study, but his mental picture seemed to allow no room for the existence of any denomination or theological view other than his own – a widespread attitude in the Greek Church at that time. One of those students did receive a scholarship to study in the USA for a year, and must soon have had to confront a more complex ecumenical reality than in his home diocese.

An imperative necessity

Those of us who, like that Greek Orthodox bishop, exercise our role in the predominant church of our area always run the risk of marginalising minority denominations and brushing aside views with which we are not prepared to engage. For much of the time we think and act as if our own church was 'the only show in town'. Yet the reality of broken Christendom cannot simply be ignored. No church can afford to live in isolation, or regard itself as exclusive and self-sufficient. A closed-circuit ecclesiology does not fit the facts, and ducks the challenge that we are called into a single communion of faith and love. The 1920 Lambeth Conference in its *'Appeal to All Christian People'* described the reunion of Christendom *'not as a laudable ambition or a beautiful dream, but as an imperative necessity'.* Disunity between Christians has to be faced and lived with, penitently and constructively, in accordance with Christ's prayer *'that all may be one ... so that the world may believe'* (John 17, 21)

A positive vision of unity

A particularly enlightening experience for me was to attend the WCC Assembly in New Delhi in autumn 1961 as an interpreter. When this large international gathering was not in plenary session, it did most of its work in smaller sections and committees, and I was attached to the Unity section and the department of Faith & Order. Here detailed debate took place about the nature of the Church's unity, and a historic statement was hammered out describing the sort of unity for which Christians should work and pray. It was a thumb-nail sketch of what Christian unity might look like in each locality if taken seriously, and became a landmark in the quest for visible unity.

> *'We believe that the unity*
> *which is both God's will and his gift to his Church*
> *is being made visible*
> *as all in each place who are baptised into Jesus Christ*
> *and confess him as Lord and Saviour*
> *are brought by the Holy Spirit*
> *into one fully committed fellowship,*
> *holding the one apostolic faith,*
> *preaching the one Gospel,*
> *breaking the one bread,*
> *joining in common prayer,*
> *and having a corporate life reaching out in witness and service to all*
> *and who at the same time are united with the whole Christian fellowship*
> *in all places and all ages*
> *in such wise that ministry and members are accepted by all,*
> *and that all can act and speak together as occasion requires*
> *for the tasks for which God calls his people.'*
> ('The New Delhi Report', SCM Press 1962, page 116)

This statement was approved by the whole Assembly, and 'commended to the churches for study and appropriate action'. It has provided a firm foundation for much subsequent ecumenical endeavour, and an inspiring vision of the goal towards which we should continually aspire.

All bishops need to have deep and well thought-out convictions about the nature of the Church's unity, and allow these to inform and guide their ministry. For example, chapter two of "Porvoo" (*'Together in Mission and Ministry'*, CHP 1993, §14-28) provides a solid theological foundation for all ecumenical engagement, not just between Anglicans and Lutherans. Some other key ecumenical texts are suggested towards the end of this chapter for the benefit of new bishops.

Engaging at various levels

In order to translate ecumenical vision into practical action bishops can get involved at four main levels in respect of their own territory:

- building personal links with their counterparts in other churches
- sharing oversight at county level
- encouraging and supporting local ecumenism
- sustaining diocesan links with ecumenical partners overseas

Some of the tasks that bishops may be asked to undertake at national or international level have a mainly ecumenical focus. Others contain at least a significant ecumenical dimension, even if they have some other principal focus.

a)   Building personal links with counterparts in other churches

The most obvious way for bishops to live out their ecumenical calling is to relate positively to their counterparts in other denominations. One of the best-known examples occurred in Liverpool in the 1970's and 80's, as described in *'Better Together'* by David Sheppard and Derek Worlock (Hodder & Stoughton 1988), but even this illustrated some of the problems involved. What was widely perceived as a duo of church leaders was actually a trio – Anglican, Roman Catholic and Free Church – though the last element often got lost from public view. To the media a bishop tends to be more visible than a moderator, district chair or regional minister. The onus rests on bishops to correct this imbalance whenever possible. These different titles are well explained in Bishop David Hawtin's valuable booklet *'Bishops Behaving Ecumenically – courtesies and practicalities'*, page 10. The functions and powers of such office-holders are by no means identical within each denomination, and it must be borne in mind that leadership and pastoral oversight have to be exercised in subtly different ways depending on the church in question.

It can send a positive signal if the leaders of different denominations appear together or speak jointly in public from time to time, but this by itself is not enough. Mutual relations need to move beyond superficial courtesies into personal friendships that spill over into deeper mutual understanding and committed partnership. The graphic imagery of Psalm 133 pictures the blessings that flow from religious leaders and their people living in a covenanted relationship:

> *'Behold how good and pleasant it is to dwell together in unity. It is like the precious oil upon the head, running down upon the beard, even on Aaron's beard, running down upon the collar of his clothing'*
>
> (Ps 133, verses 1-3)

Rather than the literal image of chrism oil trickling down the high priestly robes, it is more appropriate in today's ecumenical situation to consider the beneficial 'trickle-down effect' that occurs when senior church leaders trust and respect one another, setting a model of collaboration for ministers and laity to follow. If the leaders get on well together, it certainly oils the wheels for their co-workers.

Close friendship at this level is more difficult to achieve than appears at first sight. All those concerned have full diaries, and may live many miles apart. Unless church leaders are prepared to spend quality time together as a priority, at least occasionally, their hearts and minds are unlikely to meet at any real depth. A good example was set by Bishop James McGuiness (the former Roman Catholic Bishop of Nottingham) when in 1982 he invited leaders of the six main denominations in Lincolnshire to a two-day retreat at Mount St Bernard monastery in the Charnwood Forest. Through the daily round of services, corporate meals and Bible discussion groups we were drawn closer together. During the office of Compline, in the presence of the Cistercian monks, we each signed a covenant of ecumenical solidarity. In the spirit of the well-known 'Lund Principle' of 1952 we pledged to act together as far as possible *'except where deep differences of conviction compel us to act separately'*, and did so with a sense of personal engagement. In due course our successors in office have been invited to enter into this personal covenant. Inevitably, the task of sustaining mutual acquaintance and commitment within this ever-changing group is perpetually ongoing.

A relationship of trust between bishops and their counterparts can make a real difference when ordained ministers wish to transfer between denominations. Misunderstanding and conflict can be minimised, and difficulties resolved with goodwill and compassion. Similarly, when disciplinary procedures need to be applied within an ecumenical partnership, this can be done along clearly agreed lines without fuss or confusion. Bishops are often well placed to keep their fellow church leaders in touch with Members of Parliament and County Councillors.

b) *Sharing oversight at county level*

Operating within the safety of one's own familiar denomination is more comfortable than living ecumenically. When Church of England bishops function within the Anglican set-up, they know the rules and expectations. They still feel broadly at home whatever internal difficulties have to be contended with. This is not so in the wider ecumenical scene, where they step into other Christian sub-cultures where different assumptions and traditions hold sway. It requires a conscious decision on a bishop's part to contribute fully and actively to the ecumenical scene at county level.

Any ecumenical initiative needs to be properly resourced and managed on a shared basis, and this is the purpose for which so-called 'intermediate structures' exist, such as Churches Together at county level, the Regional Forum or Assembly (where one exists), the Sponsoring Body for ecumenical partnerships and local covenants, the consortia that provide ecumenical chaplaincy services, and so forth. These instruments enable pastoral oversight to be shared, and only if bishops and their counterparts participate in them conscientiously can these bodies stay connected with the denominational authorities that provide stipends, housing, pensions, etc..

This is one more network, indispensible if the bishop's ministry is to be effective ecumenically. David Hawtin has rightly said of 'intermediate' structures that they are *'only effective if everybody is willing to collaborate, and if they are properly resourced for the work to be done. Poorly attended groups which are poorly resourced are unlikely to deliver'* (see *'Bishops Behaving Ecumenically'*, page 5). Their work tends to be unexciting and technical, and is subject to the frustration that diocesan and other similar territorial boundaries rarely coincide. This calls for much travel, patience and persistence. Wasteful re-duplication of meetings has to be avoided. I used to feel pretty reluctant to turn out on Saturday mornings for county-level meetings, but what chastened me to attend was the comment of a fellow bishop during the Lambeth Conference 1988. During a Bible study group I asked Barnabas from Burma how important he thought it was to attend ecumenical church leaders' meetings. Through his interpreter he replied simply: 'I always attend. It takes me a fortnight to walk there, and another fortnight to walk back'. Faced with such commitment, who would dare to complain of his or her own minor inconveniences.

The linchpin of the unity network is usually the Ecumenical Officer, whose role is found in two distinct forms – either as a denominational officer responsible for ecumenical affairs within his or her own church, or as an ecumenical post-holder serving several denominations jointly. In some dioceses both types of post exist side by side, and work hand-in-glove. Though professional support is available at national level through the Council for Christian Unity (CCU) and Churches Together in England (CTE), it remains essential that bishops should take a direct interest in the work of their Ecumenical Officers and give them strong personal backing, especially with projects that push beyond the boundaries of congregational life. Frontier ministries are underappreciated by many who pay the diocesan 'quota', and are vulnerable in times of financial stringency. The bishop needs to be aware of a particular role in seeing that the Ecumenical Officer is adequately resourced, and has access to the senior staff meeting and key committees of the diocese when necessary.

c) *Encouraging and supporting local ecumenism*

The bishop's own personal vision and understanding of the quest for visible unity are vital elements in encouraging local initiatives. The Ecumenical Officer usually negotiates with local congregations and accumulates expertise in what makes for 'good practice' or otherwise, but bishops cannot delegate all this work. They are necessarily involved in giving written approval of certain permissions required under the Sharing of Church Buildings Act 1969 and under Canons B.43 and B.44, or in extending or terminating such arrangements. A merit of these so-called 'ecumenical canons' is the discretion they confer on the bishop as to whether adequate local soundings have been taken, and whether special circumstances justify a departure from usual practice. The bishop must be satisfied that serious pastoral need is being met, and that the doctrine of the Church of England is not being compromised in any essential matter. These factors call for careful discernment and a willingness to be flexible over sensitive situations. It is the bishop who is ultimately the signatory to an ecumenical agreement on behalf of the Church of England.

When assessing a local ecumenical situation it is useful to check out people's expectations. Local congregations often assume that the higher authorities of the church are stopping things from happening, yet they themselves may have no clear idea as to what they actually want to do or whether anything stands in the way of doing it. The main limitation is often their own, or their clergy's, lack of vision, imagination and flexibility. A great deal more is already possible within the six currently recognised types of Local Ecumenical Partnerships (LEP) than many congregations have ever dreamed. The impetus for ecumenical progress can come from below or above, or a combination of both. Where there is sufficient understanding and goodwill, bishops can grant permissions generously. However, there is little point in struggling to open some door that nobody actually wants to go through. Periodic review is an important requirement, since vision can often fade when key personalities move on. If a once thriving project withers on the vine, the reality must be faced and acknowledged.

The *'Code of Practice for Ecumenical Relations'* abounds in practical advice, and is updated from time to time. Another useful guide is *'Telling the Story'* by David Hawtin and Roger Paul (Archbishop's Council, 2012), which tells the story of how LEPs began and developed. Custom varies between dioceses as to which bishop handles particular matters. In Lincoln the diocesan normally dealt with LEP's under Canon B.44, whilst the area suffragan handled other ecumenical issues under Canon B.43 applicable to any parish.

Bishops can sustain their direct link with an LEP in two particular ways. The first is by co-operating actively in making joint appointments and sharing in the public licensing of new ministers. The other is through ecumenical services of confirmation. Though the House of Bishops first approved these in 1975, a few bishops still seem to find these services beyond their comfort zone. Such occasions can become edifying and inspiring as long as the points mentioned in the Code of Practice (paragraphs 113 and 114) are carefully heeded. Bishops need to be willing to enter whole-heartedly into a variety of worship styles, and useful resources are available to them through the Council for Christian Unity, including David Hawtin's check-list of arrangements (see *'Bishops Behaving Ecumenically'*, page 23). By whatever means, bishops should make a conscious effort to keep a direct personal link with ecumenical partnerships, and not leave them to float off into no-man's-land as if they were virtually a separate denomination.

d) Sustaining diocesan links with ecumenical partners overseas

Beside the links with Anglican dioceses abroad already mentioned, many dioceses also have well established partnerships with sister churches of other traditions, especially in continental Europe. Ecumenical twinnings have long been in operation with several French and Belgian Roman Catholic dioceses, and in Lincoln's case there has been a fruitful three-way link with Brugge and Nottingham for over 30 years. Residential consultations have regularly been held every few years with representatives of all three dioceses, and joint courses for junior clergy held alternately in Belgium and England.

Since various ecumenical agreements were signed – Porvoo (with Nordic and Baltic Lutheran Churches), Meissen (with the German Evangelical Church) and Reuilly (with French Lutheran and Reformed Churches) – most English dioceses have set up interchanges and partnerships with these churches in continental Europe. On two separate occasions the Bishop's Council in Lincoln hosted a visit from the equivalent body in a Swedish diocese, whose members were keen to explore amongst other matters how we recruited voluntary church workers, and how we managed our glebe and *forests*! During my Grimsby years we seconded two ministry officers to conduct lay training courses in Estonia, and sent a curate from Grimsby to work under the Bishop of Iceland for three months. Conversely, the diocese received the services of several Lutheran clergy from Iceland and Sweden, usually as team vicars where they could fit in easily without having to run a whole parish or in three instances as incumbents. A key element in getting these ventures off the ground was the direct link from bishop to bishop.

e) Ecumenical tasks at national level

From 1992 to 1998 I served as chairman of the Council for Christian Unity (CCU), the General Synod's main ecumenical arm, and it was a great joy to work with the Council's staff under the talented leadership of Dr (later Dame) Mary Tanner. I also served from 1986 to 2002 as one of the so-called 'Ecumenical Bishops' – a group which assists the Archbishops of Canterbury and York in reviewing policy annually across the entire spectrum of relations with other Christian traditions.

Soon after the General Synod's decision to ordain women to the priesthood, Archbishop George Carey and Cardinal Basil Hume set up a joint group to advise on the pastoral and practical aspects of clergy transferring between the Church of

England and the Roman Catholic Church, and I was one of the three Anglican bishops who met several times in 1993-94 with three members of the R.C. hierarchy to work out guidelines.

In 1995-96 Brian Beck (Secretary of the Methodist Conference) and I co-chaired preliminary talks between the Methodist Church and the Church of England, paving the way for formal conversations to be re-opened and for the Anglican-Methodist Covenant eventually to be signed in November 2003.

These are examples of the kind of ecumenical tasks which a bishop may be asked to undertake. Others would be serving within the structures of Churches Together in England, such as the Enabling Group or its Group for Local Unity (GLU), or of Churches Together in Britain and Ireland. It always has to be borne in mind that these responsibilities are undertaken on behalf of our Church as a whole.

f) *Ecumenical tasks at international level*

Often a bishop is sent abroad to represent the Archbishop of Canterbury at some event such as the consecration or funeral of a foreign church leader, or a major anniversary or festival. It is important that the English bishop who is sent should be properly briefed about the background, and should afterwards send back a full report of proceedings and other intelligence to Lambeth Palace.

From time to time bishops are invited to join, or lead, a delegation on behalf of the Church of England or the Anglican Communion Office, which provides the opening for local visits and contacts abroad and dialogue on current issues. In 1983 I led an English delegation to six dioceses of the Greek Orthodox Church. It was a good opportunity for the clergy who accompanied me to get into discussion with their opposite numbers in each diocese we visited. I was fascinated to discover how far church life had moved on since my studies in Athens 25 years earlier, and glad to brush up my Modern Greek. This portfolio then passed to another bishop so that I could give more attention to Anglican-Lutheran relations, in which I had already been involved since 1956.

The Anglican Communion Office asked me in 1986 to co-chair the Anglican-Lutheran dialogue body at world level, and over the next 20 years this role took me to Canada, Malaysia, Brazil, Zimbabwe, South Africa, the USA, Iceland, Tanzania and various parts of continental Europe – usually for just a few days each year. These were years of fruitful teamwork, which gave birth to the Niagara report on *Episcopé* (1987) and the Hanover report on *'The Diaconate as Ecumenical Opportunity'* (1996). Anglican-Lutheran relations opened up considerably in Southern Africa, and it was a particular joy to share the chairmanship with two excellent Lutheran bishops from that region – Sebastian Kolowa (Tanzania) and Ambrose Moyo (Zimbabwe).

In parallel with these commitments at world level Archbishop Runcie invited me to lead the English delegations to two different sets of theological conversations with European neighbours. First was the dialogue with the Protestant Churches of East and West Germany (1986-87), leading to the Meissen agreement in 1991. Secondly, we held talks with the episcopal Lutheran Churches of the Nordic and Baltic region (1989-92), and this led to the Porvoo agreement establishing full communion between the ten churches that initially signed in 1996, together with the Church of Denmark which signed in 2010. During the phase of reception and initial implementation (1992-98) I also co-chaired the Porvoo Churches' contact group.

This type of work has to be in the service of unity in several senses. In the first place there is the duty, when acting as a delegate, to be loyal to the viewpoint of one's own church and express it accurately – often in another language. If serving as leader, one must try to draw on the talents of everyone in the delegation and weave their contributions together. At the same time the intention of ecumenical dialogue is to enter into the mind-set of one's partners from another tradition; to clarify misunderstandings, discover common ground, and grasp some vision of a new way forward. This cannot happen if people only argue from fixed positions, or simply air their own pet theories, or fail to achieve a real meeting of minds. Moreover, any new understanding has to be articulated in a joint document that will not simply paper over the cracks, but make plain, honest sense in other languages. A further constraint lies in not promising more than can be delivered. It would be irresponsible to agree on proposals that stand no reasonable chance of commending themselves to the authorities of one's own church, not least because of the negative consequences. All these constraints are part of the burden of unity that has to be borne. This bridge-building theological work is not without its frustrations, disappointments and complexities, but is mentally challenging and spiritually fulfilling if well founded.

RESOURCES FOR NEW BISHOPS

New bishops already possess much working knowledge through their previous experience, but where there are gaps they need know where to turn for help. On ecumenism a classic statement of Anglican policy was the *'Appeal to All Christian People'* by the 1920 Lambeth Conference (see *'Resolutions of the twelve Lambeth Conferences 1867-1988'*, ed. R. Coleman, Anglican Book Centre, Toronto 1992). The section report on ecumenical relations at the 1988 Lambeth Conference gives an excellent overview of the subject (*'The Truth shall make you Free'*, ACC 1988, pages 125-150). Much valuable clarification regarding the nature of the Church's unity has been carried out by the World Council of Churches, especially in its

Toronto Statement (1950) and the Canberra Statement (1991). The Lima text on *'Baptism, Eucharist and Ministry'* (1982) was already cited briefly on page 54, and abounds in illuminating exposition of sacramental theology. Pope John Paul II's encyclical *'Ut Unum Sint'* (1995) is a fine document, setting out an irrevocable commitment to ecumenism on the part of the Roman Catholic Church. It was warmly welcomed by the House of Bishops of the Church of England in their occasional paper *'May They All Be One'* (GS Misc 495, 1997).

David Hawtin's booklet entitled *'Bishops Behaving Ecumenically'* is full of useful tips on good ecumenical practice, especially on the questions that a new bishop needs to ask and suggestions on whom to approach for an initial briefing. It contains a sensible list of books and websites, and a clear summary of the ecumenical agreements to which the Church of England is committed. Bishops should be aware, when authorising an occasional service in a building closed for regular public worship, that this may include worship 'by persons belonging to other Christian Churches' (Mission and Pastoral Measure 2011, sections 57 (9) and 61 (2)(c)). On LEPs *'Telling the Story'* (D. Hawtin and R. Paul) gives a clear orientation.

On collegiality *'Bishops in Communion'* (GS Misc 580) is probably the best starting-point.

When a bishop is planning a sabbatical, it is worth considering whether an overseas study visit could form part of it, such as my own short trips to the USA and the Baltic States in 1989. Valuable opportunities of ecumenical study are available through the World Council of Churches, especially in the form of consultations and courses at the Ecumenical Institute, Bossey.

Summary

All that I have written in this and the previous chapter leads me to sum up the unifying element of episcopé in these terms:

> **It engages** with the secular world, and has a special concern for the outcast and needy;
> **it unifies** diverse views and contributions;
> **it minimises** and overcomes divisions; and
> **it promotes** ecumenism and catholicity.

CHAPTER 17

Review & Personal Development

ANSWERABLE TO GOD

Introducing the eleventh vow at the service of consecration, the archbishop asks the candidates:

> 'Will you then, in the strength of the Holy Spirit, continually stir up the gift of God that is in you ...?'

In echoing the words of 2 Tim 1,6 this question reminds new bishops of the obligation to take stock of the gifts God has given them and the use they are making of them. It implies an ongoing process of review in which bishops confront their personal accountability to God. This chimes in with Bernard's advice that consideration of yourself should cover three areas: your nature, your role and your character. It is not just about how well you are doing your job, but also whether you have advanced or regressed in Christian virtues (see earlier quotation, page 46). It also connects with the questions which the Niagara Report posed in regard to the reform and renewal of episcopé:

> 'Do those exercising episcopé show in their own personal lives Christ-like qualities? Do they give an example of holiness, love, humility and simplicity of life? Are they generous and hospitable? Is their style of life influenced too much by the patterns of leadership that are dominant in the culture where they live? Is it evident that they are dedicated to unselfish service, and are open to be touched by the suffering of others? Do they give the time and space needed for prayer, study, rest, recreation and family life, and avoid being devoured by unreasonable public expectations of their office?
>
> (Niagara Report, CHP 1988, §108 – see also the whole of §§99-109)

A PATTERN OF REGULAR REVIEW

During my first seven years as a bishop I had a two-hour review session with Simon Phipps every six months. That was his particular style, and something he did for each member of his senior staff. Our conversation covered personal and family agenda as well as my actual job. I gave him a summary of what I had been doing, what I was planning to do, and how I felt about it. His critique and affirmation were immensely helpful, and I came away with a sharper sense of direction in my ministry. He was of an older generation, and when he retired I realised the need to work out my own pattern of review.

The method to which I later switched was one of annual self-review, adapted from the one I already used with clergy for their work reviews. It contained these elements:

    a)   Look back over the year's diary, and ask myself: What have I accomplished of particular note since my last review? What do I see as the four or five most important areas of my ministry? How much time was actually spent in those areas? What criteria exist for telling whether my work is effective, and how do I get the feed-back? In the light of that, what are my strengths and weaknesses?

    b)   What factors frustrate or hamper my ministry? How far could they be changed? Which of my talents / skills are underused or underdeveloped? What training or professional support could help my ministry to develop?

    c)   Cast an eye over the current state of the eight networks identified earlier:

episcopal (p 108)   teaching/learning (p 159-161)
synodical (p 108)   ministry (p 176)
pastoral (p 123)   secular (p 179-180)
worship (p 142)   ecumenical (p 194-195)

How far is my ministry being shared with others in these fields? Is the balance right? Should I consult more? Should I delegate more? Where are the gaps?

    d)   Reset targets for the next period. Which two or three things, if done well, could have the most beneficial result for the diocese? What should I cut back on? What should I do more of? What specific objectives do I plan to achieve by the date of my next review?

    e)   With whom shall I now share the results of this review?

AN ALTERNATIVE FRAMEWORK FOR REVIEW

From time to time I have chosen to use the following check-list instead, based on Bernard's work *'On Consideration'*. This approach arose from an idea suggested to me by the Revd Vernon Brooke, a former industrial chaplain:

- Reset sensible boundaries for my life / work balance
- *What* am I?   [Quid?]   the real me
- *Who* am I?   [Quis?]   handling office and role
- *What sort* of person am I? [Qualis?] remedying my faults
                                          developing my character
- Under me   those *for* whom I am responsible
- Around me   those *with* whom I live and work
- Above me   those *to* whom I am responsible
                          God whose servant I am

MUTUAL ACCOUNTABILITY

The question 'With whom shall I share the results of this review?' permits of various answers, not necessarily the same every time. Some findings may be appropriate matter for confession and absolution. Many aspects will be talked through with one's spouse. Bishops will probably wish to share much of the outcome with their spiritual director, or confessor, or work consultant, or support group, and to invite their comments. I shared my findings on various occasions with my diocesan bishop, the archdeacon with whom I worked, a suffragan from elsewhere, my wife, or a wise friend. At all events there does need to be a testing for reality, and self-delusion must be dispelled.

Roman Catholic bishops are required to make an 'ad limina' visit to Rome every five years for a group interview with the Pope and to render an account of their diocesan life to the appropriate Vatican department. Nothing so formal or centralised occurs within the Anglican Communion, though the possibility of an ecumenical dimension to such a visit was hinted at in *'The Gift of Authority'* (ARCIC II, 1999). In recent years the Archbishops of Canterbury and York have taken to holding regular periodic meetings with each of the diocesan bishops in their province. The Anglican Church of Canada has developed, in response to the Niagara Report 1988 and the Waterloo Agreement 2001, a procedure for evaluating a bishop's ministry after several years in office.

In general, the main emphasis for Anglicans lies on the sense of mutual interdependence and accountability between bishops, clergy and laity, which was spelt out by the 1988 Lambeth Conference (*'The Truth shall make you Free'*, pages 61-

62). Bishops have a personal responsibility to uphold the discipline and corporate life of the church, and to be obedient to it themselves.

BISHOPS' NEED OF TRAINING

For generations bishops simply learnt their job as they went along, and the first Lambeth Conference to express the hope that they should get some training before taking office was in 1968 (official report, page 109). This suggestion was taken further by the 1978 conference, when Resolution 19 asked each member church to make provision for induction training and continuing education. The general content of initial training was sketched on pages 78-79 of the report, together with a wise emphasis on wholeness in four particular areas:

    a)   the integration of intellectual and devotional life, linked with adequate attention to physical and emotional health;

    b)   sound home and family life on which to rely for support and deep mutual sharing;

    c)   good 'give and take' in the context of mature adult-to-adult interaction;

    d)   integration with other executive leaders (not necessarily episcopal) with whom to share the concerns of work and family.

A number of Anglican Provinces set up schemes, in some cases including bishops' spouses. There was, and still is, no standard pattern throughout the Communion owing to the diversity of cultural contexts and financial resources. In addition, Resolution 41 of the 1988 conference added two further recommendations:

> a break of one month for initial preparation after completing one's previous job; sabbatical leave for study and refreshment after six years in office.

As new bishops are not appointed *en bloc,* but come on-stream in a continuous trickle, induction has to be tailor-made on an individual basis. It is usually hard to fit it in at short notice, and depends on people being available to act as mentors. The stressful process of responding to the call, leaving one's former post and changing gear was described in an earlier chapter, where I spelt out my understanding of the aims of initial training. Only when the previous job has been completed is it generally possible to do much study or go on retreat. The receiving diocese can make plans to welcome the new bishop and induct him or her into the relevant networks and aspects of episcopal ministry, as well as setting up a local support structure. Not until bishops have been in office for several months is it feasible to bring them together in viable numbers for their first residential consultation, usually lasting for a week. Ideally they should attend a second one a year or so later, whilst still in the early and formative years of their episcopate. These courses often include participants from smaller sister churches that have too few new bishops to run their own training scheme (e.g. Lutherans, Old Catholics).

Over the three decades since I was consecrated in 1979 the provision for bishops' training has changed a number of times. It may be worth looking back at what was available to those of my generation, and reflecting how far it was useful. This may assist new bishops and their current Training Officer in the quest for training that matches present-day requirements.

Training courses for bishops

a)   St George's House, Windsor

In England the main initiative in providing residential courses for senior church leaders was taken by St George's House, Windsor, where I attended three courses in 1980, 1981 and 1982. The participants in my first 8-day course were mainly English suffragans, but also included a moderator of the United Reformed Church, a Dutch Old Catholic bishop, a German Lutheran Oberkirchenrat and a deputy secretary of the Church Commissioners. The theme was 'Authority', and visiting lecturers explored its meaning in scripture and church history, as well as in politics, law and business management. Each of us brought a case-study on the exercise of authority in church life, and in group work we thrashed out the implications for our own ministry. Time was also spent on comparing our experiences of other practical issues, such as diary control, the impact of being a bishop on our family life, new devotional patterns, initiatives in pastoral care, etc.. The content of the course was highly relevant at that stage, and most helpful.

My second Windsor course was not just for bishops. Five dioceses sent a mixed team comprising a diocesan bishop, a suffragan, an archdeacon and the diocesan secretary. We spent five days together focussing on the teamwork of the Bishop's Staff, and became more self-aware about our corporate decision-making processes and the interaction of our diverse roles.

Another short week-end course, including wives and a leading Jewish rabbi, was interesting and enjoyable, but failed to engage with the experience of the participants.

b)   The Urban Ministry Project (UMP) & William Temple Foundation (WTF)

I also attended an experimental course run jointly by these agencies (1982-83), both of which had had long experience of running clergy courses on issues of social justice. They mounted two pilot projects: the first was only for C. of E. bishops, and the second – in which I took part – was for an ecumenical mix of senior church leaders. Both courses extended over eighteen months, and were interwoven with our normal work. In the first phase each participant was given a personal tutor, who visited him (we were all men!) at home for a substantial interview every month and helped him to set up a local support group. For three months we kept a careful log of our time-use in certain agreed categories, and began discussing with our support group the issues raised by the log. Each church leader analysed the emerging picture, noted the perceived pressure points, and began drafting his own understanding of the essence of episcopé. Having worked separately up to this point, we then shared in our first week-long residential. Taking part were two Methodist district chairmen, one United Reformed moderator, one Roman Catholic auxiliary bishop and several Anglican bishops (diocesan and suffragan).

We challenged and supported each other in equal measure, learning a great deal in the process. After re-formulating our findings we moved into to the second phase, which involved working out three profiles: a social profile of the area we served, a church profile of it, and an overview of the institutions within it. During the next few months we prepared this material in consultation with our support groups. At our second week-long residential we compared notes, and explored the significance of what we had discovered.

Finally, each of us formulated "What I see as the 'Signs of the Times' and what I believe God wants me to be doing about them". The issues we judged important had to be ranked in priority, according to the degree of our personal involvement, viz.:

- issues in which I am directly involved with others, and carry a main responsibility (e.g. as chairman)
- issues on which I am keen, but for which I carry no main responsibility (i.e. keep myself informed, and give active encouragement when possible)
- issues on which I feel that more should be done, but cannot quite see what; (i.e. put on the back-burner, and stir occasionally!)
- issues that are undoubtedly important, but are not on my plate (i.e. someone else is looking after these, so I leave them well alone)

This yielded a great deal of well-grounded material. Spreading the course over an extended period assisted our integration of experience, reflection, learning and putting into action – an excellent educational model. I rated this project pretty highly. It helped us to crystallise our ideas on how a Christian leader could relate to the secular world. We tried to interpret God's presence in the contemporary scene, and to perceive what others may easily miss. We wanted to say, like an artist:

"See what it looks like from where I stand".

This course also helped me to pinpoint a number of tensions which, irrespective of workload, are inescapable for senior church leaders:

a) *Local / regional* As individuals and families our identity is local, but professionally we function at regional level – something which many people fail to grasp. The principle of subsidiarity must operate, whereby the bishop declines invitations to do what would be more appropriately done by a local minister, such as an area dean or team rector, rather than 'upstaging' them. Nor can bishops afford to be sucked too greatly into the claims of deaneries or parishes near where they live, to the detriment of the claims of other deaneries further away.

b) *Roles past / present* Some invitations may arise on account of one's experience in a previous role, or one may become over-involved through relying on earlier skills. When under pressure it is tempting to revert to the safety or familiarity of an earlier role. However, one may need to resist acting as if still in a former role.

c) *Deciding / consulting* In conversation with a bank manager whom I once met whilst camping in France, we were talking about our respective jobs. He wanted to know what a bishop did, and his main question was: 'What kind of decisions do you make?' He approached it in a clear-cut, simplistic way: 'If a loan of less than x thousand pounds is requested, I decide. Above that figure, the next manager up must decide. That's what a manager is for – to make decisions. So what does a bishop decide?' It seemed impossible to answer purely in those terms, since the mission of the church is about so much more: teaching, caring, perceiving, motivating, etc. None the less, it *is* about deciding some things, even if a good deal of consultation goes into the process. So one has to come clean about the element of decision-making that episcopal ministry necessarily contains, and say – mentally if not aloud – 'Are you asking *me* to decide? If not, after we have talked it through, *you* decide.' If a decision or definite 'steer' is required, one needs to get on with it in the hope that it will prove more often right than wrong, without losing too much sleep.

d) *Reactive / proactive* One needs to be clear about the boundaries of availability, and what initiatives to take. If no limit is set on responding to some demands – e.g. by referrals, by pre-arranged schedules, by rationing systems, by saying No, etc – what is urgent is likely to push aside what is really important.

c) *The need for new provision*

When these Windsor and UMP/WTF courses ceased being offered, alternative provision was urgently needed. The House of Bishops set up a working-party under Bishop Alec Graham (Newcastle) on the 'Initial and Continuing Ministerial Education of Bishops'. This body, on which I served, met six times in 1986-87, and built on what had been learned from earlier pioneering efforts. Our main recommendation was the creation of a new half-time post, eventually known as the Archbishops' Adviser for Bishops' Ministry, to oversee the induction of new bishops and organise residential courses during their first eighteen months in office. For a few years in the 1980's and 90's new bishops had received a booklet of briefing notes on various practical aspects of their role. To replace this so-called 'Jackdaw Kit' we drew up a list of issues for the Adviser to go through with each new bishop soon after appointment, so as to discover what extra knowledge was required and what areas of weakness would need sustaining. We also sketched out the contents of the residential course. The first Adviser, Dr Norman Todd, took up post in 1988.

The establishment of induction training paved the way for other forms of continuing ministerial education (CME) for bishops. The working party defined the aims of subsequent CME as:

a) to reflect on experience and register new insights;
b) to monitor and re-set targets;
c) to provide collegial support in the exercise of leadership and guidance in the sphere of Christian belief and teaching;
d) to deepen appreciation of the social setting in which ministry is exercised, and to improve skills in operating outside the institutional church;
e) to attend to areas of skill or personal development that are either lacking or not fully realised.

The rather scrappy day meetings for bishops at Lambeth Palace were discontinued, and from 1991 an annual residential gathering of the whole college was held, in which professional development was a basic ingredient. Regional bishops' meetings and sabbatical leave were encouraged, and became the norm. As diocesan provision for the costs of Continuing Ministerial Education (CME) for clergy became more widely available, bishops were able by this means to fund their own attendance at retreats, conferences and training courses in particular skills. This emerging framework was confirmed in a policy paper of the House of Bishops in 1999, and marked a major step forward. In recent years the role of Adviser has been replaced by that of Bishops' Training Officer.

d) The Grubb Institute

The most challenging and stimulating training event I experienced was a research project by the Grubb Institute. Its former director, Bruce Reed, conducted separate consultations in London with the Bishop of Lincoln and both of his suffragans over a several months in 1989-90. This approach, called 'Organisational Role Analysis' (ORA for short), offered no blue-print or fixed package of solutions, but focussed on each bishop's own agenda. It was not counselling, nor was it concerned with private and family life, but analysed the bishop's professional role in situations of his own choosing. It was valuable that all three bishops did this exercise separately, but over the same period. These confidential discussions provided a safe zone in which to address issues where we felt vulnerable, and to face openly our mistakes and limitations.

Bruce's attentive listening and perceptive questioning through the course of eight two-hour sessions per person were utterly remarkable. His profoundly spiritual approach was informed by a rich fund of biblical insights and broad experience in many fields. He got us to examine theological and practical aspects of the particular situations we identified, and challenged us to relate them to appropriate spiritual resources. For example, I recall looking at the distinctive character of Lincoln diocese not just logically but emotionally; at where I came across fears, resistances, immature dependence, projections, etc; at how I could avoid colluding with people's own negative self-image; at how I could exercise servanthood and leadership in specific dysfunctional situations, etc. I examined what my style was; how I related to congregations and the wider community; how I related to other members of the Bishop's Staff and to ecumenical counterparts; how I handled my workload; what I should look for when appraising teams or particular clergy, etc. With Bruce's skilled help each of us unlocked spiritual and practical resources that enabled us to gain fresh insight and energy for our ministry. Finally, we each wrote a paper to share with Bruce and our two colleagues, and held a three-hour joint session in which to re-focus our work together. The whole process was immensely beneficial, and subtly modified the way we perceived our roles and related to the vast and varied territory of our diocese. It was hoped that this project would be of potential value for the Institute's work with other bishops in the longer term.

e) Other courses and conferences

It became generally accepted that bishops, like all clergy, should be personally responsible for their own development and 'keeping the flame alive', and take charge of their own ongoing studies. Each person's programme of CME would reflect his or her own needs and interests, and would not be confined to events tailored for bishops. In addition to the courses already described, I undertook training on conducting job appraisals, chairing selection panels, understanding sexual abuse and its effects, media skills (TV and radio), Myers-Briggs personality types and their relevance to spirituality, marriage enrichment, computer literacy, and so on. I attended study conferences on topics such as rural and urban mission, church and state, inter-faith dialogue, international peace-making, human relations' education and the gospel, intercommunion, episcopé in relation to mission, the diaconate, Icelandic culture and the Folk Church, etc.

Summary

In this chapter I have mentioned the gradual raising of awareness within the Anglican Communion during the 1960's and 70's that bishops required initial and continuing training, and have briefly described the development of policy within the Church of England in support of this ideal. I have also tried to evaluate some of the pioneering projects that tried to help bishops of my generation. To me it is a matter of passionate concern that there should in the longer term be:

1) central provision of adequate resources for bishops' training; and
2) corporate acceptance of some procedure for helping bishops to assess the effectiveness of their own ministry at certain agreed 'milestone' intervals after taking office.

In conclusion, I would define this further important element of *episcopé* as follows:

> **It is committed** to regular review and continuing professional development.

CHAPTER 18

Stepping into Retirement

In many respects the term 'retirement' is a misnomer. When the time comes to lay aside the duties and pressures of a particular public office, it is good to remember that you cannot retire from being a bishop any more than from being a parent or grandparent, or indeed from being a Christian. Even if the public exercise of that ministry eventually becomes impossible by reason of infirmity or family commitments, the journey of faith still continues as you endeavour to live out God's purpose for the rest of your life. In Sidney Carter's apt words:

'One more step along the world I go.
From the old things to the new
Keep me travelling along with You'.

The challenge is not to retire from life, but to advance in living it as fully as opportunity permits. The privilege of having more time for family, friends and hobbies is balanced by the responsibility of working out your Christian vocation in changed circumstances.

The blessings of retirement do not come to everyone, since some die in harness and others after only a brief retirement. The bonus of 'extra time' can never be taken for granted. It is a precious gift from God, to be accepted with humble gratitude, used well and eventually handed back with life itself. Some people find retirement harder than others, depending both on current circumstances and on what lies ahead. I was hugely fortunate in being able to retire having my dear wife, Mary, with me. Both of us were still in reasonable health, and she continued working for a couple more years. We had enough to live on, and a roof of our own under which to dwell and welcome others. We could travel, and enjoy a satisfying measure of active involvement in our family, our church and the local community. For others it can be very different.

For bishops, no less than anyone else, the change from full-time work to a different mode of being in active retirement takes a good deal of adjustment, and can initially be quite a stressful process. This is not one single change, but a series of steps and stages that are explored in this chapter with particular reference to episcopal life and ministry.

Gradually letting go

What retirement may mean for a bishop was well expressed by Cardinal Cormac Murphy-O'Connor in his homily on Easter Day 2009:

'We should recall, as we rejoice today in the resurrection of Jesus Christ, that in our own lives we have to follow the pattern of the life of Jesus – the pattern of dying in order to live. And all of us die a little, perhaps every day, every year, every stage of our lives.

This is the last time that I shall be preaching to you at Eastertide. This is because I now have to move on to a new stage of my life as I go into retirement. I have, if you like, to die a little in order to follow the Will of the Lord and begin, perhaps, a new stage of living, a more abundant life. But it does mean that I have to let go of things that I have done for many, many years as a bishop: of leadership, of pastoral care, of responsibilities, and so many other things, and reach out to begin again and follow what the Lord wants.

Each in your own life has to die a little to the past. Sometimes we carry resentments, grudges, prejudices, hurts and angers – like security blankets in our lives. This may be particularly pertinent at the present time, when many people are feeling stress and anxiety due to the difficulties resulting from the economic situation locally and globally. But negative feelings and negative attitudes are bundles of death that stand in the way of life. Jesus said that love was the greatest commandment. So it is because of Jesus's love that we are able to forgive and pass over the things of the past, and die to pride and selfishness, and begin anew a choice for life ...'

This begins to explain why the process of moving into retirement is such a curious mixture. There is parting and loss, but also a sense of relief. Alongside the wisdom of experience and maturity comes the challenge of learning new skills, and of operating in new social situations without your customary role. A major factor is being cut off from previous support structures.

Step 1 – the 'run-down period'

Time eventually runs out for trying different ways of being a bishop. In the run-down to my retirement from the suffragan see of Grimsby at Easter 2000, soon after my 65th birthday, the first step was to let go, and tie up the loose ends of the main job I had been doing for 21 years. As soon as my retirement date was announced many factors subtly changed. More than a decade earlier Simon Phipps had announced his retirement twelve months in advance. With hindsight this was too long, and six or seven months' notice would have been better. In my own case I remember what a strain it was to work through a whole string of tasks for the last time, and have to carry on whilst feeling chronically worn out. I would recommend any bishop approaching retirement not to draw out this abnormal period unduly, though it does take a few months to achieve an orderly phase-out. Because of the corporate momentum involved, it is like berthing an oil tanker or landing an airliner. Forward thrust reduces long before the final destination.

When the Revd David Deeks was about to retire as General Secretary of the Methodist Church, he wrote to all Methodist ministers explaining that his attention was concentrated on leaving and letting go. He set out a helpful agenda of the questions and feelings that he was having to address at this stage, including:

- *What is essential for me to complete before I move?*
- *As to what cannot be completed – if it will need continuing action by a successor, how do I hand things on adequately? If not, how do I draw a line under it?*
- *What has accumulated that needs to be thrown out? What must be carefully recorded and stored?*
- *What relationships need attention, to be put right or rounded off appropriately?*
- *In the midst of the sanitised farewell speeches, how do I acknowledge my faults and inadequacies, and the actions – or failures to act – that have hurt some people?*
- *How do I leave behind in a safe way any resentments, regrets, jealousies or anger that have focused on particular people or situations?*
- *How do I say Thank You to the multitude of people who have encouraged me, prayed for me, supported me, told me the truth (even when it was unpalatable) and loved me into a continuing fascination with the gospel and a deepening discipleship of Jesus?*

Many of my own ongoing tasks, especially to do with parochial appointments, were handed over to colleagues. I stood down as president of Grimsby hospice and chairman of the Diocesan Pastoral Committee, and brought the working party on Ministry Development to a conclusion. Mary and I held a final series of dinner parties and buffet suppers – twelve events in all. We attended farewell services at Lincoln cathedral and three other regional venues, and a village hall party at Irby-on-Humber where we had been residents for ten years. These occasions were heart-warming, though emotionally exhausting.

I thinned out the contents of my bookshelves and filing cabinets, and disposed of about 100 books and 170 black sacks of shredded paper! I left a selection of files and memoranda for my successor, who would not be taking over until several months later. BBC Radio Lincolnshire did a 'Desert Island Disks' interview with me, and broadcast it on my last day in office – which felt curiously symbolic of being cut adrift from the networks described in previous chapters.

My commitments outside the diocese, such as the House of Bishops, the General Synod and all their committees, ceased automatically with my retirement, but decisions about when to relinquish three other ecumenical tasks were not needed until later.

Step 2 – taking a real break

Mary and I moved to the village of Wrawby in the adjoining county of North Lincolnshire. For family reasons we needed to be not too far from Grimsby. Bob Hardy was most understanding about this, and I gave him an assurance to honour the long-standing clerical etiquette of leaving a clear field for my successor. My second step was – as they say in Methodist parlance – simply to "sit down"! This meant having a good rest, making more time for the family, and stepping back from active ministry into a more leisured and less cluttered way of being. It was a huge relief to lay down the burden of so much preaching, travelling and pastoral administration, especially the unrelenting task of filling vacant benefices. Several episcopal colleagues had suggested a fallow period of at least six months, and I would heartily endorse this advice to bishops approaching retirement. In fact, I took a gap of nearly a year before becoming an honorary assistant bishop. This was a good way of escaping the treadmill, and discovering a slower and gentler pace of life.

Many clergy fear retirement, and find it hard to adapt to it. Ordained ministry is not so much a job as a way of life, as indicated by the solemn words of the 1662 ordinal for priests:

'We have good hope that ... you have clearly determined, by God's grace, to give yourself wholly to this office ... and that you apply yourself wholly to this one thing, and draw all your cares and studies this way ...'

With such words echoing in their ears, it is little wonder that many clergy feel guilty at the idea of taking a break and developing other interests. They wonder whether retirement will be like stepping into a black hole. Having spent many years responding to other people's pastoral needs, they may suffer withdrawal symptoms when no longer needed themselves. The story is told of a retired bishop who prayed: "Lord, use me ..." (adding under his breath) "but only in an advisory capacity!" It is good to take a substantial pause, and wait to discern what doors may open for a different kind of life and ministry.

STEP 3 – REFRAINING FROM PUBLIC COMMENT

The natural sequel to "sit down" must surely be "and shut up!" This comes hard when, for years, a bishop has lived in a state of perpetual readiness to respond to the media on numerous topical issues as a spokesperson of the Church. From my days on the staff at Lambeth Palace I recall how irritated even the saintly Archbishop Michael Ramsey was by the many public letters and utterances of his predecessor, Geoffrey Fisher (see Owen Chadwick's biography of Ramsey, pp 114-115). In my view all retired bishops – including archbishops – should exercise a self-denying ordinance to refrain from public comment for most of the time on matters of current policy or controversy. This is not to rule out sharing their expertise through lectures, articles, books or sermons on specific subjects where they have wisdom to offer, but interference in issues for which they no longer carry the main responsibility is quite a different matter. To discern the difference requires discretion and tact. At retirement you step outside the networks, and quickly get out of date. Events move on, and access to the whole range of current factors becomes reduced. At the same time there is also a sense in which, by watching from the touch-line, you see more of the whole game. Of course I continued to hold my own opinions about all sorts of things, but had to keep reminding myself: "I have had my go. Now it is somebody else's turn, and time for me to stand back. If my advice is sought, I can offer it discretely and privately."

STEP 4 – FINDING ONE'S PLACE IN THE LOCAL COMMUNITY

The fourth step, after moving out of church-provided accommodation, was to live in the greater privacy of our own house in an ordinary road, and to take our place as local residents and members of a congregation. It took several months to complete repairs and modifications to our retirement property, settle into our new home and garden, and discover the pattern of local life in a different village. It was a joy to get to know our neighbours, and make a host of new friends many of whom are of a younger generation. For years I had rarely had the chance to sit with Mary in the pew, but now this could become the norm. In the first twenty years of our marriage I had taken the main public role, and Mary a more domestic one. Later, as her professional life developed, our roles became more evenly balanced. In retirement I could take more of a back seat, and support her in taking an up-front role locally in church and community. It was the right juncture to re-negotiate our mutual obligations and wider commitments, and so to discover a new identity and a slower tempo in which time with our own family could take a higher priority. I found it a real treat to have space for more activities than were possible in a tight episcopal schedule. I could play the piano and organ much more often. I could attend concerts, go swimming, read novels and belong to a book club. We could watch more television together. I could do some writing. I could attend my local branch of horological colleagues and mend more clocks. We could take short breaks to look up our friends and relations, and so on.

Such activities have to be be tailored to the constraints of a reduced family budget and ageing bodies, but retirement is not just about growing older. It is not like being an old donkey turned out to grass. It is also about staying young at heart, and still engaging with what one enjoys and cares about passionately. It involves fostering the health of body, mind and spirit, and seeking appropriate ways to give Christian service. As to retirement in general, many helpful books on this broad theme are already available.

STEP 5 – DISCERNING WHAT DOORS ARE OPEN FOR ACTIVE MINISTRY

After an initial pause of several months the time seemed ripe to re-assess how much ministry to undertake. I found much value in taking part, with Mary, in a retreat at Ampleforth Abbey for married couples on the brink of retirement when we could address our concerns and hopes. Some useful lateral thinking was sparked off by a group Bible study on the raising of Lazarus (John, chapter 11). Christ granted him a new lease of life. Lazarus emerged from the tomb, his winding sheets stripped off. Untrammelled by these ties, he discovered that God had not finished with him yet. The retreat was a chance for me to clarify how much of my former working life to take with me. There was more to life than an office I once held. What mattered was: Who am I now? How can I exercise my freedom of choice wisely and unselfishly? As one participant aptly remarked, "God is not somewhere else, at the end of the rainbow. The challenge is to serve Him now in changed circumstances, and continue to offer our lives as a living sacrifice."

To put some shape on this process, my approach was to group possible channels of ministry in the categories shown below, then to set priorities and limits, and subsequently to review the whole picture annually.

a) *Phasing out previous responsibilities*

I set provisional deadlines for handing over various responsibilities that had continued from before retirement. In 2002 I withdrew from the annual meeting of 'Ecumenical Bishops' which I had attended since 1986. In the following year I handed over the chairmanship of a committee that awarded scholarships for Anglican clergy and ordinands to study Eastern Orthodoxy. The Anglican

Communion Office asked me to continue as co-chair of the body at world level for dialogue with Lutheran Churches until our report *'Growth in Communion'* (2003) had been published. An important element in serving such bodies is holding their corporate memory through changes of personnel, and contributing to consistency and continuity of policy. Nevertheless, the time eventually comes to stand down. Nobody is indispensible, and change can be beneficial.

b) *Invitations from bishops*

From time to time I have been glad to represent the Archbishop of Canterbury in several European countries on different types of occasion. Sometimes this involved delivering a paper on behalf of the Anglican tradition. A number of retired bishops assist the archbishop from time to time, e.g. by advising on the grant of faculties under Canon C.4, by hearing appeals for the withdrawal of licences under Canons C.12, E.6 or E.8, by looking into local difficulties, etc.

Within the Lincoln diocese I have usually been asked to conduct a few Confirmations each year. The bishops' other requests have included licensing an ecumenical youth chaplain, reviewing of a team rector's licence, leading a supervision group for spiritual directors, representing the diocese at celebrations in Brugge (our twin diocese in Belgium), attending clergy funerals, and occasionally mentoring priests who faced particular difficulties. My priority has been to support and assist the current episcopal team, and I have declined a few requests where a conflict of loyalties might have arisen. I have joined in most diocesan events to which I have been invited.

Recently, in another diocese where the bishop did not ordain women, I was delegated to ordain a woman priest, but this was a unique occasion arising from a personal link and is unlikely to recur.

Episcopal consecrations are strongly collegial occasions, and I have been glad to share in them about once every couple of years – usually at York rather than in the southern province for reasons of cost. A specific network for retired bishops is the annual briefing session at Bishopthorpe hosted by Archbishop Sentamu, which I have enjoyed attending. A few years ago I greatly valued taking part in a week's conference for over 100 bishops (mostly Roman Catholic), held in Rome by the lay community of St Egidio who exercise a remarkable apostolate, not least in cherishing and encouraging church leaders on many continents.

c) *Requests for help*

Subject to the limits of time and energy, I have done my best to respond to particular requests for help. Two examples arose in the sphere of education. The ecumenical chaplain to the Scunthorpe Colleges asked me to chair her support group, and I did so for six years once per term. My local vicar asked me to be a Foundation Governor of the church primary school in our village, which I did for a standard four-year period. Though I had served as a governor in other settings over some 30 years, it was valuable to re-train on the excellent governors' course provided by North Lincolnshire Council.

On the ecumenical front I was asked to be secretary of the 'UK Friends of Bossey', a role I carried out for three years – a welcome chance to repay some of the debt I owe the Ecumenical Institute (Geneva) for the benefits received from courses there. Locally the Methodist circuit of Barton & Brigg became desperately short-staffed on account of illness, and for five years I was authorised by the Methodist Conference to act as an Associate Minister, and normally conducted two or three services on each quarterly plan.

One of the greatest joys in retirement has been to resume some normal priestly ministry without the pressures of senior leadership. The need for this arises mostly during vacancies and when local clergy are away on holidays, sabbatical or sick leave. I try to set my limit at celebrating and preaching on no more than two Sundays a month (including all the commitments mentioned above). After twelve years of active retirement I conduct weddings and funerals only very occasionally, and have cut down preaching engagements to an average of a dozen a year. I also see several clergy for spiritual direction, but am gradually reducing this too.

As one gets older, things take longer. It is a bonus to have time to do things carefully and properly, without constantly chasing one's tail, and an even bigger bonus to be able to say 'No' – something I am gradually getting better at. One strategy for thinning out public engagements, suggested to me by Bishop David Shepherd, is to block off three months each year when none will be accepted. I normally keep February, June and September free of church duties, though of course there can be no let up for any Christian from the demands of daily discipleship.

d) *Other invitations*

All invitations have to be judged on their merits, and many have to be declined. A few years ago I agreed to cover a continental chaplaincy for two weeks, but it turned out to more exhausting than I had imagined. It is doubtful whether I would ever do that again.

Here are my criteria for responding to opportunities for active ministry that may arise:

1 What preparation will be needed?
2 How long it this likely to take?
3 Does it meet a real need?
4 Whom will it benefit?
5 Is there any financial cost or gain?
6 Will it entail follow-up?
7 What are the boundaries?
8 What impact would my doing this have on other people?
9 What consultation will be required?
10 Is it a responsible use of my particular gifts or experience (i.e. a moral obligation on me)?
11 If it involves travel and being away from home, is this manageable?
12 Would I enjoy it, and do I really want to be doing this?

By answering these points honestly I can generally get a clear sense of what my answer ought to be. I test this out on Mary, whose wisdom on such matters is considerable! Two votes are needed for a 'Yes' response.

Closing comment

None of us knows the day or the hour when our active ministry will cease. It may be curtailed suddenly or unexpectedly. In the mean time we may serve God thankfully and joyfully, and live life as fully as health of body and mind permit within the limits of diminishing strength, gradually drawing in one's circle and learning to be content with what is possible. Not long before the death of Bishop Edward King (who never retired) he wrote to an old friend:

'We must keep quietly to the old ways, and trust. The great comfort is knowing that the Church and the world are both under the eye and control of our Blessed Lord. He is Head over all and over the Church. One's only anxiety should be to know and do His will, then calmly, thankfully and lovingly to trust.'

('Spiritual Letters of Edward King', page 173)

EPILOGUE

Amongst the books on my horological bookshelf is one that deals solely with the escapement – the bit in a clock that goes 'tick-tock'. The book in question goes into fine technical detail about the inner workings of clocks, but no reader would ever imagine that the escapement mattered more than the clock. Largely unseen, the escapement makes all the difference to the clock running smoothly or not all. The ultimate test is: does the part enable the whole to fulfil its maker's design and be of service to humanity in telling the time?

By the same token I trust that nobody who reads this book on the ministry of a bishop could possibly run away with the idea that the episcopate mattered for its own sake. The inner workings of how bishops carry out their particular function must be judged by how far they enable the church as whole to fulfil its divine mission and share the gospel with all humankind. Though this specialised topic, its consequences are very far-reaching.

These pages, whilst containing some personal memoirs, consist mainly of systematic reflections and pointers to those resources that I have actually found useful on the main aspects of episcopal ministry which are outlined on page 60. Several chapters take their starting-point from the relevant clause in the revised ordinal of 2006, which articulates the Church of England's current understanding of bishops' ministry. This understanding cannot, however, remain static since the episcopate – like the church itself – must constantly adjust and evolve in relation to the times, places and cultures in which it takes root. It follows, therefore, that these reflections are offered not in a spirit of *'This is how it should be done'*. Rather, it is a question of one bishop describing what he thought he was meant to *be* and to *do* in his particular situation, and how he tackled it – however imperfectly and whatever his limitations.

It would be good to hear from other bishops about the different ways in which they have carried out their ministry, or are still doing so. I hope that some will feel moved to share their wisdom and experience by spelling out their own theological model and praxis of bishop's ministry, and identifying what resources they have found most useful and inspiring. Most of all, I would encourage the church as a whole to continue exploring – ecumenically and internationally – what styles, structures and methods of *episcopé* are best suited to carrying forward its mission in today's rapidly changing world, and how its leaders can be properly equipped for their ministry.

Appendix

SERMON

Westminster Abbey
25th January 1979
(Feast of the Conversion of St Paul)

Consecration of Bishops:
Conrad Meyer, to be Bishop of Dorchester
David Tustin, to be Bishop of Grimsby
John Waller, to be Bishop of Stafford

Preacher: **The Revd. Michael Mayne**, MA
(Head of Religious Programmes, BBC Radio;
Honorary Canon of Southwark)

When in 1885 Mr Gladstone appointed to the See of Lincoln the saintly Edward King, King's friend Scott-Holland wrote to him: *"Blessings, blessing, blessings! It shall be a bishopric of love"*. And so it proved. Edward King was so loved in his diocese that a certain Master of Foxhounds kept on his bedside table two photographs: one of the bishop and one of his favourite hound.

But expectations are not always so happily fulfilled. As a one-time bishop's chaplain I know the expectations Parochial Church Councils have of potential incumbents, demanding a family man in his early forties, a gifted preacher, patient with the elderly and expert with the young. Rarely do parishes actually ask for a man who is in his own unique way will exercise a ministry of love: a ministry in which the Eucharist is at the centre; a man who will listen and pray and heal and reconcile because his eyes are fixed on the Lord and his Kingdom.

No doubt the expectations made of a new bishop are greater and more threatening than those made of a parish priest. Cardinal Hume, preaching at Ampleforth after his appointment to Westminster, said:

> *"The gap between what is expected of me and what I know myself to be is considerable and frightening. There are moments in life when a man feels very small, and in all my life this is one such moment. It is good to feel small, for I know that whatever I achieve will be God's achievement, not mine".*

I hope – Conrad and David and John – that you will be wary of what you imagine or discover the churches in your diocese <u>expect</u> of you; for paying overmuch attention to people's expectations is not a good way of developing your sensitivity to God or the world or yourselves, which is your proper business. The whole emphasis in this consecration service is on your relationship to God, and it is His expectation of you alone that matters. And His expectations are quite simple: they are that you will open yourself to his Spirit; and that you will trust Him.

The fact that you are made bishop on the day of St Paul's Conversion should be a humbling reminder of the singularity of God's choice of church leaders. Paul quite rightly never stopped ruminating on the strangeness of <u>his</u> being chosen for such a task. *"You have heard how savagely I persecuted the church of God,"* he writes to the Galatians, *"until God chose to reveal His Son <u>to</u> me and <u>through</u> me"*. And I believe you should take into your bishopric a sense of astonished wonder: that you, with all your funny ways, all your failure to love (like Peter), all your betrayals of Christ, have nevertheless been called to this office because (also like Peter) you can say: *"Lord, you know all things. You know I love you"*. It is that which carries the day. Do not doubt that, amid all the fears and self-questioning which I guess you faced when that letter came from No.10, the inner compulsion which in the end prompted you to say 'Yes' was the urging of the Holy Spirit. This thing you do <u>is</u> of God, and He does not play practical jokes. And do not forget that to believe in the Holy Spirit is to believe that all of us can find resources in ourselves beyond all our expectations, and surprise ourselves and others by what we can accomplish.

But, above all, do not forget that you have been called not in spite of what you are but <u>because</u> of what you are. Don't let your office or people's expectations of your office change you. It's <u>you</u> we still want, not a de luxe version of you.

The difference is that your own particular insight is now to be exercised in a wider sphere. And it is that word '<u>insight</u>' which goes to the very heart of what a bishop is. Episcopé means oversight, literally the act of 'looking round' or 'looking over' like a look-out on a tall tower who can view every building in the city. And this whole group of words: insight, oversight, vision, perception, all have their roots in that seminal New Testament word 'to <u>see</u>'. Jesus comes so that men may see. He comes to open the eyes of the blind, and that covers the whole spectrum from a blind man regaining his sight to the post-Easter vision of the world transfigured and redeemed. Like Paul, at first blinded, and then with restored sight, in Christ we see the world and each other with new eyes.

The oversight and insight we demand of our bishops is rooted in this vision of how things truly are. We need you to be <u>seer</u> and an overseer: to look not just at the Church but at the world: with one eye to see its disorder and confusion, and with the other to discern the glory and the activity of God within it. To speak of God and what He is doing in His world; to show people they are loved and valued and forgiven; and to do it in language which relates to real life and in terms all can understand.

And for some of us who speak and write and preach that will mean joining the human race again: seeking to discern in the world about us the hidden presence of God pervading the scene, and pointing it out. It will mean, in the words of Simon Barrington-Ward, *"scanning the broken surface of the world and discerning hidden connections like an artist, a scientist or a novelist".*

It will mean, above all, an <u>attentiveness</u> to what the world is saying. And therefore, I beg you, in ordering your life as a bishop, to make your first priority the creating of a proper space. Time to be still. Time to contemplate the world around you. Time to look at, and listen to, your wife, your children, your neighbour. Time to read novels and poetry. Time to look at pictures or listen to music. Time watch television and listen to the radio. Time to think and to pray and to see ...

If you forget you are first and foremost a seer and an overseer, that is to say a <u>contemplative</u>, you will be tempted to justify your existence by working yourself to death. And that you have no right to do. As Father Herbert Kelly, Founder of Kelham, used to say: *"I wish the clergy would do ten times less and <u>think</u> ten times more. What we want of the prophet is not work, but vision, sight and prayer."* More than anything else it is that serenity, that space at the heart of you, that will clear your vision and allow you to be an effective pastor to the many who look to you as a reconciler and interpreter: one who points men to Jesus as their true centre and to the Spirit of God active in their midst.

And finally, lest the thought of the gravity of your office overwhelms you, I beg you to retain the gift of laughter. To sit light to yourself: to take neither yourself nor your office with a seriousness it does not deserve. In T.S. Eliot's words: <u>"Teach us to care and not to care"</u>: to care passionately that we sing the Lord's song in a strange land; to care passionately for people and for the Kingdom; but still to be able to laugh at yourself with that laughter which is healing and redemptive, for it means viewing yourself with a sort of loving forgiveness which is an echo of God's loving forgiveness of you.

Blessings, Conrad; blessings, David; blessings, John: and may it be a bishopric of openness to the Spirit, of shared insights, of a stillness at the heart of you; for that is to say with Scott-Holland: *"it shall be a bishopric of love".*

SELECT BIBLIOGRAPHY

Avis, P. – *'Beyond the Reformation?'* (T. & T. Clark, 2006)
Benedict, St. – *'The Rule of Saint Benedict'*, transl. D. Parry, OSB (DLT, 1984)
Bernard, St. – *'Five Books on Consideration'* (Cistercian Publications, 1976) transl. J.D. Anderson and E.T. Kennan
Bernard, St. – *'On the Conduct and Office of Bishop'* (Cistercian Publications, 2005) transl. M.G. Newman
Bernard, St. – *'The Letters of St Bernard of Clairvaux',* (Burns Oates, 1953) transl B.S. James
Bonhoeffer, D. – 'Ethics' (SCM Press, 1955)
Bursell, R.D.H.- contributor to *'English Canon Law'* (University of Wales Press, 1998)
Chadwick, O. – *'The Victorian Church'* (A. and C. Black, 1966 and 1970, and SCM Press, 1987)
Champ, J.- *'William Bernard Ullathorne – a different kind of monk'* (Gracewing, 2006)
Countryman, W. -*'Mission and the Reform of Episcopé'* – see Niagara Consultation (below)
Dale, R.W. – *'Nine Lectures on Preaching'* (Hodder & Stoughton, 1877)
Elton, Lord – *'Edward King and our Times'* (Godfrey Bles, 1958)
Evans, G.R. – *'Bernard of Clairvaux – selected works'* (Paulist Press, 1987)
Evans, G.R. – *'Bernard of Clairvaux'* (OUP, 2000)
Frere, W.H. and Illingworth, A.L. – *'Sursum Corda'* (Mowbray, 1898)
Gregory, St. – *'Pastoral Care'* (Paulist Press, New York, 1950) transl. H. Davis, SJ
Grundy, M. – *'Leadership and Oversight'* (Mowbray, 2011)
Hahn, C. – *'The Minister is Leaving'* (Seabury Press, 1984)
Halliburton, J. – *'The Authority of a Bishop'* (SPCK, 1987)
Hamel, J. – *'A Christian in East Germany'* (SCM Press, 1960) transl. C.C. & R. West
Hastings, A. – *'A History of English Christianity 1920-1985'* (Collins, 1986)
Hawtin, D. – *'Bishops Behaving Ecumenically'* (Council for Christian Unity, 2007)
James, E. – *'Bishop John A.T. Robinson: Scholar, Pastor, Prophet'* (Collins 1987)
King, S.D.M. – *'Training within the Organisation'* (Tavistock, 1964)
Machin, D. (ed.) – *'Simon Phipps – a Portrait'* (Continuum, 2003)
Marshall, R.J. – *'Episcopé and the Mission of the Church in the 21st Century'* – see Niagara Consultation (below)

McCullum, H. & MacArthur, T. (ed.) – *'Into God's Hands – Common Prayer for the World'* (World Council of Churches, 2006)

Mead, L.B. – *'The Developmental Tasks of the Congregation in search of a Pastor'* (Alban Institute, 1984)

Moore, P. (ed.) – *'Bishops, but what kind?'* (SPCK, 1982)

Morgan, E.R. – contributor to *'Bishops'* (Faith Press, 1961)

Neville, G. – *'Free Time: towards a theology of Leisure'* (University of Birmingham Press, 2004)

Norris, R.A. – *'The Bishop in the Church of Late Antiquity'* – see Niagara Consultation (below)

Podmore, C. – *'Leadership and Oversight'* (Mowbray, 2011)

Podmore, C. – *'Aspects of Anglican Identity'* (Church House Publishing, 2005)

Ramsey, A.M. – *'The Christian Priest Today'* (SPCK, 1972)

Rogers, C. R. – *'Freedom to Learn'* (Penguin, 1969)

Rogers, C.R. – *'Encounter Groups'* (Penguin, 1973)

Sheppard, D. and Worlock, D. – *'Better Together'* (Hodder & Stoughton, 1988)

Somerset Ward, A. – *'A Guide for Spiritual Directors'* (Mowbray, 1957)

Wright, N.R. – *'Lincolnshire Towns and Industry 1700-1914'* (History of Lincolnshire, vol. XI, 1982)

Yon, W.A. – *'Prime Time for Renewal'* (Alban Institute, 1977)

REPORTS

All are Called: towards a theology of the laity (Church House Press, 1985)

Anglican Covenant – see *Windsor Report 2004*

Anglican-Lutheran Agreements 1972-2002 – documentation no. 49, ed. S. Oppegaard and G. Cameron (Anglican Consultative Council / Lutheran World Federation, 2004)

Apostolicity and Succession – House of Bishops occasional paper, GS Misc 432 (General Synod, 1994)

Baptism, Eucharist and Ministry – Faith & Order paper 111 (World Council of Churches, 1982)

Bishop, Priest & Deacon in the Church of Sweden (Swedish Bishops' Conference, 1990) English translation

Bishops in Communion – House of Bishops Occasional Paper, GS Misc 580 (Council for Christian Unity, 2000)

Called to be a bishop – overview of the roles and activities of the bishops of the Church of England (Church Commissioners for England, 1999)

Called to be Adult Disciples – report of the Board of Education, GS 794 (Church House Bookshop, 1987)

Called to Common Mission (U.S.A.) – see Anglican-Lutheran Agreements

Called to Witness and Service – the Reuilly Common Statement with essays on Church, Eucharist and Ministry, GS 1329 (Church House Publishing, 1999)

Cameron Report – see *Episcopal Ministry*

Criteria for Selection for Ministry in the Church of England – ABM Policy Paper No. 3A (Central Board of Finance of the Church of England, 1993)

Documents of Vatican II – Abbott W.J. (ed.) (Chapman 1967)

Ely Report – *'Christian Initiation: Birth and Growth in the Christian Society'*, GS 30 (Church Information Office, 1971)

Episcopal Ministry – report of the Archbishops' group on the episcopate [GS 944], often referred to as the Cameron Report (Church House Press, 1990)

Growth in Communion – report of the Anglican-Lutheran International Working Group (ACC and LWF, 2003)

Lambeth Conference 1968 – Resolutions and Reports (SPCK & Seabury Press, 1968)

Lambeth Conference 1978 – Report (Church Information Office, 1978)

Lambeth Conference 1988 – 'The Truth shall make you free' (Church House Press, 1988)

Lumen Gentium – Dogmatic Constitution on 'The Church' – see Documents of Vatican II

Lund statement – 'Episcopal Ministry within the Apostolicity of the Church' (Lutheran World Federation, 2007)

May They All Be One – House of Bishops Occasional Paper, GS Misc 495 (Church House Press, 1997)

Meissen Agreement – see 'On the Way to Visible Unity'

New Delhi Report – report of the 3rd Assembly of the World Council of Churches (SCM Press, 1962)

Niagara Consultation – 'Episcopé in Relation to the Mission of the Church Today', background papers for the Niagara Report (Anglican Consultative Council and Lutheran World Federation, Geneva, 1988)

Niagara Report – report of the Anglican-Lutheran Consultation on Episcopé 1987' (Church House Press 1988)

On the Way to Visible Unity – the Meissen Common Statement, GS 843 (Church House Press, 1988)

Ordained Ministry Today – report of CACTM (Church Information Office, 1969)

Ordination Services (study edition), (Church House Press, 2007)

Pastoral Office of Bishops – Decree – see Documents of Vatican II

Porvoo Agreement – see 'Together in Mission and Ministry'

Reuilly Agreement – see 'Called to Witness and Service'

Something to Celebrate – report by the Board of Social Responsibility (Church House Press, 1995)

The Church as Communion – ARCIC II (Catholic Truth Society/Church House Publishing, 1991)

The Final Report – ARCIC I (Catholic Truth Society/SPCK 1982)

The Gift of Authority – ARCIC II (Catholic Truth Society /Church Publishing, 1999)

The Lutheran Understanding of the Episcopal Office (Lutheran World Federation, 1983)

The Nature of Christian Belief – statement and exposition by the House of Bishops (Church House Publishing, 1986)

Today's Church and Today's World (Church Information Office, 1977)

Together in Mission and Ministry – the Porvoo Common Statement with essays on Church and Ministry in Northern Europe, GS 1083 (Church House Press, 1993)

Ut Unum Sint (1995) – Encyclical of Pope John Paul II, 1995

Visitation – a study by the Theological Committee of the United Evangelical Lutheran Church of Germany, ed. M. Lasogga and U. Hahn (VELKD, Hanover 2011) English translation

Waterloo Agreement (Canada) – see Anglican-Lutheran Agreements

Windsor Report 2004 – report of the Lambeth Commission on Communion (Anglican Consultative Council, 2004)

Church Legislation

The text of current Acts, Measures and Canon Law affecting the Church of England is accessible through the website www.churchofengland.com.

INDEX *of subjects and key words*

accessibility   79, 83-84, 90, 117-120, 180
accountability   14, 36-37, 60, 108, 118-119, 201-203
aims   26, 46-47, 85, 134-135, 202
ambition   19-20, 73
apostolicity   32, 53, 147, 149-150, 152, 163-164
appointments' process   16, 21-22, 100, 121, 154, 173-176
archdeacon   38, 42, 59, 91, 99-103, 108-109, 121-126, 156, 173-174, 203
authority   27-28, 32-33, 50-51, 70, 115, 205

Bernard, St:
  -- On Consideration   4, 11, 17-18, 46, 62-64, 74-75, 100, 203
  -- On the Lifestyle & Duties of Bishops   4, 11, 14-15, 19-20, 72-73, 115
bishop's family   23-24, 41-43, 81-86, 118, 204-205, 211, 214-215, 219
bishop's lifestyle   10-11, 44, 51, 69-80, 84-85, 87, 93, 95, 159, 214-216, 218
bishop's role as:
  -- bridge-builder   55, 180-183, 208
  -- focus of unity   53-55, 106-107, 180-182, 190
  -- hospitable host   44, 84-86, 213
  -- guardian of the faith   50, 53, 152-153
  -- link with the wider church   15-16, 151, 187-189, 193-198
  -- manager   106-107
  -- member of episcopal college   15, 183, 185-187
  -- pastor of laity & clergy   49-50, 54-55, 60, 110-112, 115-116, 118-124
  -- pioneer and enquirer   15-16, 152
  -- preacher / teacher   9-10, 18-19, 50-51, 60, 146-158
  -- reconciler   60, 178-179, 182-184
  -- successor of the apostles   76, 163-164
  -- theologian   17, 150-153, 199
  -- worship leader   9, 50-51, 60, 132-141
bishop's senior staff   38, 43, 100-104, 123, 173-174, 205
boundaries   85, 98, 180, 183, 195, 206-207, 219
buildings   99, 139-140, 144

canon law   50, 60, 64-65, 76-78, 84, 124, 126, 134, 136, 139, 142-144, 146, 168, 170, 174, 195-196, 217
cathedral   38, 139, 171, 183
churchmanship   136, 144-145, 182
churchwardens   108, 126, 165
civic leaders   38, 128, 180

clergy & their families   39, 50, 58, 101, 118-120
clergy discipline   9, 50, 112-113, 115, 119, 130-131, 173, 194
collegiality   15-16, 34, 51-53, 152-153, 184-189, 200
communion, being in   15-16, 34, 55-56, 108, 188
conflict resolution   9, 14, 60, 121, 130-131, 144-145, 178, 182-184
consecration rite   30-36, 53, 61, 69, 110, 132, 146, 163, 178, 190, 201
consultation   52, 60, 120-121, 137-138, 184, 207, 219
continuing development:
   -- clergy career path   121, 175-176
   -- moving jobs   21-22, 23-24, 121, 175-176
   -- review of ministry   47-48, 59-60, 118, 121, 128-129, 196, 201-203
   -- training courses for bishops   204-210
county level   6, 28-29, 194-195
criteria for selection   10, 13-14, 168-170

deanery:
   -- chapter   39, 109, 119
   -- day visit   127-128, 180
   -- lay chair   43, 102-103, 109
   -- rural dean   38, 43, 102-103, 108-109, 121-123, 139, 173, 176
   -- synod   109
   -- time share-out   92
debt   119
demography   28-29, 116, 124, 206-207
discipleship   106, 161
diversity   181-183

ecumenical:
   -- agreements   31-32, 54-56, 197
   -- co-operation   6, 60, 139, 142, 144, 153, 173, 192-198
   -- counterparts   43, 193-196, 205-206
   -- dialogue   6, 198-199
   -- local partnerships   195-196
   -- officer   195-196
   -- overseas partners   197
   -- vision   190-192
education, church's role in   6, 59-60, 159-160
encouragement   60, 76, 124, 129
Episcopal Ministry (Cameron report)   28, 49, 97, 180-181, 187
evangelism   54, 134-135, 156, 163-164
experience, drawing on   5-6, 26, 32, 40, 44-45, 97, 153-154, 158, 218, 220

fostering vocations   60, 165-166
Free Churches   6, 43, 193-196, 198, 206, 213, 218

Gregory, St – Pastoral Rule   4-5, 9-10, 18-19, 61-62, 69-71, 112-114, 148, 178-179

holiness   61-68, 79, 133-134
housing of bishops & clergy   24, 119-120

international responsibilities   90, 188-189, 198-199

Kingdom of God   106-107, 129-130, 156

laity (all the baptised)   33, 38, 53-57, 65-66, 108, 116, 123-126, 143-145, 149-153, 160-161, 183-184, 203
Lambeth Conferences:
  -- 1920   191, 199
  -- 1968   51-52, 204
  -- 1978   52-53, 134, 151, 174, 204
  -- 1988   54-55, 179, 182, 199, 203-205
Lambeth Quadrilateral   49
legal issues   139, 144, 169, 173-174, 177, 189 (see also 'canon law')
licensed lay workers   118
local community & leaders   38-39, 43, 58, 116, 124-129, 179-180, 215
Lund statement 2007 (LWF)   49, 56, 125, 133, 147, 187
Lutheran churches   6, 13, 35, 55-56, 67, 125-126, 149, 197-199, 205, 217

magisterium   56, 188
marital breakdown   59, 101, 118, 120
marriage   42, 81-84, 119, 210
media   25, 154, 156, 210, 215
mission   53-55, 60, 150, 177, 179, 185, 189, 210, 220
models of episcopacy:
  -- Cyprianic   187
  -- Ignatian   132-133
  -- Irenaean   147
  -- Lincoln   57
  -- oversight   13, 55, 60, 120, 158-159, 179-181, 194-195, 222
  -- pastoral imagery   111-112, 116
  -- re-stated shape   60
moral issues & standards   9, 50, 78-79

national responsibilities   90, 185-186, 197-198
networks   108-109, 122-123, 141-142, 159-161, 176, 202
new bishops:
    -- expectations   11-12, 17, 26-27, 36, 120, 130-131, 135, 153, 196, 221
    -- induction process   25-26, 38-39, 204-205, 208
    -- mentors   26-27, 75
    -- preparing for consecration   23-25, 35
    -- recommended reading   28, 107, 145, 157-159, 161-162, 177, 199-200, 210
    -- support group   43, 47, 79
    -- vesture   25, 76-77, 139-140
Niagara - consultation & report   9, 34, 35-37, 49, 54, 107, 133, 135, 153, 164, 180, 198, 201

office administration   25, 43-44, 89
ordinands   165-166, 168-170, 185-186
Orthodox churches   13, 33-34, 77, 81, 190-191, 198, 216
overseas partnerships   188-189, 197-199

pastoral re-organisation   40, 104, 172
patchwork scheme   102-103
patronage   12-13, 173-175
personality   8, 13-15, 17-21, 45-47, 113, 148
policy making   103-107
Porvoo Common Statement   6, 31-34, 107, 164, 192
pressure points   90, 122, 130
priorities   121, 206
public affairs   55, 60, 179-180, 215
public worship:
    -- preparation for   25, 92, 136-140, 219
    -- regulation of   143-145, 196

readers, licensed lay   142
record keeping   45, 47-48, 88-89, 122, 155
retirement   211-219
Roman Catholic church   6-7, 11, 13, 20, 32, 40, 59, 81, 107, 115-116, 150, 157, 193-194, 197, 200, 203, 206, 212, 217 (see also 'Vatican II')
rural ministry   52, 126-127, 154, 172, 176

sabbatical leave   5, 160-161, 200, 208
sacraments   50-51, 60, 133, 135, 140-141
schools & colleges   157, 159-160, 218

Scripture   15, 61-62, 65, 137, 147
sharing ministry   13-14, 60, 82-83, 96, 100-103, 106, 127, 138, 142, 151, 165, 167, 173, 194-195, 202
social concerns   9, 52-54, 58, 60, 66, 116, 128-129, 149, 151, 185, 206-207

spirituality:
 -- contemplation   64, 222-223
 -- daily office   64-65
 -- in broad terms   67-68
 -- intercession   41, 53, 65-66, 120
 -- lectio divina   61-62, 65
 -- meditation   41, 62-63
 -- private prayer   41, 60-62, 223

start-up list   121, 175
suffragan bishop   6, 52, 57, 97-99, 186-188, 205
Sweden, Church of   35, 55, 125, 197
synods   40, 103, 108-109, 157

time use:
 -- diary control   26, 87-95, 120-121, 206, 218-219
 -- holidays   91, 93
 -- kairos (opportunity)   94-95
 -- time off   26, 83-84

titles:
 -- forms of address   77
 -- training curacies   171

travel   77-78, 93

unity   6, 60, 178-179, 183, 187, 190-192
urban ministry   52, 124, 172, 181-182, 205

Vatican II (Second Vatican Council)   28, 50-51, 79, 115-116, 133, 150, 182, 187
visitation   50, 124-126
vocational discernment   16-22, 32, 165-167, 216

www.ingramcontent.com/pod-product-compliance
Lightning Source LLC
Chambersburg PA
CBHW081847170426
43199CB00018B/2838